# CAIRNGORM RANGER

# CAIRNGORM RANGER

A fascinating walk in the Cairngorms
with the Ranger

## Nic Bullivant

Participation statement: By their nature the activities described in this book have an unavoidable
element of risk of personal injury or death. Anyone undertaking any activity as a result of any perceived
recommendation in this book must accept full responsibility for their actions. Precautions to be taken
in undertaking these activities may be recommended in this text, but may not be exhaustive nor complete,
and participants will need to satisfy themselves on all matters of safety at all times when undertaking any activity.
It's a big world out there, take care!

Front cover: Cairn Gorm and Loch Morlich
Title Page: The Long Walk In, on the path to the Chalamain Gap.

Matador
9 Priory Business Park,
Wistow Road, Kibworth Beauchamp,
Leicestershire. LE8 0RX
Tel: 0116 279 2299
Email: books@troubador.co.uk
Web: www.troubador.co.uk/matador
Twitter: @matadorbooks


ISBN 978 1788039 437

British Library Cataloguing in Publication Data.
A catalogue record for this book is available from the British Library.

Printed and bound by CPI Group (UK) Ltd, Croydon, CR0 4YY
Typeset in 11pt Gill Sans by Troubador Publishing Ltd, Leicester, UK

Matador is an imprint of Troubador Publishing Ltd

*For those who would come this way*

# Contents

This story is a personal recollection of a long relationship with the Cairngorms, especially the time working as Head Ranger on Cairn Gorm itself.

I want to show you the natural aspect of the mountains. The way Nature has the upper hand.

I want to explain how fragile the arrangements are that keeps things natural, and how easily and thoughtlessly this arrangement is upset.

I want to express the historic step change represented by the Cairngorm development, and remember the immense amount of pleasure and the livelihoods it brings.

# 1 | Hello, I'm your Ranger for the day

I'm Nic Bullivant, 20 years Head Ranger at Cairngorm and one of those annoying people who tell you that they had the best job ever. So I'll try not to be annoying any more.

I'm going to be introducing you to the places, wild things and ideas I think are important. I hope that once you've been introduced, you get a feel for the importance of this place, and you want to keep it prospering and healthy.

It might help you to know that Rangers on Cairn Gorm work from a Ranger Base at 635 metres, (2150 ft) adjacent to the highest car park on the hill. The Base is part of a large modern stone-clad building which houses the Base Station of the Cairngorm Mountain Railway – a funicular – which was developed as a ski lift and tourist attraction. Close by is a second large building, known as the Day Lodge. The Cairngorm Rangers' parish covers the Cairngorm Ski Area, which you could walk round in a day, and the rest of Cairngorm Estate, which would take a long day to walk round, covering 1400 hectares, or 14 grid-squares of the

map. It's all mountain country; the lowest point is at 500 metres, the highest at 1245 metres. (That's 1800 to 4000 feet).

It's best for this introduction if we imagine our day to be a fine one. There is plenty of time later for foul weather. If your first visit to a place is shrouded in mist, or pouring with rain, it creates a poor impression, and we would hardly see anything. Walks in the rain are not to everyone's taste, and you probably wouldn't have thought of reading about a place that started in the pouring rain.

One reason for enjoying working as a Ranger is this stroke of luck: If the weather is good, the Ranger needs to be outdoors, because that's where things are happening; people are enjoying themselves. Some of the work depends on dry conditions, it can't be done in low cloud or rain. Even if it could, it wouldn't be as good. There are hardly any people out there when it's wet, and binoculars, camera and electronics get wet in the rain. On the other hand, when it is raining, the Ranger is quite often found inside. I can think of only one outdoors job that's better to do in the rain, and that's observing and improving the drainage on the paths. Why anyone should be doing this, I'll explain later.

Gales are a completely different class of inclement weather. The saying

# "There is no bad weather, just inappropriate clothing"

is all very well, but it was coined for places that don't have really bad weather.

Cairn Gorm has some really bad weather, when the only reason for going out in it is to experience it at first-hand. If you want to know what a 100 miles-per-hour wind feels like, this is the place to do it. No other work gets done outdoors in conditions like these.

It doesn't stop the weather being bad weather just because the clothing is appropriate.

During difficult weather it is good to be indoors catching up on reports, setting up a new slideshow or something equally pressing. When these kinds of jobs crowd around, any beautiful weather is actually quite distracting. The Ranger should be out in it, not adjusting somebody's timesheet. Then again, after a long spell of good weather (ha!), the opportunity to catch up on entering data to a spreadsheet or planning school visits is something which has had to wait for a wet day, and when it comes, it can be quite welcome.

Before you come away with the old joke about being a Lone Ranger, there is more than one Ranger at Cairngorm. Usually there were two Seasonally-employed Rangers but numbers have dwindled lately, and I can't tell what will happen next. There are some days when there are no Rangers available, and someone else will open the Ranger Base, so I hope you pick a day to visit when one or other of us is present and can help you, or at least say hello.

## So, what would be a typical day?

That depends on the season. In summer, the timescale can be quite relaxed. Rangers are at work from 8.30 am, preparing for the day, answering visitors' questions and adding to the information available in the Ranger Base. When the Rangers go out, often from about 11am, the Ranger Base has to operate on its own, so the weather forecast and weather headlines on the whiteboard are displayed, and there is a place for leaving messages about route plans.

We used to have a wildlife diary on the desk for public entries as well. I tolerated several of the *"Saw a yeti on the ridge having a pint"* nature but what killed it off were the *"This is a lovely/terrible place and it should be better known/closed down"* comments and finally the ones from colleagues keeping in-jokes going.

Since the 1970s, the Cairngorm Rangers have performed a daily reading of the weather instruments at 0900 GMT (this is 1000 BST in summer). The long run of data is very valuable to the Met Office, to whom we send it, and is a daily ritual. If you like, I'll share some of the results later on.

There may be a guided walk, a school group or a media visit to lead. There might be a path repair contract team working that needs a visit. Rangers could be training with colleagues, carrying out monitoring (which, again, I'll explain later) or downloading data from people counters.

Every day is different. Nearly all involve a snatched lunch sometime, and there is always a fair degree of pleasure in the surroundings realised and shared.

On return, the journal diary is updated, observations recorded, and a map annotated to note where the day has been spent. Rangers download the weather forecast for the next day and prepare and tidy up for the next day.

Winter sees a different world at Cairngorm. People tend to start their day earlier, limited by an early dusk. So the day starts around 8.00 a.m., the weather

readings made and then a good bit of time is spent in the Ranger Base talking to people who are asking for advice before they set out.

Nobody is obliged to ask for advice. This is not one of those Ranger stations where everyone has to sign in before they can be allowed to proceed.

Most people feel better having heard the Ranger's view about what is happening or has happened or might happen, to the weather, snow and ice conditions or something else. Two most important allies in this are the mountain weather information service, mwis, for their weather forecast, and the sportscotland Avalanche Information Service, for their avalanche report and forecast. Both are available on the Internet, but people appreciate an interpretation of the technical information.

Daytime expeditions to the hills are necessarily shorter in winter than in summer. I have performed regular counts of the numbers of people in the Northern Corries, particularly Coire an t-Sneachda. In a good winter, most of the things a Ranger might have been going out to look at during the summer are buried in snow. Wildlife is still around, in small numbers. People are climbing or schlepping around in totally unsuitable clothing and footwear. Sometimes they even alarm and entertain us with their antics. It is never a waste of time going out to look.

In truth, there isn't really a typical day when you look at the detail, but the strands of looking after the place, welcoming and assisting visitors and promoting understanding about the environment are ever-present.

# "There isn't really a typical day"

# 2 | Cairn Gorm, Cairngorm and the Cairngorms

This is a tale of the Cairngorms, and of Cairngorm, and Cairn Gorm.

Let's start with Cairn Gorm, the name of the blue mountain.

For once, the English language, that precise and dispassionate expression of every last nuance of meaning is outdone by another language. In the same way that the Inuit have many ways of describing snow, Gaelic has diverse and considered ways of describing mountains. Many of these names have been rendered into English. Ben is the most widespread, Stob is another. So Cairn (from the Gaelic Càrn) is not only a pile of stones, but also a style of mountain found in the East of the Highlands, where, by a combination of geology and weathering, a large rounded rocky hill has been formed.

There are lots of Cairn (or Càrn) names in the Cairngorms National Park, from Càrn Ban and Càrn Dearg in the Monadhliath above Laggan through Cairn Toul and Cairn Lochan in the central massif to Broad Cairn and Cairn Inks in the south-east.

Why you would think a mountain is blue might not be obvious until you see it in the hazy distance on a fine day. We need to be careful interpreting Gaelic colour names though, as the culture which gave rise to them did not necessarily adopt the same boundaries in the spectrum as we do. Light blue and grey are grouped together under the word liath. Gorm refers to the darker blue.

Gaelic consonants have different pronunciation rules, too. English rules have

6

*Carn Elrig, reflected in Loch Morlich*

become all-pervasive, and it is difficult to think of the symbols "it" representing anything but the sound "it". In Gaelic this might be nearer to "itch".

An English pronunciation of the name of our mountain might produce Cae-n Gawm. The consonants "r" would have much more prominence in Gaelic. So the words would come out as Cerren Gorrom, with a roll on the r if the speaker was feeling particularly declamatory. In practice, the letter r followed by m or n, would require separation by an additional vowel in Gaelic. This additional vowel has crept into Scots pronunciation of English words as well, two which come to mind are "fillum" (film) and "moddren" (modern). We will see an extra consonant creeping in to Coire an t-Sneachda later.

So that's Cairn Gorm, the mountain. This is the one that came first.

As with many great landscape features, they give their name to other features by reference. Cairn Gorm is unusual in that its name has been applied both to a larger-scale region (the Cairngorms) and to smaller scale places (Cairngorm). In all these cases the name has been elided – run together – into either Cairngorm (singular) or Cairngorms (plural). Only in the name of the mountain are the two words separate.

# Am Monadh Ruadh

The Cairngorms are exclusively pronounced in the English manner, because Gaelic speakers do not use this term to refer to the range of mountains at the Northern edge of which Cairn Gorm stands. They use the older term, Am Monadh Ruadh, which means the red mountains. Whereas the Gaelic name for the grey mountains facing them across the Spey has survived, Anglicised as Monadhliath, Am Monadh Ruadh persists as a romantic historical name and in the Gaelic form of the name of the National Park.

Not only has Cairn Gorm had its name applied to the whole massif which forms part of the Grampians, and stretches variously, according to opinion, to include all the high ground between the Spey and the Dee, it has now had its name applied to Britain's largest National Park.

Calling Scotland's second National Park the Cairngorms National Park was never in doubt, but gave many people a problem. Why should Deeside and Angus be lumped in, geographically, with a northern hill, arguably much less attractive than Lochnagar or the Esk glens? Well, Deeside (or more precisely, Derry) has its own Cairngorm, and, as referred to earlier, there are Cairns all over. Cairns National Park doesn't have quite the same ring, does it?

*The Northern Cairngorms rise above Glenmore Forest*

The mountains have been referred to as the Cairngorms in the vernacular for so long that some authors have been apologising for using this term for well over a century. Whatever you do, don't refer to it as Cairngorm National Park, because Cairngorm is something different.

Cairngorm is the smaller area. There are place names at the foot of many hills which reflect the name of the hill: Benmore, Morven, Creagdhubh Lodge. Cairngorm is a good example.

For me Cairngorm encompasses the buildings and Car Parks in Coire Cas. The ski area is Cairngorm Ski Area and the operating company has been Cairngorm Chairlift Company and Cairngorm Mountain Limited. So you could be *at* Cairngorm, *on* Cairn Gorm and *in* the Cairngorms all at the same time.

# At Cairngorm, on Cairn Gorm and in the Cairngorms

What's more, a cairngorm is a type of smoky quartz crystal we will find later on our walks in the Cairngorms and used in costume jewellery.

*Fiacaill a' Choire Chais*

9

And there are several other companies named after Cairn Gorm, such as Cairngorm Brewery, Cairngorm Hotel, Cairngorm Mountain Sports (in Aviemore) and Cairngorm Windows (in Inverness) and many others.

# 3 | Let's take a walk

Before we go we have to get ready.

We can check the weather and the forecast to help us decide what to wear when we step out of the door, but there's nothing as fickle as mountain weather, so even if there's something I don't want to wear just now, I might take it in case.

*Nothing as fickle as mountain weather*

As it's summertime, we can leave the winter gear behind. We still need good boots, but these are hill walking boots, not stiff boots for crampons. They have a good depth of cleated sole – that's the grooves around the edge – and they lace up onto the ankle, to give support.

This is one piece of kit I don't compromise on. My boots have to be comfortable all day, and tomorrow, and every day. They have to give a steady level of performance. I like to have a boot with as little stitching as possible, to give the water as little chance of getting in as possible. Best performance socks, too. Loop-stitched merino wool.

I don't usually bother with gaiters in the summer, unless I'm expecting a lot of deep heather, or scree. They can be useful if we have to ford any rivers, but we are not expecting anything like that today, so I'll let my legs breathe.

I like to wear shorts if I can, but I would hardly ever set out without having trousers on or in the pack. In summer I will wear a cotton base layer if it's really hot and I can expect to be really warm. Otherwise it's a clean polypropylene shirt.

*Regular gear*

I will take a jacket, though I might not wear it all the time. A fleece layer and a breathable waterproof is what I prefer, but some people have the whole thing combined in a single layer.

It has to have a hood which you can draw tightly round your face. Not a detachable one, because the join is a weak point and why would you want to detach something essential that might blow away?

Alan (left) on an average day with jacket, fleece, trousers, gaiters, boots, rucksack, walking poles and his lunch at his waist. He took his gloves off (in his right hand) to look at the map, which is in a case.

I'll take overtrousers, but not everyone likes to use them. If you are going to wear cotton trousers like jeans, then overtrousers are a must, you can't afford to get jeans wet on the hill. Even if it's just for comfort, overtrousers can make a wet day bearable.

A lot of people regard outdoor gear as comprising fleeces and shell jackets, but these are only the outside layer. If you don't get the other things right, like footwear and base layers, keeping warm is likely to be the least of your problems. It's the wind that takes away the heat, especially from your head and your body.

I always have a hat – one that won't blow off. Peaked caps and Stetsons are fine in their place, but not on a windy hill. Like the waterproof layer, you don't have to wear it all the time, but you do need something to carry it in.

That's a rucksack, not a shoulder bag or a carrier bag. All this gear is going to do some tough work, so it needs to be tough gear, not plastic and flimsy.

## So, is that us ready?

We're going to be out all day and we'll need to take lunch.

I have lived on cheese sandwiches for about twenty-five years, and I'm getting a tiny bit intolerant of bread, so I take flapjacks for lunch, followed by chocolate covered bars and an apple.

I've lost count of the number of glass flasks I've broken on the hill, so I've gone over to steel. Heavy but worth it sometimes.

I like a hot drink. It used to be coffee, but that filled me up and the milk curdled, so I went on to tea, and the milk turned to butter. So I had black tea, weak enough that it wasn't acidic, and I gradually cut out the sugar, too. I found it was the feel of the warm drink and the liquid that were the best of the tea, and as it was so weak, I decided to cut my trouble and now just take hot water. The flask doesn't go brown, and I can use the water for other things like first aid if I have to. We could drink the stream water, and in summer I usually just take a water bottle and fill it up while I'm out. Cairngorms streams are generally perfectly good to drink.

What else is in my sack? Map, compass, GPS and spare batteries, first aid kit, I'm not going to bother with a torch, but I would from August to April. Mobile phone, fully charged (it's got a good clock on it), camera, sit mat. It's a good job I've got a decent-sized sack, but the trouble with huge sacks with lots of zips and straps is they weigh heavy before you put anything in! I might take binoculars, spare specs and sunshades. Whew! And that's just a day's kit.

# What about the children?

In case you are wanting to bring young people on the hill, we had better have a think about them, because they introduce a lot of additional considerations. If children are coming on the hill, I like them to get a good experience and enjoy it. It inspires them for the rest of their lives, but if they don't enjoy their day, it can put them off and make "the outdoors" a big, scary place they want nothing more to do with, so let's do it right.

You are probably the parent(s) of the children you are thinking of taking, but that doesn't mean you can't be cruel to them by ignorance. If they are someone else's children, you need to be really careful about keeping in touch with the parents, a lesson I learned the hard way recently. Though the children were mid-teenage and strong walkers, we were delayed by our adventures and didn't keep adequate contact with their parents. There was quite a fall-out afterwards, but the worst experience was not for the children, it was for the parents who waited and wondered what we were up to.

It is impossible to generalise for all children. Lots of people can say they climbed Cairn Gorm aged four, or in a backpack aged two, or even before they were born. It seems to be a matter of pride, which reflects more on the determination of the parents than any long-standing prowess on the part of the child.

*Small people on the summit of Cairn Gorm, aged 1, 3 and 5*

*Family and dog*

The pre-natal ascents are interesting if only to demonstrate the strength and hardiness of their mothers, and should never be undertaken under duress or against advice. It might be romantic to be known as the babe born on the mountain, but it won't be at the time.

Once they have their new baby, many parents want to get back to going over mountains as soon as possible. This might lead to taking it in turn to be out or looking after the little one. There are some brilliant baby carriers that can make a little mountain activity possible at ideal times.

Small babies prefer to be on the front, but this is quite a strain on the person carrying. It seems to represent progress when you can put the child in a backpack, and the older children usually enjoy this until they get too heavy. For all of our three children their first or second word was "backpack".

A short walk in dry conditions on one of the paths on Cairn Gorm should be no problem carrying a child. The real issues start when the expedition is longer than the gap between feeds, or nappy changes. There is nothing worse than the nagging cries of a hungry baby or the smell and potential infection of one that needs cleaning and changing.

The practicalities are almost insuperable, and this is a real barrier to taking them out, even on good days. Even if the feeding and changing could be solved, what about the turns in the weather we regularly experience? We can take them in our stride, little ones can't.

One New Year I met a man with a little boy in a backpack returning down the Northern Corries Path. He had another mile to go, and the boy was tall enough to peep round the man's head. As they drew closer, I could see the grim look on the man's face and that the bairn was wearing only a woolly bonnet on his head. It was windy and trying to snow.

Nearer they came and I could see that the boy's face appeared to have snow stuck to it, though the skin was bright pink. They passed so quickly, I didn't have time to do more than raise my eyebrows in sympathy with both. Here was an adventurous walk quite well planned, but overtaken by cold, windy weather, and the man was trying to make amends as quickly as possible.

I had a radio on me. Should I radio back to base, unasked, for someone to meet these two and assist in re-warming the child? Hypothermia was a real possibility. I stalled and was distracted by a second child-carrying person coming down the path, this time with a baby in a front-pack. She just looked resigned to having to get back as quickly as she could, and said nothing. So neither did I.

Small bodies radiate heat more quickly and have fewer defences and less resilience to the cold. Getting children cold is a real life-threatener. There doesn't need to be any trauma or crisis. When conditions get cold, the children need to be considered all the time. When they are active, they keep warm better, but in a backpack, they just get cold.

Rangers lead lots of guided walks at Cairn Gorm, and set a lower age limit on them, but regularly leave it to the parents to decide whether to over-ride it. Some young people are so determined to keep up, and so interested in the unfamiliar terrain, that they astonish everyone and make it up to the summit of Cairn Gorm from the Ptarmigan building and back.

To be fair, this is only a short walk, and is not an all-day ramble. As well as having fewer defences against the cold, children have much less stamina than even a moderately unfit adult. Their energy comes in short spurts, which can see them run off ahead and then demand to be carried.

They do not have the experience to spread out their effort over the whole day. Even if they did – and young adults are like this too – they don't know how much energy they will need and how to use it sparingly. I have often been overtaken near the start of a walk by a superfast family party, to catch them at their next stop for a breather, and eventually leave them behind.

Nevertheless, children will need regular rest stops, when having something interesting for them to look at or think about adds to the fun of the climb. Story telling is great for this. So are flowering plants. They will be interested to see wildlife, but often don't have the powers of concentration to pick out a distant herd of deer or a large bird above the skyline, though they learn quickly. As I will explain later, cairn building is not a great idea.

Children, and other people, too, like to know "How much longer is this going to take?", and it is always a good idea to have a clear plan for a route and then achievable steps on the way that will act as milestones to be looked forward to, and, when passed, looked back upon with satisfaction.

*Strolling down Coire Cas*

In the absence of other incentives, there's always chocolate....

Some children will enjoy the responsibility of their own rucksack, but most won't want to carry much. Up to a certain age – which may be in their teens – taking children on the hill is to accept that the adults will have to carry most of the gear and food.

Some people even extend this to their female partner later on, but I would advise against this dependency carrying on indefinitely. What will happen if the partner that is not used to carrying a load is obliged to carry it because of an emergency? Generally the load is split between members of the party, with the adult males generally accepting more than the females, unless the latter are very strong and determined.

Kitting children out is an expensive process. Upgrades and resizing are never-ending. Boots make children feel important, and there is usually a fine trade in hand-me-downs. I would still prefer to see children in good trainers with a thick sole than thin wellies or school pumps. It's amazing how many parents think these are adequate for even quite long mountain walks. They give virtually no support and risk foot injury and blisters.

## Now can we go?

We've got the kit, are we all fit? How would you know? If you're feeling under the weather, it's probably not a good idea. See how you get on and be ready to

*Strolling down Coire Cas (2)*

turn back. If you have any medical condition, you had better let me know, and we can discuss it in private before we set out. Toilet stop? Might as well go before we leave; there are no loos out there!

We should let someone know where we are going and when we expect to be back. Then they can decide what to do if we're late. The Rangers have the luxury of good comms, but we can't rely on them everywhere. The batteries could go down, there may be malfunction, and if I was on my own, I might be incapacitated and not able to call for help, so there's no absolute fail-proof system.

I know that seemed to be an immense rigmarole just to go out for a summer walk, but if you have already collected the gear, it's one of those things that, with experience, it's easier done than said.

## Now at last, we can set out. But where shall we go?

# 4 | On the Northern Corries Path

We're going to take the path known as the Northern Corries path. This gives a good low-gradient introduction to the hill, but nevertheless climbs steadily, and eventually you could reach the summit of Britain's second highest mountain, Ben Macdui (1309m, 4296ft) if you stick with it.

Needless to say, in that space, you will pass through many different areas, several different habitat zones, and climate zones, and you may even be overtaken by a complete change of weather. So it's really difficult to say that this is all the same path. There is no official public numbering scheme for paths like there is for roads, though, if there were one, I would be happy for the whole length of this path to Ben Macdui to be classed as the same path.

## You could reach the summit of Britain's second highest mountain if you stick with it

The Northern Corries path came about when the high level car park at Coire Cas was built.

Before that, climbers and walkers made their way up by Lurcher's Gully, or the ridge next to Lurcher's Gully, or followed one of the streams coming out of the Northern Corries, depending on where they were heading. The most popular route was probably the one past the great boulder, Clach Bharraig, and on up An t-Aonach, heading for the summit of Cairn Gorm. Ben Macdui was quite a bit further away, and probably climbed more often from Derry in those days.

How those climbers reached the foot of these ridges was generally through the forest from Glenmore, and the new road and car park must have opened up the prospect of great time-savings, especially if they could pay the modest bus fare or parking charges which were levied in the early years of the road's existence.

Once out from the car park, the new path they trampled soon cut through the heather and straight into deep peat. Although peat is not quite as abundant in the Cairngorms as further West, it is still extensive. This peat is the upper edge of a blanket of the stuff, mantling the lower-angle gradients of the lowest reaches of Fiacaill a' Choire Chais.

Peat hardly needs introduction to British hillwalkers. It is almost ubiquitous, the preserved remains of sphagnum moss, a deep brown substance unlike soil, with little internal structure and no strength.

# Bare peat is really awful stuff to walk on

I did my early training in the Peak District, (the 'Peat District') where the peat has the good manners to mantle the high plateaux, giving the walker time to clean boots in puddles and streams on the way down. In Scotland, the high tops are generally too extreme and sloping, and the peat accumulates thickest in the glens, meaning that the walker may well fall in a particularly deep patch just before returning to the car.

As we cross the last stream in the ski area, there is an ancient stump on the left. This is obviously the remains of a tree of major proportions, with a trunk of at least a metre diameter. When could such a giant have lived at this altitude? We passed the last living trees of this size some 300 metres lower, down the ski road, yet this example appears to have arrived here and mouldered away quite naturally.

This is just one remnant of the higher forest that prevailed at this altitude in the warmer conditions that followed the ending of the last Ice Age. From 8,000 to 4,500 years ago mean temperatures were up to 2.5 Celsius higher than now, and all the habitats were located at higher altitudes on the hill. The Highlands' peat bogs are littered with the trunks and stumps of the larger trees that grew at this altitude, visible when the peat has recently been eroded, as here.

After this warm period came a cooler, wet period, more like the present, which favoured the growth of moss, which in turn impeded drainage and gradually changed forest soils into waterlogged ones, favouring more moss and drowning the tree roots. The associated rise in the acidity of the soils made it possible for the timber to be completely preserved, as if pickled in the bog, and this is what we are seeing now,

Some disturbance, perhaps associated with the development of the path, has exposed the timbers, and the stump can continue with the natural decompositional process. It is a bit humbling to think that it is more than 4000 years old, though.

As you probably gathered, bare peat is really awful stuff to walk on. It is slippery and wet, dirty, harbours holes where underground water courses run, and to make matters worse, it stains your clothes and rots the stitching in your boots! So everyone tries to avoid walking on it, and they walk on the remaining vegetation nearby. Then that becomes eroded away to expose more bare peat, and then the next bit, and so on, until the path, which was taking a similar number of walkers as today's path, is ten metres wide.

As this path traverses a gentle slope, walkers found a higher terrace to use, and then another higher one. The slope helped the different braids of the path to drain slightly, but standing water was as likely to lie on the fifth level as on the lowest level. The Northern Corries path turned, over the years, into an eight-lane highway. It was one of several really messy paths onto the Cairngorms, but probably the most famous.

Some walkers, seeing the way the path repulsed the attempts of ill-equipped walkers to gain access to the hills this way, termed it a "granny-stopper", perhaps reflecting a little satisfaction in its existence.

In later years, while trying to explain the concept of a granny-stopper without offending anyone (or perhaps aware of grannies who had not been stopped by this stretch), the Cairngorm Visitor Management Plan termed it a "slipper stopper", meaning that slippers were not going to make it along this path.

By the time of the Visitor Management Plan, the granny stopper was no more in any case. Apart from the unfairness of such a feature, it represented a major loss of natural habitat and a disincentive to recreation in the area. To this

I would add that the granny-stopper in question was one of many examples of poor-quality land management that spoke of how little regard was held for the quality of the place.

## Fixing the Paths

Repairs to this path started with a Job Creation team in the 1970s, and works were advised and quickly improved by Bob Aitken's pioneering work on mountain paths for the Countryside Commission for Scotland.

There were some serious professional misgivings about this work. Removing the granny stopper would give thousands of people easy access into what was known to be prime mountain landscape and wildlife habitat. I'll go into designations later on, but for now, just leave it that the Nature Conservancy Council, the Government's nature conservation agency of the day was not as positive about the work as their successors are. The path workers had to create a path using no drainage, an impossible task, as it turned out.

Bob Aitken soon recommended adopting the old Victorian path-builders' methods, basing each path solidly on crushed rock, topped with more finely graded aggregate, or gravel. A major consideration was to prevent water running across or along the gravel and thus washing it away. For this, a system of drainage was essential, keeping the water which was draining from up-slope off the path with a side drain until it could continue alongside no longer and guiding it across in a cross-drain. For sloping sections of path, water draining down the path surface was guided off using a water bar.

Where the gradient was steeper, such as at the start of the Northern Corries Path, the repairs copied the pitched-construction which the Victorian estates had used to help ponies walk up the hills and carry back down the carcase of the day's stag. The construction had the stones laid into the slope like the courses of a drystone dyke, almost like books on a shelf, so the ponies stepped on the ends, equivalent to the spines of the books. The upper surface mirrored the ground slope, with the occasional stone set proud to aid friction for the hooves.

This pony pitching became a standard technique and was popular with workers, who could lay about a metre a day, and sometimes continued it up onto flat sections, where the aggregate construction would have been feasible and preferable.

*Pony pitching at the start of the Northern Corries Path*

In the first few metres of the Northern Corries Path we can spot the standard basic features: pitching, side drains, cross-drains and water bars. There are also a couple of bridges over piped ditches (culverts), which is a technique that favours wheeled vehicles, but is more difficult to maintain.

The style of pitching in common use has changed completely as time has gone on, and you might notice this as you progress along the path. Pitched construction is now built more like step risers,

and steep sections now have what's called boulder pitching. This uses boulders like steps or stepping stones, but only when the path is steep enough to need them and people are willing to walk on them.

We are very proud of the constructed paths at Cairngorm, and appreciative of the years of hard work by the construction teams that built them. Often they coped with rain, high wind and near-freezing conditions, sometimes all at the same time, and sometimes they could not work without midge net protection. Occasionally the work had to be called off because of heavy snow.

They walked daily up to their worksite, perhaps an hour's walk carrying tools, laboured hard and long and then walked back at the end of the day. Few jobs in the modern world can compare to the physical demands on the mountain path builder.

The first works that take place might be what we called pre-emptive drainage, which just means getting the water off the path to stabilise it before it gets any worse. Then the work can begin to create a broad flat trench to line the path and fill it with hard core and gravel, or alternatively pitched stone. This material could sometimes be found on the site, by a laborious process of hand-digging pits in promising places and mining out the material. As the pits were back-filled with the useless stuff that could not be used, they became called borrow pits, although exchange pits would have been a more accurate term.

Frequently, the additional material was brought in bags slung under a helicopter. The source of the material might be nearby, or in the ski area – which was scoured several times – or from a delivery made by a quarry vehicle to the car park. The helicopter delivery days were watched with some concern for the weather, and were often postponed due to low cloud or high wind. The pilots do not like flying over anywhere there might be people, such as paths, and the contractors would hold walkers back from the drop zone while when the helicopter was nearby.

A big job might need a hundred bags, 90 tonnes, which can take a whole day of back-and-forth flying, and constant noise for other users. The bags would not all contain the same type of material – some may be stone, some may be surfacing – so it has to be carefully directed to make sure it is in the correct place.

So now, instead of watching our feet every step of the way, we can enjoy looking around at what this path can show us.

## Plants are our summer-time companions

On the peat, the heather is quite thick, but as we climb gently onto drier ground, it has to share the space with a variety of other plants. If you have not had to tell the difference between plants before, and find 'green things' all a bit of a blur, this is a good place to start.

The variety is less than in your average woodland or garden, and here the plants have a very clear link with what's going on in the ground, they can show you good ways to walk that will be easier for you. They even hold the ground together. Later on we will turn up some really amazing plants: plants that developed before flowers were seen, a wild azalea, related to the big bushes in the garden, but less than a centimetre high, a flat juniper and the world's smallest willow with only its leaves showing. So hang in there. The plants are part of the wildlife, and make any day on the hill richer.

Heather. Everyone knows heather, don't they? Or do they? Like peat, it's ubiquitous. The Speyside Heather Centre had over 300 varieties of heather on display. And they are not all derived from the common ling.

The best time to see ling flowering is August and September.

White heather is surprisingly abundant here. I once walked across the area down to the right of this path and came across no fewer than a dozen clumps of genuine wild white heather in the space of about half an hour. It made no difference – my luck never improved. In fact, my photos were all out of focus.

There are two other heathers which are very common and widespread, and

*Three heathers: Ling (above), cross-leaved heath (top right) and bell heather (below right).*

to appreciate the difference, and how they sometimes grow together, you can play the game of putting your thumb and forefinger round a sprig of all three at once.

Ling is another name for the common one, and it has the tiny leaves all seemingly squashed against the stem, and its flowers are open and tiny.

The other two both flower earlier than ling and their flowers are shaped like cow bells. So much so that the darker purple one is called bell heather. The lighter one has its leaves arranged in pairs down the stem, but each pair is at right angles to the last pair, forming a criss-cross pattern, so it gets called cross-leaved heath, and it prefers wetter places. And, yes, you get colour variants in all three, with white bell heather and creamy cross-leaved heath, as well as the white heather.

Because heather turns up everywhere, it has a strong cultural significance, nowhere better demonstrated than at the Highland Folk Museum in Newtonmore. There they have heather thatch, heather rope, heather bedding, heather pot scrubbers, and that's before you get on to consumables like heather honey and the legendary heather ale.

We will eventually climb so high that the heather gets left behind. The highest in Britain is at 1100m, and these mountains go on for over 100m above that. So the notion of heather covered hills is a romantic idea that doesn't apply to the summits. Who knows, though, with climate change, we might be back into the realms of heather right over the tops again?

There are only a few plants that I would describe as pretty flowers on the hills, and two grow right by the path here. The best time for seeing them is July and August.

The first is heath spotted orchid. This is usually pink with delicate magenta detail on the petals, but, like the heather, you can get completely white ones. The leaves are a bit of a give-away, even before they come into flower. For some reason, they have a few dark spots on them.

Like most of our orchids, a new plant will spend years building a pair of underground bulbs, when the only evidence of the species is these spotted leaves, then after all that time a ten-centimetre stem will grow with this amazingly intricate flower head, a cluster of really delicately-designed flowers on top to attract pollinating insects and produce microscopic seed.

I met a French family along here once, and the little girl was carrying a big bunch of the flower heads. They can't have known the damage they were doing, nor how short a time the blooms would survive before browning.

The other "pretty" plant is another tall stalk and group of blooms, but this time it's yellow. I really like the name asphodel, and why we can't leave it at that, I don't know, but someone has decided that it's to be called bog asphodel, and that rather spoils the effect.

It grows on the edges of blanket bogs, but it also spreads out thickly on the hillsides to cover perhaps a square metre or so with tightly packed plants that can be mistaken superficially for grass. Not in autumn, though.

This is one of the few plants on the hill that put on a good display in autumn. The chlorophyll breaks down from green into an amazing pinky-orange that can be seen from the opposite hillside.

There's another surprise, too, because, unlike almost everything else, these plants don't lie down when they are dead. Not straight away. The dried skeletons of the dead plants can stand for a year or more, even through the snows of winter, and dot the heath when the next year's blooms are up and blooming.

One more plant, then I promise we'll get a move on.

It's one we've seen already, but this time it's on the way back, and it's bringing about a significant change in the habitat and might even bring back wildlife that's become extinct in this country. I'm talking about the little Scots pines that are everywhere in the heath above and below the path. Not in the blanket bog, you'll notice. It's still too wet for them. But everywhere else, in singles, mostly very widely spaced, and none more than a couple of metres high.

When you look at these plants, try to work out the direction of the prevailing wind. It's not difficult, is it? The ones that have branches coming out of the stem on the West side have had them whipped round to the East and bent permanently into a flag on the downwind side. Most have very few on the windy side at all. The brown needles have been frosted last winter, and haven't had time to fall out yet. And the stems almost all slope away from the wind. A lot of them seem to be growing along the ground, with just a single stem providing a bit of height.

# Bent permanently into a flag

When you realise that each tree grows at its upper tip and sends out a whorl of new shoots each year, you can soon work out a way of estimating the age of the trees. Try counting down from the top. Count one year for each gap between the whorls of branches. There won't be many older than twenty years, and even the tallest are hardly taller than I am.

When I first started coming here, I don't recall there being any little trees, and they have gradually been invading, the seed blown in from the Glenmore forest to the north. As this hillside is so popular with walkers, any deer that might have eaten the seedlings have been scared off, and the seedlings have survived. Now with much lower deer numbers, seedlings are spreading onto many hillsides around Glenmore, and we are witnessing the tree-line rising in a process recent enough for us to notice.

If you look over to the hills to the right of Loch Morlich, the seed rain has been particularly rich on Meall a' Bhuachaille, and the lower elevation and better ground conditions there have produced a cohort of young trees over six metres tall. I don't think our trees will get as tall as that. If they did, they would be blown over. That might not kill them, they will grow along the ground. We could be seeing the return of a genuine mountain scrub here on the Northern slopes of Cairn Gorm.

Scrub is a rather derogatory term for any vegetation. I prefer the Australian 'bush', but mountain scrub, whatever it's called, is a natural component of Northern mountain forests. It makes a bit of a mockery of the notion of a tree 'line', as if the trees march up to a certain contour then stop.

You can sometimes come across trees at extreme altitudes, such as in Coire an Lochain and even on the Head Wall of Coire Cas, in excess of 1000m. This mountain scrub might one day attract back some of the native wildlife that we lost when it became too insignificant to support such species.

The bluethroat, a colourful thrush, only now appears in Britain as a migrant, but occupies mountain scrub habitat in its breeding range in Scandinavia. With a bit more birch in the mix, the bluethroat could be able to recolonise the Cairngorms. That would be a real headline event, but behind the headline, there is bound to be a myriad of insects, spiders, lichens and fungi that might also return. It's certainly worth thinking about.

After six hundred metres along the Northern Corries path there is a junction, where a path leads off left, gradually gaining height on us and heading for Coire an t-Sneachda.

This will have to wait for another day. We are going straight ahead across the hillside on the Northern Corries path, the way most people go in the summer. It's a good broad path, it has almost enough room for two people to walk side by side and chat.

# Aliens

These boulders beside the path are nearly all granite, but there are some stripy ones as well. These are aliens. Well, perhaps that's a bit dramatic. They are erratics. Still no wiser? They have had a ride on a glacier.

All the solid geology here is granite, so you would expect only granite to appear at the surface. When anything else appears, it must have been carried there somehow. Until we in Britain caught on to the idea of glaciers, we were ready to accept that the Biblical Flood had put them there, but there was no such problem for our European neighbours. They still had glaciers, and they could see that they moved, though very slowly. The only force that could move some of these rocks across the surface is ice.

So, where did these aliens come from? The nearest outcrop of schist, which

*Spotty rock*

*Stripy rock*

is what they are, is down in Rothiemurchus. This begs the question how did any force, glacier or otherwise, bring them up the hill, against gravity? The actual climb is something of the order of 300 metres. To explain this we have to have a mental picture of what was happening when the glaciers were here.

The build up and flow of ice in Scotland was not uniform. A huge dome of ice, perhaps 2000 metres high stood above Rannoch Moor and extended in a ridge to the North and South. On the West side of the ridge, ice flowed freely to the West, carving not only the deep narrow grooves we now recognise as glens, but continuing out to what is now sea in immense basins in the sea bed. Further West still, the ice floated on the sea, overrunning the Western Isles and even reaching Rockall.

To the east, things were more complicated. Precipitation was lower in the shadow of the ice ridge, the ground sloped less steeply and there are valleys running in a different orientation, especially the Great Glen and the Spey, which drew much of the ice in a more Northerly direction. There was also a significant ice dome over the Cairngorms, which also served at times to deflect the main ice around these more eastern mountains. Further complication arrived across the sea basin from Norway, when Scottish and Scandinavian ice met in an almighty traffic jam that caused the Easterly flow of Scottish ice to stagnate for long periods.

There were many times, then, when the glacier moving North eastwards down the Spey was very much bigger than anything else in the vicinity, and when it emerged from the relative confines between the Cairngorms and the Monadhliath, it spread into Glenmore and up towards the Northern side of the Cairngorms. At the time, the Cairngorms may have had only small glaciers; there may even have been extensive bare ground. The upshot was that these stripy schist stones were picked up and bundled along by the Spey ice and dragged up the hill to here.

# An almighty traffic jam

If you have a difficulty with the idea of ice travelling uphill against gravity, remember that it is a slightly flexible solid, like plastic. The glaciers that have come and gone from the world are pushed along from behind by the weight of ice following. It would be a small hill to climb to here for a glacier that had its origins at 2000 metres, some 50km to the West.

## Stopping grannies again

Shortly along from the junction of the Sneachda path there is the beginning of a view of the crags on the skyline at the head of the corrie. When I started here in 1997 there were two posts here known as the Turning Posts, because people were supposed to turn round and go back at this point, as the granny-stopper no longer had any effect. The notion might have worked on whatever planet the person who dreamed it up thought they were on, but no-one I asked had a clue what the posts were for, and I managed to get rid of them a few years later.

I actually had a complaint about this from a member of the Rescue Team, who said that in really bad conditions of blizzard and deep lying snow, it was good to come across these posts when descending from Coire an t-Sneachda, because it confirmed their position.

Most people that get this far want to continue at least as far as the next stream, which we can see ahead, so it is pointless trying to induce them to turn round in the middle of nowhere.

The stream is the Allt Coire an t-Sneachda, the stream of the corrie of the snows. It is a delightful splashy burn, now crossed by stepping stones. A couple of rowan trees overlook the crossing, one of which has had a hard time in the past from the deer, and is growing over the water and away from the rock which protected it a little from its tormentors. It looks quite healthy now.

The stepping stones have taken over as the granny-stopper, and there's no ecological reason for making it easier to cross the stream here, so those timid folk who fear falling and wetting more than missing out on an adventure turn back here and we carry on.

It was very slow work repairing the path, and it wasn't until about 1986 that the repairs reached this stream, about a mile from the car park. On the far bank

there is another slope of peat, and the path workers moved massive boulders to create stepping stones across it. Most walkers either didn't recognise the stones as part of the path, or deliberately stayed off them, so this was never a successful strategy. In 1996, another attempt was made on this section, which involved digging right down through the peat to stones four feet below the surface, building up the stonework and constructing the classic pony-pitched path we walk on nowadays. The massive boulders ended up in the stream as the stepping stones. I have never seen them submerged by running water, but in winter they are sometimes lost under the snow.

## Steady progress in the middle section

A little further, a second path diverges to the left. This would take you to Coire an Lochain, the second of the rugged Northern Corries. We will have a good view of this corrie from our straight-ahead path, so we will not take it today. Our path continues for another two kilometres to the next stream. On the way we will climb nearly 200 metres, though the steepest bits are short, and most of the path feels quite easily-angled.

After the first climb, we might take another look at the plants. Already the heather is thinning out, sharing space with a couple of grass-like plants, and there is more bare ground, too. The grass-like plants are mostly sedges. There are bright green tussocks of deer-grass, with the little brown flowers right at the tip of the stem. This is another distinctive plant in autumn, as it turns the hillsides brown in places where it is abundant. The other grass-like plant is common sedge. It has quite a big black flower at the top of the stem, and slightly hairy leaves drooping to the ground all round.

Several berry-bearing plants grow on the heath, too, and get a chance to spread out a bit when the heather isn't so dense. You might have noticed some already, but I should introduce them properly.

Most familiar is the blaeberry. Bilberry if you come from England, or blueberry if you are buying cultivated ones from America. *Vaccinium myrtillus*, if you need to be precise. The leaves and stems are green, but some of the fruit pigment leaks into their cell structure and give them an attractive pinkishness, which becomes browner as autumn comes on and the leaves fall. The birds love the fruit, and leave tell-tale indigo spots on the rocks where they perch after feeding on them. There are hardly ever enough to be worth you collecting here, you would be much better to go into the woods, where they grow much more profusely.

The blaeberry has a close relative with the unfortunate name *uliginosum*, making it look like the ugly sister, but the name means bog-living. I prefer to call this Northern blaeberry, and look for the more blue-green leaves edged with a dark line. It takes a warm summer to bring these to fruit, but they taste even better than their relatives, though much less prolific.

Two more berry plants are cowberry and bearberry. Cowberry is not common on the hill, as they grow better in the forest, but the bearberry are unsung heroes. From a single plant, a bearberry can gradually spread and cover a bare patch a square metre in extent, holding the ground together and preventing it washing away. It's an important food species for the netted mountain moth, which is quite rare, and there is still fruit left in the autumn for the birds. You can try it if you like; I find it too bitter.

Cowberry leaves and bearberry leaves are almost indistinguishable from

*Blaeberry*

*Bear-berry*

above. Turn them over and cowberry leaves have a faint pock-marking. Bear berry leaves are net-veined. You might catch a bear in a net, and maybe even catch cow-pox? Far-fetched, maybe, but it's a way of remembering the difference.

One more berry, and this is quite different. It looks a bit like a shiny green heather and has black

berries only of interest to the birds. It is crowberry, and it climbs much higher than heather, being one of the few plants to accompany us all the way to the top.

I was on the hill one day with my elder son, who was suffering from slight toothache. He convinced himself that the crowberry took away the pain of the toothache. He may have stumbled on something, but I don't want to have to try it.

*Cowberry*

What's that bird? It's a little brown job. Well – that's what a birdwatcher would call it. It flew up from the heath with the most insipid "tsweet", but then took off on a song flight up to about ten metres. The song is pretty insignificant too, but the return to earth, parachuting on stiffly-held wings, is a pleasure to behold.

*Crowberry*

We're crossing the territory of a meadow pipit, and he's telling us about it. Dowdy and brown he might be, a cluster of brown flecks at his throat, but he's a real mountaineer. And a beachcomber, and a cow-herd, an insect-eater. These birds are everywhere, except towns and woods, one of the most successful bird species, and completely modest with it. The winters here are too hard for them, so they go down to lower ground, perhaps even the coast, but their return in the spring is a sure sign of things moving on.

## Diverted by a mystery

Now because we're curious and could do with a short rest, I'm going to take a brief diversion off the path to show you something that started as a mystery. Just ten metres up to the left, on the north end of a gently rounded hill is a shallow pit which has been hastily dug and the stones thrown out in all directions. See, they are still sitting on top of the plants, although the plants are pretty dead now. Some are quite big stones, some several metres from the pit.

There are two deeper parts of the depression, only 15 cm or so, separated by a boulder that looks as though it has been dislodged but not displaced. It's still pretty bare, but the vegetation is creeping back in and in a few years it'll just be another odd dip on the moor.

# A shallow pit has been hastily dug and the stones thrown out in all directions

When I first saw this in 2002 the pit wasn't the first thing I noticed, it was a cairn made by someone on the vague summit of the hill, 30 metres distant. They had used some of the stones that had been dislodged at a similar pit. I followed a very distinct crack in the vegetation, a wiggling line connecting the pits and running on beyond to the shallow hollow where the ground is damp, but there is not enough surface water for a stream.

Another hundred metres down this hollow, I later found another oddity, and you can still see it, a boulder in the boulder field down there has been turned over. This is not something that any person could have done, the boulders weigh several tons each, and they are very stable in their hollow. This had been done with tremendous force.

Thinking about all these things happening in the same area made me dismiss one or two theories. Not one of our path contractors looking for stone (too untidy), nor crystal hunters (no quartz), nor animal (too big), nor fire. I had to come to the conclusion that this was a lightning strike, and I was witnessing two stroke sites, possibly opposite ends of the same cloud-to-ground contact, with the line of passage seared out, stones cast aside in confusion and, at each end, truly massive power turning or dislodging some really heavy boulders.

There were quite a few electrical storms in 2001. While my son Duncan was sailing on Loch Morlich one strike hit a tree in the forest. Another zapped all the phones and computers at work. My office at the time was in a metal box, a temporary structure. In the area which gets the fewest electrical storms in Britain, 2001 was quite exceptional.

By the time I found this in 2002, it had had time to settle down a bit, and some kind person had built the cairn out of the debris. I have returned the stones whence they came, as far as possible, and no doubt I will have a bit of a rant about cairns later on.

We don't usually think much about lightning strikes in this part of the world, but there are a few trees in the Strath that show the distinctive spiral-scar, and the lightning must strike somewhere.

The fact that the lightning struck so low down and so close to the path makes everyone that comes to look at this spot feel rather uncomfortable. I have only run off the hill once, from Bynack Mor, when an electrical storm approached from the North-east. There is no shelter on these hills whatever, and any person is bound to be the highest point for miles around.

I well remember watching the Ben Macdui plateau on a day when a big storm was playing out to the South, in 2003, and being amazed at the casual attitude of people – families with children included – continuing stolidly with their route up to Ben Macdui, a sure invitation for more than a tingle.

Now let's return to the Northern Corries path for most of the rest of the way.

After a few yards, we come to a big rock slab. Here I can point out where the path used to go before it was realigned in 2002. The direction taken by a path is nearly always chosen first by the users. Until 1999, everyone seemed to be quite happy heading for the foot of the ridge that divides Coire an Lochain from Lurcher's Gully. This was despite some pretty dreadful boggy ground, and a crossing of the Allt Coire an Lochain at a wide and difficult point. Then there was quite a long plod up the ridge on an eroding path.

In summer 1999, which was very wet, a lot of people had spotted and followed an apparently more direct route onto the ridge and it had turned into a trampled avenue on the wet moor up to seven metres wide in places. A wet summer can see more erosion on the paths than a dry one in which there are more people using them. The big problem with this short cut was the incredibly wet bouldery hillside it crossed.

So when we were coming to repair this path I had to choose which of these two routes to follow. If I chose the lower, original, one, people would still take the short cut. If I chose the new route, no-one would use the old route but the big problem with the new route was the bog it crossed.

This is a formidable bog by any measure. It is on a moderate slope, with a considerable flow of water across it all year. In common with many wet places, the surface will not support a walker's weight, and it would be possible to go in over your knees. So everyone trying to cross the bog would use the few dry bits and the scatter of boulders as a way across, almost like following a route through a maze.

In winter it freezes solid, producing a wide, long sloping sheet of blue water-ice, which can develop into quite a dome in a long winter. In these conditions, only crampons will allow the walker to cross, and most people would avoid. Our

*Which way to go?*

path creation couldn't be allowed to interfere with the hydrology of the bog, and the ice would still reform in the winter, perhaps as another slipper-stopper.

As you can see now, we took the bog route, and our path builders created an ingenious series of stepping stones and gravel sections through it, with hardly any disturbance to the bog. The old route up the foot of the ridge has started to heal over, and even the ridge itself is recovering. Compare the picture of the junction with the previous one of cross-drains on this path (p.22). They show the same patch of hillside, but the big eroded path to the right has disappeared in 15 years.

At last we reach the second stream, Allt Coire an Lochain, the stream flowing out of Coire an Lochain. It is crossed by a single massive stone which the doubters assured me would not last one winter because it sits across the direction of flow of the river. It's still there.

Now for the approach to the ridge. We have a choice here, and we could take a rough path off to the left. This climbs the side of the ridge very gently at first, crossing steep ground and finally popping up steeply onto the plateau next to the headwaters of this stream. It's not one for people who suffer from vertigo, nor when the snow lies deep and prone to avalanche, so we'll take the main path and continue up onto the ridge.

There's another plant you might not recognise here. It's small like all the others, sometimes straggling through and round other vegetation, and it's a lighter shade of green than most of the other plants. The upright stem is covered with tiny pointed leaves, like a miniature monkey-puzzle stem, but these are as soft as ferns, and evolved at about the same time.

When the club-mosses first flourished, there were no flowers, and they grew to massive dimensions and contributed in places to our coal deposits. These ones here are the descendants of those ancient plants, making no fuss, just getting on with life, four species competing successfully with all these more modern flowering plants.

The first to stand out are the little clumps called fir club-moss. Then the two straggling ones are stag's horn club-moss, which has strange two-pronged fruiting bodies, and interrupted club-moss, which has a section of the stem where the leaves are smaller, and it looks as though it's

*Fir club-moss*

been pinched and constricted. Lastly, there is a club-moss which looks as though it's been woven from a thinner thread, the alpine club-moss, and this can be rather straggling as well. And you can collect the set on a short walk on Cairn Gorm!

*Interrupted club-moss*

*Alpine club-moss*

If anyone has an older name for the ridge we shall be climbing, I would be very pleased to hear it. The Ordnance Survey marked it Miadan Creag an Leth-Choin, but a miadan is a meadow, and there are two excellent meadow-like areas nearby, this can be treated as a slight mistake on their part.

The Rangers at Cairngorm have resorted to the ugly compound name

*Stag's horn club-moss*

taken from the adjacent hollows: the Lochain-Lurcher's Ridge. Such a compound has a precedent in the Tearlaich-Dubh Gap in Skye, but hardly anyone uses our neologism. Some try to name it Fiacaill Coire an Lochain, but this is truly absurd, as a Fiacaill is a tooth, and anything milder than this would be difficult to imagine.

By the time we've puffed through this argument, we're halfway up the ridge anyway.

There are several places where the path gets suddenly a bit steeper, then settles back again, as if we are going up a series of very large-scale steps. This is ground creep on a massive scale, lubricated by permanent ice (permafrost) under the ground. There isn't any permanent ice here any more, but when this was periglacial – when there were glaciers nearby – and possibly even in the Little Ice Age in the Middle Ages, permafrost was widespread and effective in creating this landscape.

In winter, of course, the whole slope was frozen solid, but in the summer, the surface layers would melt and slip on the frozen layer underneath. Where the material is mostly smallish, all the top layers would move together, perhaps causing some rumpling as though a carpet were on a slope. With bigger stones and boulders in the mix, though, the slipping layer would sometimes get held up behind them. Sometimes the melting would be deep enough to make even the larger boulders move a bit, but they always provided more friction and gradually gathered at the front of terraces or lobes, behind which finer material gathered, so producing the classic stepped formation here.

# A series of very large-scale steps

If you look over to the right from the ridge, you gaze across the most celebrated of these slopes in the country, the Lurcher's Gully side of Creag an Leth-choin. Here terraces in the finer, smoother material to the left give way in the centre of the slope to lobes of coarse boulders, with heather growing on the well-drained steps behind them. It's almost reminiscent of the effect you get when running water down a glass. The centre of the stream has less friction and travels faster, leaving the edges to be held back by the dry areas of glass. Here the centre of the boulder creep has the greatest weight of material behind it and the edges of the lobes, having been held back perhaps by a particularly immovable rock, have fallen behind in the slow progress down the slope and now experience all the friction from being at the sides.

Notwithstanding the current search for contemporary permafrost in the ground, there is generally agreed to be none in Britain, and these features are not active, they are all fossilised and would only become active again if the climate got much colder. They are still visible because nothing else has happened to the ground since they were forming. In particular, no glacier has over-ridden them, or they would certainly have been wiped away. These terraces and lobes are surprisingly common over the highlands, and I recently walked down a staircase of about fifty terraces that had developed on a particularly suitable slope.

*Terraces of upper Lurcher's Gully*

# Which way to go?

At last we reach the top of the slope. The path — several paths — carry on, of course, but become less obvious. Which way to go?

I often have to tell people that there are no signs, waymarks or painted rocks telling people which way to go. Even at the start of this trail, there is no destination marker. People point to this path and say "Where does that path go?", and the answer is that it has not one but many destinations. The alternative could be that we advertise a really exciting, super-sounding destination and everyone crowds along the path, causing congestion and disturbance, only to find that the named destination is a very long way off, the route is difficult, the weather changeable and their preparation, equipment and ability to use it inadequate for the task.

There is a good chance that they arrive at the end of the constructed section of path and the cloud level at the same time. If they looked at a map they might be able to make the connection onto the next part of the path, but the rules have changed, and their approach needs to change likewise.

When I was preparing for path works on the Lochan-Lurcher's ridge, I walked up the path with my son Duncan and the contractor and we marked the positions of the drains we planned with a painted number on the rocks. Later on, having finished the site meeting, the contractor returned and Duncan and I continued on towards Ben Macdui. We stopped at some point on the way and were caught up by a large American walker and his son who wanted to know what had happened to the painted numbers, why they had stopped, and how they could be expected to find the way to Ben Macdui without them.

I'm tempted to say they were navigating with a road map of Scotland, but that would be to conflate more than one story. I'm sorry to say they had no map at all, and as the day was clear and set fair, it was easy to point out the objective in the distance and assure them that the path, although stony, did continue to the top, but they would find no more numbers.

Things change so fundamentally at the point we reach the plateau, I think that's a new story, and we'll pick that one up later.

# 5. Exploring Cairn Gorm's Northern Corries

One remarkable feature of the Northern Cairngorms is the array of corries which ranges across the view, from Coire Laogh Beag in the North East to Coire an Lochain, and then after the gap of the Lairig Ghru, an even greater suite on Braeriach, from Coire Beanaidh right round to Coire Odhar above Loch Einich.

So, reasonable question:

## "What's a corrie?"

*Coire an t-Sneachda*

Corrie is the English version of a Gaelic word, written coire, but pronounced the same way. It's a hollow place, perhaps originally a deep pan or kettle. In more familiar modern usage the word refers to a medium-scale glacial feature on the upper slopes of high mountains. The Welsh have cwms, the English coves, the French cirques. They are all the same thing.

A corrie is generally the birthplace of a glacier at some stage in its history. Before that, it may have been a gentle valley-head cut by a small stream into which winter snow was prone to accumulate. There is an example of one of these next to Coire Beanaidh on Braeriach, which just goes to show that the story of corrie development is a really complex one, as highly-developed corries exist close to one where the development has stalled.

*"How much snow do you get?"* is a question visitors often ask.

Many visitors, especially Americans, have an idea that the snowiness of a place is measured in the depth of a straight fall. They find it difficult to come to terms with the situation in a windy place like Scotland that snow depth can be extremely variable across the mountains. While the windward side of the hill is being blasted by winter gales, the snow is being stripped from there and re-deposited on the lee side, often reaching tens of metres depth at the same time as other areas are showing bare.

In most snowy mountain ranges, the heads of high valleys accumulate enormous depths of snow blown from the windy side of the hill. It is possible for the wind to blow it all back again, but not likely when a prevailing wind blows for weeks on end. The effect on a simple valley head is that the snow begins to start a process of movement and erosion which tends to become intensified and self-perpetuating.

The first snow slips down the slope under its own weight, accumulating at any slightly flatter section through friction. The slow melt through the summer provides a constant source of water for the streams which remain active (and eroding) for longer than streams in valleys without a big snow build-up.

The slippage of the snow is considerably easier on any patches of long-lived snow which has lasted from the previous winter. This is usually compact and icy, and within a few years of accumulation, the snow crystal structure progresses through névé and firn into glacier ice, each stage providing more effective slip-planes for the snow above.

The critical stage is when the glacier ice itself has built up sufficient mass to start slipping on the ground below. There needs to be an enormous build up for the initial friction to be overcome, and, especially in the early years, any slippage will be very intermittent, and only on steeper slopes.

It is common for mountain valleys to be steepest at the top, where water is actively wearing into the mountain side. The valley is typically less steep further down as some of the rock and gravel dislodged comes to a rest and the stream is slightly less active.

As the combined weight of the compressed ice slips most readily on the steepest ground, the first and the most slippage is near the head of the valley. The moving ice will then come to the less steep ground and grind to a halt. More will eventually slip down behind and increase the pressure on the ice that went before, building up a thick and very dense mass.

Eventually the pressure from behind will be sufficient to move the front ice over the lower-gradient ground and a glacier starts to slide down the valley, always pushed from behind.

The process I have described involves enormous pressures and weights, especially where the ice from the steep ground is catching up and being amalgamated with the slower ice in the flatter ground.

All the time it is moving, the glacier is bulldozing everything before it: plants, soil, rocks, lumps of bedrock and anything else that gets in the way. Where it is under more extreme pressure, even the bedrock can be ground away, scraped along and removed, and the first hollows are formed by the glacier, as it grinds down in the high-pressure areas and rides up over rock that has resisted it in lower-pressure areas.

A pattern of slippage is often established which sees the ice describe a course similar to the shape of an italic capital *J*, and around the lower part of that course, the ice could be described as rotating almost as if around an imaginary axle. This rotational slippage is what gives corries their distinctive shape.

The rock remaining on the lowest edge of the hollow it forms is called a lip. Some of the corries in the Cairngorms have a lip, but many more don't. They have been bulldozed away by moving ice under great pressure. The rotational slippage is effective in producing a steep back-wall, a less steep slope and a flattish floor to the corries. These features are so characteristic of glacial corries, that we will use them to accept or reject the theory of glacial origin for the ones along the North face of Cairn Gorm.

You might find trying to imagine what the hills were like before the glaciers came along quite a challenge, but hang in there – at a later part of my story you won't have to imagine it, you can see it for yourself. For now, we're going to take a bumpy ride through some big features made by the glaciers, starting in the North.

## Coire Laogh Beag, the little calf corrie

The actual hollow of Coire Laogh Beag is so small it is difficult to imagine it being ground out by a full-sized glacier, and it could be one of the early-stage hollows I described before.

You will hardly ever meet another person round Coire Laogh Beag, but there are still plenty of paths. These were probably made by deer. Red deer used to be more common on these hills, and, having the run of the forest as well, they produced some fine specimens. When they were excluded from the forest by fences, the deer became exclusively confined to the inhospitable and less nutritious grazings of the hills.

Further woe was to befall them, because their numbers rose unchecked and starvation loomed every winter. In an attempt to reduce the nuisance they caused, and for their own welfare, national policy recognised the need to reduce deer numbers by culling. Local efforts by land owners Forestry Commission Scotland and Royal Society for the Protection of Birds (RSPB) have had the effect of reducing the local herd down to almost sustainable levels. These deer paths are still used, but almost always at night, and by very small numbers compared with former times.

Out to the North of the hollow of Coire Laogh Beag is a collection of scrappy pines high on the mountainside. This is all that is left of a high-level forestry plot planted as an experiment in the 1950s by the Forestry Commission to see if commercial species would grow this high up. By the time the land was transferred back to their ownership in 1999 it was decided that the experiment had ended.

*Plantation near Coire Laogh Beag*

The conclusion was yes, they do grow, but the growth rate was far too slow for it to be a commercial prospect. So the non-native trees were felled to waste and removed by helicopter, leaving a few unsatisfactory clumps of Scots Pine.

These pines, surrounded by brash which is slowly naturalising and rotting, was home to a singing willow warbler last time I was there, which is an unusually high location for this woodland species.

Numerous seedlings of the pines, spruces and larches that used to stand here can be found on the moor, and at times a small team of people comes over this part of the hill to weed out non-natives. This is likely to continue for the best part of a century before the weeds are all gone.

From here, let's traverse round the hillside to a much more impressive hollow.

# Coire Laogh Mor, the big calf corrie.

This is much more like it: A steep back wall, becoming gradually less steep as it falls to the sloping floor of the corrie, but it has no lip to hold back a lochan. Streams just gush out and down into the lower corrie to become the Allt Ban, which means the fair stream.

On one of my early visits I found a complicated system of pipes and plastic boxes arranged to catch some of the stream water in Coire Laogh Mor. This, I guessed, was a University fieldwork installation, not notified to the landowner, and now clearly derelict and defunct. I tried to find out who knew about it over

the Internet, but I drew a blank. I even tried a round-robin message to as many University geography and hydrology departments I could think of, to no avail.

So, the next spring, when the snow was sufficiently depleted for me to expect to find the stuff, I resolved to return and rip the whole lot out. I puffed my way up to the corrie and there it was, gone. Someone had beaten me to it! Any pleasure I might have felt at this remarkable piece of clearing up was tempered, however, by finding another, smaller installation in Coire Laogh Beag, which I had not known about. I ripped it out anyway.

No-one has ever been in touch to complain. I think this illustrates an ignorant and cavalier attitude prevalent in some academic departments, one of which I witnessed personally, from the other angle.

As a geography undergraduate in 1975, I was part of an enormous group of students under the guidance of my University Department. We descended on part of the Peak District National Park with spades to dig soil pits. A Ranger came along to inquire who we were and whether we had sought permission to dig up the land. The member of staff with us confirmed that we had not sought such permission, and thought it would be all right.

I am sure I was not the only one to be deeply embarrassed by the affair, but the passage of time seems to have had little influence on the behaviour of those wishing to dig, bore, scrape and sample the earth wherever they please, and believe it will be all right to do so.

I have come across rows of pins, flags, metal spikes in the ground, a floating device on a loch, uncovered pits and even a senior academic with a power drill. The people responsible all thought it would be all right, and had not cared to ask for permission, nor even found out who might be interested.

Almost by default, now, any junk – because that's what it is – Rangers find on the hill they remove. I'll come on to the biggest most scandalous academic junk later, and have to admit, my organisation was responsible for permitting it.

Coire Laogh Mor is steep and snowy in winter, a good place for experiencing steep snow and practising techniques to deal with it. The most frequent visitors are from Glenmore Lodge, the National Outdoor Training Centre, which lies at the foot of the slope, in the forest.

I wonder if anyone else has explored the moderately steep ice which forms before the snow accumulates on the back wall. The whole edifice can look like a fancy wedding cake. I enjoy winter climbing, which I will revisit later. Here the trick is to find a sporting line with a continuous run of ice. It forms on steps and levels in the stream all the way up and can be quite a delight. I expect someone else has already been here. These are well-known and accessible mountains, and just because no-one has claimed or named a route, is no guarantee they haven't been there.

The shape of Coire Laogh Mor produces a spring snow patch which curls far down on the right wall, looking to me, from a distance, like a lizard – a salamander, I've decided – with a long tail. It's very distinctive in spring, and the tail gradually shortens and the head becomes detached as the body thins away.

There are no crags in Coire Laogh Mor, but a single enormous boulder the size of a caravan, on which some boulder climbing can give good sport on a summer evening.

Traversing round to the next corrie brings us across a stray fence line, an offshoot from the ski area, and an intrusion into the wild scene. This gathers a good drift of snow in most winters and has become known as the "Lui Mor fences". It makes a good tour for skiers, but at the time of writing, return to the main ski area is necessarily by bus from the Ciste car park, as the uplift in Coire na Ciste is no longer functioning.

The ridge running up the side of Coire na Ciste makes a good walking approach to Cairn Gorm from the Ciste car park, and a good descent if you prefer to avoid Coire Cas.

On this ridge has been found a very rare lichen *alectoria ochreoleuca,* also known as Arctic Sulphur Tresses. This was for long the main location in Britain, the other plant being located on the slope overlooking the Day Lodge on the next ridge. It is also found in a very strange circumpolar distribution in Japan and the Urals, and that's it.

# A very rare lichen

It is very rare and has legal protection, and the academic who found it was very concerned that it had no designated protection and was in a ski area. He proposed netted cages over the plants to ensure its survival, whereas before it had to put up with the combined effects of hare and deer grazing and walkers and skiers trampling it, not to mention getting blasted clear of snow every winter. That it survived at all was a wonder but he believed there was no way it could be sure of surviving without our intervention.

Some years later we did have cause to erect small cages over small plants and found that snow covered and filled the cages preferentially, interrupting the natural conditions significantly. The lichens would probably not have survived our ministrations, so I'm glad we did the easiest thing – nothing.

Better still, Andy Amphlett, Ecologist at the time with RSPB discovered thousands of the plants on the Meall a' Bhuachaille range, and we can all relax that the ski area is not the only repository of this mysterious lichen.

At a couple of places on the Ciste ridge the smooth skyline is interrupted by a sudden notch. These must have been made by a strong flow of water across the ridge from the Ciste side into Coire Laogh Mor, but the water would have to have been supported on ice on the Ciste side of the notch for this to happen.

Skyline notches are actually quite common across ridges in the Northern Corries. There are several of these channels on the next ridge from Coire Cas to Coire na Ciste; and the Chalamain Gap and Eag a' Chait between the Lairig Ghru and Glenmore are well-known meltwater channels.

## Coire na Ciste, the kist corrie

Ciste is Gaelic for box, which comes into Scots as kist. This usually refers to a storing-box, or possibly a coffin.

There is the persistent legend of a girl named Mearad (Mairead, rhymes with pirate) who died in the snows, her resting place being called Ciste Mhearad, which is just East of Coire na Ciste. Coire na Ciste itself could on the one hand

be the corrie leading to where she died, or, just as likely, the corrie up which those bringing back her body carried her coffin, and by which route she made her last journey. Better still, it could be both, each meaning reinforcing the other.

However, kist could just as easily be a reference to a long narrow box in which grain or corn is kept, or, in this case, snow, because that is the shape it presents to the north.

Coire na Ciste is a strange corrie that doesn't fit in to the general pattern on Cairn Gorm, and raises more questions than almost anywhere else.

The notches I mentioned on the Ciste ridge complicate the explanation of how Coire na Ciste evolved. For sure the corrie was occupied by ice, but the profile of Coire na Ciste is completely different from the others.

Instead of having a classic long-profile of a steep headwall, becoming less steep to a lip and then a moderate hillside below, Coire na Ciste has a very mild dish-shaped upper valley which then suddenly narrows into a vee-shaped gully before settling down to a gently-inclined but deeply enclosed valley, narrowing again towards the point where it emerges from the high mountains and merges with the lower hillside. To add further complication, a massive blocky crag lies on the east side of the lower slopes, completely contrasting with everything else.

I haven't got a full explanation for all this, but I'll try anyway. The headwaters gather in such a shallow valley, I believe it resembles more the plateau valleys rather than the steep Northern Corries; what I term 'old ground', and I'll explain that later. The vee-shaped gully is a classic water-cut channel. The lower valley is much broader, and may have been enlarged considerably by a moving stream of ice, but this ice has not produced a classic bowl-shaped corrie in Coire na Ciste, and may not even have come from there. I think it possible that it might even have come over from Coire Cas.

The big cliff has some of the characteristics of a tor. I'll introduce tors later, but for now, I'd say it's unusual to find a tor down in a valley, but not unique. As the slope is gradually being eroded back, the region of massive granite has resisted the process and become progressively more exposed. It has few clefts dividing it into smaller blocks. Some parts seem to have been forced away from the main mass slightly, as if a glacier has pressed on it but not removed it completely.

In the biggest rift, on the upstream side, a cave has formed which has been added to in recent times to provide a little shelter. At the back of the cave, the massive blocks of the cliff can be seen to have been riven away from the main hillside blocks, creating a rare through-route (a tunnel).

This is the only through route in granite I know, and the forces that created it must have been enormous, but insufficient to pull the whole lot down into a heap of boulders.

# A rare through-route

The narrows at the foot of the corrie provide another mystery, and appear to show evidence of a great deal of loose material: Sands and gravels. If the glacier was continuing through here and on down the slope, this narrowing of the valley would have been bulldozed away. The fact that it survived as a moraine at the mouth of the corrie almost suggests that the glacier coming down the valley was held up here, and was prevented from travelling any further.

I'm proposing another traffic jam of ice, limiting the capacity of this downhill-moving glacier to erode and causing it to drop some of its load in this low-speed area. What could have done this? Only another, even larger glacier, and there certainly was one to hand. I have already invoked the Strathspey ice as the bringer of aliens, and I think this must be the main suspect here, too.

When you arrive at Coire na Ciste, the first thing that comes to your attention is the car park. It's enormous, with a capacity of about 600 cars, and stretches down the slope parallel to the access road, visible quite clearly from Tullochgrue in Rothiemurchus. There have been discussions about landscaping the car park, and this may be done naturally for us as trees on the lower slope grow taller and shield it from view.

Lots of visitors arrive here first, thrown off the Hill Road at the bend at the entrance to the car park. They just trundle on ahead, not noticing at first that they have in fact turned off. Most of them find their way back onto the intended route, but some don't.

The second group of features to assail the eye at the time of writing is the derelict development at the foot of the former chairlift. Nearby are rows and rows of double chairlift seats, replaced in 1998, funded by public money, but hardly used more than a dozen times since.

We found an Emperor Moth cocoon in one of them once. It appeared that the animal had hidden away in a hole which something had eaten in the rubber of the seat. Neither this chairlift nor the one which continued from it to the top of the steep slope will carry passengers again, as they are due for demolition as I write.

All this is very disappointing to those who would benefit from using the lifts. The alternative – catching a shuttle bus back round to Coire Cas – doesn't suit everyone, especially when there are long queues and foul weather. A campaign group is urging "Save the Ciste", and have advanced interesting plans which await someone with money to commit to them, and the necessary planning permissions, but until then, the best we can hope for is a general tidy-up of the dereliction.

A sewage treatment plant is concealed nearby behind some successful tree planting – which also attracts willow warblers – and there is an area where our outside squad park anything that needs to be parked for a while, such as a snow blower, or rolls of fence.

Behind the chairlift unit a set of broad steps leads down to a useful bridge.

The river here, Allt na Ciste, is quite deep and swift and would be difficult to cross without the bridge. Beyond this the path divides: Left towards the experimental plantation, straight on to climb steeply up the ridge which divides Ciste and Laogh, and right to follow the burn up Coire na Ciste.

I would never suggest walking all the way up Coire na Ciste as a way of gaining the high ground, as you would spend a lot of time and energy struggling through peat and heather in the lower reaches and the interminable slopes of the Ciste Gully higher up.

Much better would be to climb by the Ciste ridge on the left above the crags, pass the two water-cut notches and join the broad slope above. Once, in winter, I did this and came out through the top of the cloud. Just at the same point the reindeer herd was happy to be resting. It was a magical day from then on.

The path by the stream takes you to a special place beside the crag and through-route I've already mentioned. In the 1980s the Royal Botanic Garden was looking for a mountain plot to give some of their plants a more rarefied atmosphere than they could provide in Edinburgh and obtained permission to set one up in Coire na Ciste near the crag.

The plot is not a public facility, and does not exhibit the high standards of presentation the RBG likes to maintain, but it is a fascinating place, nevertheless. It is surrounded by a deer fence and access is by locked gate. There are three terraces on the hillside in which are planted exotic plants from mountains around the world. They were chosen because they would not set seed or spread out onto the hillside.

Many of them exhibit cushion growth-forms producing small flowers, sometimes on long stalks, which disappear for the winter. Unlike many popular Alpines, though, these are not flowering under the snow, and take their time to develop even at these relatively low altitudes.

Another group of plants here is the acyphillas, which I called bayonet plants before knew the real name, because of the shape of the leaves. The biggest one occasionally produces a flowering and

*Bayonet plant, or acyphilla*

fruiting stalk nearly two metres long. Every part of the plant is so covered with long needle-sharp spikes it is impossible to touch it safely. Although this plant catches the attention, there are actually several smaller species of acyphilla here, all similarly armed to the teeth, presumably to deal with a very hostile environment.

*Ciste Gully and walkway to West Wall chairlift and tow*

Coire na Ciste is a favourite place for skiers to go. To look down the throat of the Ciste Gully, the steep West Wall on your left and the imaginatively-named Number 1 gully and Number 2 gully coming in on your right, you know you are going to have to ski well to enjoy the run in style. I once counted 100 turns I put in to skiing down Ciste Gully. A good skier would do it in a dozen or fewer.

Above all this are the shallower slopes where so many have learned to ski, and above even the highest uplift on Cairn Gorm is the quiet hollow of the Marquis' Well, the highest spring water on the mountain. We will come by this way when we climb to the top.

The ridges between the corries are bigger towards the West, and are given names on the Ordnance Survey maps. The one between Coire na Ciste and Coire Cas is named An t-Aonach, which means The Ridge.

Although hardly anyone goes here, An t-Aonach is a delight, with good walking, interesting windswept vegetation, glacial meltwater channels and a

*Clach Bharraig*

superb view of Glenmore. These quiet places are the best for mountain hares.

On the lower part of An t-Aonach, overlooking the ski road is Clach Bharraig, a granite boulder of some 200 tons which has been edged into place, like everything else, on a glacier. When the road builders surveyed the route they seem to have had cold feet about this monster and twice resorted to explosives to attempt to dislodge it or reduce it to smithereens. The blast marks can still be seen on the back of the boulder, having had no more effect than to slice off a couple of flakes. The boulder sits quietly, massive, unmoved.

Close by the rock passes the old route to Cairn Gorm, the path by which Victorian picnic parties, Great Depression flat-caps, wartime trainees, Post-War photographers and growing numbers of recreational skiers walked – *walked!* – up from Glenmore.

The path was worn into a broad bouldery highway down which the rain washed, causing an erosion scar on the hillside easily visible from Aviemore. Skiers, aiming for Coire Cas, split off to the right on one of many braids, or carried their skis right up high, depending on where they were aiming.

Next west from An t-Aonach is Coire Cas, which means the steep corrie. It's a rather odd name, as it's not as steep as any of the other large corries.

## Coire Cas. The steep corrie

Coire Cas is probably the most famous of all the Northern Corries, of interest to skiers and walkers; location of the high-level car park that gives them all easy access to the high Cairngorms.

It's a broad, open corrie, with a gravelly head wall and a steady slope below, steepening slightly into a secondary bowl and then becoming narrower, bouldery on one side and eventually losing its identity as it reaches the mountain front.

Hundreds of people climb Cairn Gorm now from the car park, perhaps 8,000 per year. The two most popular routes diverge just above the main

buildings at the car park, opposite the old red telephone box. I will come back to the Windy Ridge path when we climb Cairn Gorm later.

The obvious route up the coire is the broad vehicle track. It goes up by the railway, back and forth on the zig-zags and on up towards the headwall. Then, when all sense of direction has been dispersed, the road takes a sharp left-hand, flattens out on the Traverse and finally rises in a last mind-numbing climb to the Ptarmigan building.

This was my first experience of climbing Cairn Gorm from Coire Cas, and it is for many other people, too. It is not what I would consider a good route onto the hill. If you are too early in the year, you will find the road holds more snow than everywhere else, packed down for the skiing, and soft and yielding to walk on.

*Lower Coire Cas*

There are several saving features, though. You follow the highest interpretive trail in the country. It's known as the Coire Cas Mountain Trail. You don't need to buy a map or guidebook to do this; the trail is explained on small panels which fold out of upright posts on the side of the track, a little like railway signals.

The walk passes close below the boulderfield in lower Coire Cas. I have shown pictures of this to friends who think they know Cairn Gorm, and they are amazed that such a wild and unruly part of the hill is located right next to some of the most popular ski runs.

All along here, the mountain railway passes close by. You might get a toot and a wave from the driver. It would be churlish to ignore them.

# A wild and unruly part of the hill

The track takes a turn uphill, which might come as a bit of a shock after the first easy section. This is the Kassbohrer Brae, which leads up to the Kassbohrer garage.

Kassbohrer? It's a strange name for a vehicle manufacturer, but that's what it is. The piste grooming machines are great terrain-huggers, they go anywhere if the snow is right. They pack down the snow and make it perfect for snowsports, producing the "corduroy" effect with the tiller on the tail of the machine. There are usually one or two vehicles parked next to the garage.

The hillside above the garage has a small pine plantation, another experimental plot which has produced some specimens of doubtful value. This patch is popular with ring ouzel in summer. These birds are also called mountain blackbirds, because that's what they look like, except that their throat shows a patch of white like a bib or a chain of office.

Ring ouzel has become scarce across Britain as agriculture has been improved and plantation forestry has taken over their upland habitat. At Cairngorm, up to three pairs may be found in Coire Cas, a remarkable concentration. Another pair might be busy at Coire na Ciste and another in one of the other corries. I suspect that they like the grassy patches in Coire Cas, because they can forage for invertebrates just like blackbirds. There is a fair bit of grass here because the seed was used to repair the effects of development and disturbance.

The Cairngorm ring ouzel has even been known to nest in the stonework of the building at the middle station, which is very unusual for this shy species. The other advantage they gain here is the fine song perches on the ski equipment. The best ever was on the crane towers used to build the railway, giving the male bird a commanding view, and podium, from which to declaim his territorial rights with his distinctive three-note whistle.

Beyond the garage, the walk up Coire Cas passes in quick succession the site of the White Lady, then the Shieling, the middle station and the Coire Cas tow, all of which we will come back to. Our walk up the corrie now follows the zig-zag track back and forth across a steep area. A more pleasant path joins from the right. The walk up on this other path is worth exploring, so we will have a look at this one before we go any further.

The reason we didn't come this way to start with was because it is not as obvious as the main track. From the car park, we have to cross the burn just by the Day Lodge and go uphill across a peaty slope on a well-built path.

Visitors often point out cloudberry, which is a good sign of the recovery of the vegetation on peaty ground. It can grow spontaneously from small cuttings

*cloudberry in flower*

and damaged pieces. It puts out big flat leaves, unlike anything else in the vicinity. Small white flowers appear and the fruit is held upright on a short stalk. And what a fruit! Superficially it's like a raspberry, without prickles, and the fruit is not ripe until it has passed beyond the raspberry colour to a delicate gold. There are parts of Norway where it is illegal to pick these fruit until it is fully ripe, as they are so highly prized.

Dippers occasionally forage in the stream, even in deep snow conditions, but they seemed to be declining, visiting only infrequently, until a pair enchanted us by nesting near the Day Lodge and feeing a chick by the burn in 2015.

The heath is dominated by heather and then by deer-grass. A few small pines struggle to show up here and there. Cairngorm Mountain has recognised the value of this mountain scrub, and encouraged planting of additional native trees all the way up here, taking part in the Action for Mountain Woods campaign. The trees are planted small, mostly by local school children, with species including native pine and juniper, birch, dwarf birch, rowan and willow. It will be a long time before they make much impact on the landscape and habitat.

The path splits, the lower branch passing a memorial bench and joining the main track on the far side of the railway.

The upper branch continues uphill to pass the drive unit of the Shieling tow. The original Shieling tow was bought second-hand from a failing ski development at Mar Lodge. Situated at between 400 and 500 metres above sea level on a South-facing slope, the original location had its problems, so the machinery came here in 1963 and was converted to a low-speed button tow in a trench. It was well-used by beginners.

The tow which replaced it in 2015 can be raised and lowered according to the snow depth, and more easily groomed. The smoothing-out of the bulldozed trench was more difficult than expected, and caused some controversy at the time. You can judge for yourself whether there is any lasting scar on the landscape.

The trail up Coire Cas crosses the track of the Car Park tow before snaking a completely new route up to another bridge.

Just beyond the bridge, a rectangular concrete foundation marks the original site of Jean's Hut. This was erected as an advance base and a memorial to skier Jean Smith by enthusiasts who carried the materials up from Glenmore, in the days before the building of the road.

Their enterprise and energy were commendable, but by the time I came to work here, their efforts were worse than in vain. Quite apart from what happened after the hut had been moved to Coire an Lochain, and through lack of care, it had become a decrepit hovel, the original site in Coire Cas was a mess, too.

Bare peat was exposed by the trampling of countless boots for a large area around, and in that peat was all the detritus that users had not wanted to take away with them: Bottles, tin cans, and even a pair of boots. It had survived as a mess until the Rangers, spurred by Heather Morning, got round to making a big effort to tidy it up.

Now the bare peat has largely been covered with a mulch of heather and moss cuttings, in an operation also carried out by schoolchildren led by the Rangers in 2014, and the scene can return to a more natural one.

An interesting installation in 2016 was a device which weighs the snow as it falls, and calculates its water content. Although it is still on trial, it is possible this will become a permanent fixture in the effort to warn of possible flooding downstream, especially in Aviemore.

A short distance uphill is a flat area where a former ski tow, the Fiacaill

Tow started. There was an operator's hut here which I had hoped to use as an interpretive facility, but it was blown down, rebuilt and blown down again a few years later in a particularly ferocious gale.

Climbers heading up in winter regularly used to walk up the track of the Fiacaill tow as it offered a direct route towards their goal – the climbs in Coire an t-Sneachda. It was annoying to the ski area operators at the time, but now it doesn't really matter – the tow has been removed – and the climbers go a different way in any case.

After joining the main track in Coire Cas, the walking is pretty unforgiving, all the way up the zig-zags and the sections beyond. One sign even encourages you to "Take A Seat at 3000 Feet", but where the road gets steep again, the Mountain trail turns off it to the right.

Very soon after this, the trail crosses a shallow groove which runs straight down the hill from near the summit of Cairn Gorm. I had this pointed out to me as a debris slide track, where small stones, lubricated by water, may have been prone to flow in intense weather, particularly when the ground underneath was frozen.

The mountain trail crosses the upper part of the Coire Cas tow one last time and reaches 1000 metres above sea level near the return wheel, and turns at last to descend.

# A shallow groove

Here you are very close to the headwall. The steep gravelly slope above is loose and dangerous. A short detour towards the foot of the head wall takes you above all the ski development. Here Coire Cas shows a smooth and peaceful greenness that is in great contrast to the rocky corries further West.

Why did Coire Cas remain so smooth, with a gravelly head wall, when Coire an t-Sneachda and Coire an Lochain are so dramatically craggy? Actually, Coire Cas is not completely smooth, as a small disintegrating crag frames the Headwall to the right of the main slope, but this is trivial in comparison with its neighbours.

The likely reason for this contrast was explained to me by Ness Kirkbride, who worked for Scottish Natural Heritage on earth sciences at the time. The end of the last ice age was not a single event, but a warming of the climate around 12,000 years ago. The destabilising effect this is thought to have had on the sea currents could have brought on a new wave of cold climate. Small mountain glaciers re-formed. In the West, some of these advanced as far as Loch Lomond. The moraines left by these late glaciers suggested the name Loch Lomond Readvance to those first studying them.

This short intense cold period lasted around 2000 years, after which the warmer climate was re-established.

In the Northern Corries of Cairn Gorm, only Coire an t-Sneachda and Coire an Lochain were occupied by these resurgent glaciers. Coire Cas was subject to intense cold, permafrost and wholesale summertime creep of the steep back wall. Any remaining crags were frosted to smithereens, overwhelmed by summer washout, broken down and incorporated into the detritus in the corrie. The only crag partly remaining probably survived because it was more massive and steeper. Even so, the rock that has fallen from it has been transported down the corrie a short distance, possibly sliding on ice and snow.

A ski run has been bulldozed through the toe of this rock field. This also permits the summertime trail to descend gently westward to join the main Fiacaill path for its return.

The return is hinted at by the guide posts leading down the path back towards the car park. I should mention at this point that all these posts and signs have to be put out in the spring and brought in again before they get frozen in for the winter. This is one of the Rangers' jobs. It would be too difficult for people to use these trails in winter unless they were equipped for mountaineering, and in any case, the signs refer to summer conditions, would get in the way of the snowsports and would freeze and weather badly in the winter.

The Fiacaill path is the main route by which walkers approach Fiacaill a'

Choire Chais, the blunt peak at the right hand side of the headwall. The name means the tooth of Coire Cas and is also sometimes applied (in error) to the whole ridge leading up to it.

Fiacaill a' Choire Chais forms the western boundary of Coire Cas, and I have to suppress a smile when I hear geography teachers declaring to their classes that this is a glacial arête. The term brings to mind razor-sharp Alpine ridges between plunging serac-strewn glaciers, not this mild, blunt ridge. Technically they are correct, of course, but there is a much better arête in Coire an t-Sneachda, which we will come to later.

The ridge leading North from Fiacaill a' Choire Chais is blunted partly by the effects of the weathering that has smoothed Coire Cas, but probably also by being overrun by glacier ice. Although there is the remnant of a tor on the ridge, at around 940m, the great granite slabs have clearly been tipped over, making a fascinating place to visit, shelter or hide. Only glacier ice could have done this, possibly during maximum extent of the ice coming out of Coire an t-Sneachda and spilling across the ridge into Coire Cas.

Further down this blunt dividing ridge, a scatter of boulders runs in two distinct lines across the ridge, reminiscent of tide lines on a heathery hillside. These, I believe, were pushed up by ice in Strathspey, and because they survived, this must be one of the last things that was done by the ice here.

Coire Cas is the most heavily developed corrie in Britain, and is a great sadness to so many who see ski development as a scar on the landscape, or a hazard for grouse and ptarmigan. It's time to head out to the contrasting corries further West.

*Coire an t-Sneachda*

# Coire an t-Sneachda, the snow corrie

If Coire Cas is the most developed corrie in Britain, Coire an t-Sneachda can have a claim to be the most popular winter climbing destination. It is very accessible, close to a convenient car park, the routes climbed are of modest length but range in difficulty from easy snow-gullies to hard rock-dominated routes only recently popularised.

Tales emerge of "200 people in the corrie". It is the winter climbing area that has had the most observation of activity. The regularity of accidents here make it a likely place for the Mountain Rescue teams to locate a box of equipment, the only man-made object in the inner corrie. But Coire an t-Sneachda is not only for winter.

You remember, about 600 metres along the Northern Corries path, we noticed a path taking a higher line on the left which I said leads to Coire an t-Sneachda. Many people decide not to take it because it looks rougher than the main path.

The roughness is more apparent than real. The path is a little narrower, and the first few metres are of pitched construction, that is, stones set into the surface a bit like cobbles, not just gravel to walk on. There is no particular need for this type of surface here, but a little psychology is going on.

This is a path with the potential to lead the unwary into danger. The general ease of use and construction of the Northern Corries Path is not unlike a path in a Country Park. It leads directly from the car park to intriguing moorlands where dogs and children might be exercised.

It is difficult to provide support or a filtering system to protect people

*The Sneachda Path junction with the Northern Corries Path*

from the consequences of setting out too rashly. Signs, though provided, are ineffective. Artificial "granny-stoppers" are out!

In designing the upper path as a rough surface, I tried to hint that the lower path, the Northern Corries path, is the easier and therefore preferable. The upper path, which leads more directly into Coire an t-Sneachda and the steep ground around the Goat Track, is less preferable, as it has a surface more suited to boots. It's not altogether successful, but it's worth a try.

Until 1999, you probably wouldn't have noticed the upper path at all as you walked along. It joined the main path at a diffuse eroded area no different from anywhere else along the way. If you had been heading to Coire an t-Sneachda, you would probably have gone on nearly to the Sneachda burn and turned uphill there. There followed an energy-wasting slither through several peat bogs, eventually coming up close by the burn and actually between two channels of the stream on ground which regularly flooded. I thought the path and the stream were fighting, and only the stream could win.

In addition there were some really exciting plants getting trampled and eroded away.

On the way down from the corrie, walkers were successfully finding a higher, drier and shorter line. Perhaps they were trying to avoid the peaty mess they had come up. This upper path still had some pretty unpleasant peaty sections too, and it was a typical boulder-strewn passage down through the heather. There was, in practice, a one-way system in operation. I wanted to repair only one of the paths, but which one?

When I considered the length of bog that was traversed by the two lines, it was obvious that the stream-side one had just as much peat and considerably more drainage problems than the upper path. If the start of the upper path was obliterated and everyone used the stream-side path, would this be effective for both up- and down-hill traffic? I thought not. If instead the lower end of the stream-side path was obliterated, would anyone continue to use it? Only if they had missed the start of the upper path, which by then would be much more obvious.

The scale of the paths was also a factor. The upper path traversed open slopes. The environment of the stream-side path was more intimate, with lots of delightful details and stopping places. People could still walk the stream-side even if the upper path was promoted, but the stream-side path would be more like a country lane, with little traffic and plenty of local detail and interest. The upper path would take the bulk of the traffic, in the same way a motorway relieves the village of the juggernauts. Most people going off to Coire an t-Sneachda weren't wanting the detail of the journey – they just wanted to get there.

The path to Coire an t-Sneachda is so familiar in summer, I could walk it in my sleep. Recently, I was hurrying to reach a casualty, and realised I could not recall one of the stepping stone sections at all, yet, on second thoughts, I had definitely passed it.

The trail starts through the familiar bouldery landscape populated by small regenerating pines that we saw on the Northern Corries path. One granite boulder beside the path has a hollow upper surface, reminiscent of a quern or corn pestle, but it is natural. It was discovered when the path was being rebuilt, and placed hollow-uppermost to hold a small pool of rainwater.

A little further on two enormous boulders below the right hand side of the path could almost offer shelter to someone if they were prepared to crawl in between them. When the path was first rebuilt there was some evidence that the gap between the boulders had been filled with stones and turf as if someone was trying to complete the roof. I still call it a howff, but it's a poor one, roof open and entrance facing South to catch the wind and rain. Much better shelters exist not far away.

As the path climbs to a level section, a huge boulder overlooks it and a good swathe of open countryside in the lower part of the Northern Corries. This was used as a regular observation point by my predecessor, Neil Baxter. He was trying to account for activity in different sectors of the area in view. He regularly reported reindeer and sheep. Nowadays the reindeer's owners encourage their herd to use more remote areas and sheep are never seen. The grazing is so poor, they would need supplemental feeding. I still think of this as Neil's boulder.

# Neil's boulder

Shortly further on, the path dips into the start of a section that was built on peat. At least two members of the original path building teams gave up when they reached this point. Digging black, sticky peat day after day in the rain, and carrying it home on all your clothes and boots is not much fun.

A short series of stepping stones crosses a

spring where, for a moment, the heather gives way to grass and lots of different herbs, flowering plants. There is starry saxifrage here, and if I had the time and patience, I might use a botanical key to make out other saxifrages as well. There is opposite-leaved golden-saxifrage, too, no relative and not even similar.

The next little stream supports a small stripe of grass-dominated vegetation among all the heather. Where these streams can dissolve out a tiny contribution of mineral nutrients from the underlying granite, other plants can compete with heather and provide a little contrast.

Immediately beyond, an old braid leads off right. This might be useful for access to the popular ridge-line on the right, and possibly also Coire an Lochain on the far side of this ridge. Unfortunately, this braid developed on peat and became horrible, wet and wide.

I had ideas that it might be obliterated and re-instated, but found in 2002 that my colleague had instructed path contractors to line it with huge boulders which had been brought in expensively by helicopter. This effectively encouraged more use, and directed walkers to an area where they were unsustainable. It took seven years before I had the opportunity to correct this error of judgement. It will take another decade before the ground recovers.

The main path climbs more steeply for a brief moment, and arrives at the top of a glacial moraine decorated with a crest of boulders, a good point to rest and look at the view back down the way we have come, and on up to the headwall of the corrie.

Shortly further on a huge grey boulder reminds me of a gigantic blue whale, and across the stream there are several big boulders, the biggest of which was introduced to me as the Dinner-time boulder by my instructor on a Nordic ski course.

The next section of the path through a boulder field has been constructed as a causeway of flat-topped rocks. Some people can't see the advantage of these and insist in walking on the lower, softer ground.

An interesting detail is the tideline which appears on boulders denuded of protecting ground or vegetation. The lichens that grow on the rock are so ubiquitous that they become

*Tideline on a boulder: lichen above, granite below*

accepted as the normal surface of the granite. In places where the ground has been worn down, especially on a path, the brighter, bare surface of the stone is exposed. This is possibly whiter than it would be, as burial in this acid ground bleaches the colour out of the feldspar minerals in the granite.

Although the Sneachda path is a helpful companion to climbing into the corrie, the walker may still have to contend with a gale, or torrential rain, lightning, low cloud or any of the normal weather that Cairn Gorm experiences.

There was one summertime visit by a school party led by one of the Seasonal Rangers and me which reached the top of the path easily and looked round. At the other side of the corrie, no more than 200 metres away, the view was completely blotted out by a wall of water, falling as very heavy rain. Unfortunately, it was advancing slowly towards us, and there was nowhere to hide. I advised the children to get ready for it, put on any clothing and hoods, fasten zippers and buttons and stand straight with their arms down by their sides. When it came on it was quite heavy, like being under a shower, rather than impossibly heavy like a waterfall, and we realised that we would be no worse than wet through. After a few moments, the rain didn't relent, and we started walking briskly back down the path, which had turned into a stream.

In winter, of course, things change completely. The path is often lost under drifts of snow, and you might be grateful to those going before who have stamped out a trail and made the route feasible. The first person to do so has a daunting task.

This is one of those places where I can point to an innocuous spot on the slightly sloping moor and say, sadly, "Someone died here", and you might look round and wonder "What was the problem?"

The problem for the two young men I'm thinking of was that, during a day of blizzards and gales that had already sent everyone else home hours previously, they had became overwhelmed by struggling up one snow drift and falling down the next. In an exhausted and famished condition, they sat down to rest and found it easier to remain there than fight on. These unlikely spots are home to tragic tales just as the steep cliffs overlooking them.

By the time we cross the burn on the way to Coire an t-Sneachda we have climbed to the altitude of low-growing vegetation, where only in well-favoured hollows and places beside streams does the plant life show much vigour. In a habitat impoverished by lack of nutrient, these spots harbour a richer and more diverse growth. The clue lies in the soil, of course.

The stream sides have marsh marigold, which extends right up to the corrie.

*Marsh marigold*

I can't pass this flower by without telling you my favourite Gaelic name, which I've only recently discovered. *Brogan each-uisge* means kelpie's shoes. If you thought a kelpie was a cute little water sprite, think again. People really used to believe that these water-monsters in the form of beautiful horses could carry a person off and drown them. Their "shoes" grow by the water as a reminder to youngsters to keep away from the edge.

There is also globe-flower, a buttercup whose flowers stay all curled up and round.

An interesting woolly plant, a little like a thistle is alpine saw-wort, which produces a blue-purple flower, rarely above 4 centimetres high.

If you tried to find these plants in a flower book you might be puzzled that the ones here don't grow as tall or have as many flowering heads as the ones described. Later in the year the goldenrod which pops up here

*Globe flower*          *Alpine saw-wort*

and there can have as few as one flowering head rather than the panicle (loose spike-shaped cluster) it achieves at lower altitudes. This is because of the poor nutrient regime and short flowering season.

A last rise and the path guides us across the middle of a low-gradient gravel slope which, until recently, supported a heath composed almost entirely of moss. The grey racomitrium moss is common on the tops of the mountains, and is the most fragile widespread habitat. It is easily damaged by trampling. The moss here had been transformed by boots into a broad black splodge of peat, widening again as people found their way round it. The path repairs here are light-touch, the path almost merging into the general stony waste. Most people seem to follow it, though, and there is hope for the recovery of the moss heath.

As you approach the big boulders, the path peters out completely. This may well be a temporary situation, because wherever the path stops, the damage starts again, posing the question: "How far up the mountain do we repair before we stop?" If we did not mind having constructed paths everywhere, and money and labour were infinite, we needn't bother with this question, but there are strong financial, practical and ethical reasons for calling a halt at some point, and that point is being reached in some places.

The boulders are magnificent. The first one is located some distance from the others, almost like an entry marker to the corrie. It is often used for shelter by walkers in windy weather, and the ground nearby shows the trampling, and, sometimes litter, that goes with that.

The spread of boulders beyond is the moraine of the last glacier here, the one that re-advanced over the millennium until 10,000 years ago. This most recent readvance freshened up the corrie features, re-ground the headwall and spread the debris in a thick unweathered layer on the floor of the corrie, just as far as the glacier reached. Little gravel came with it, so few of the gaps between the boulders have been filled in, little soil has developed, and the boulders stand as they were left, now weathered and lichenous.

Near the edge of the boulderfield is a particularly high pile of impressive rocks, and a little howff, or shelter, has been constructed underneath one of them. I have made many visits here and found it provides good shelter on only a few occasions. There is not room to lie down in it, and the opening faces South, but it does make a good spot from which to observe the climbers on the cliffs opposite. We can look at them later.

It would be an unusual visit to Coire an t-Sneachda if you didn't come across the real heroes of the mountains. These medium-sized birds live here all year, thrive in the snowy wastes of winter, and are a characteristic part of the wildlife of the mountains.

# The real heroes of the mountains

Ptarmigan are not unique to the Cairngorms, and there are related species all round the Northern hemisphere. An elderly Japanese visitor once told me he had visited every ptarmigan sub-species in its natural habitat, and this was the last on his lifetime's list.

In an ecosystem with little diversity among the vertebrates, the Scottish ptarmigan is a star. They advertise their presence by making a harsh open-mouthed croak which can be heard right across the corrie, and this is how you will probably detect them first. You might hear them in winter, but it is more common during the preparation and course of the breeding season in early summer.

Another remarkable feature of the ptarmigan is its complete change of colour from pure white in winter to a fantastically-detailed mottled plumage in

*Female ptarmigan in summer*

summer, though still retaining some white on their feathered legs and feet. And what distinctive feathers. The main body feathers are double, having two quills, which instantly identifies odd ones that you might find during the moult period.

The birds maintain such control of their body heat and energy that the only place it can leak out is at their eyes and mouth – when they are open.

As another energy-saving tactic, they are often seen to walk slowly along the ground, or to hunch down and rely on their excellent camouflage to avoid having to move at all. In summer plumage, you might even step on a hen bird when she is laying, so well hidden is she.

The reason for all this camouflage is the natural selection of birds that are white in winter and not white in summer. The birds would be concerned about land predators, of which wolves, and now dogs, are the least welcome, but the main concern is eagles.

*Male ptarmigan in winter*

# Savour the incredible presence of this unsurpassed survivor

Fortunately for the ptarmigan of Coire an t-Sneachda, but unfortunately for you, the chances of an eagle coming over this way are very slim. It has now been accepted that the Northern Cairngorms are not prime eagle habitat – it is just too barren, and there is too little prey.

So observe the ptarmigan from a distance. If you come across one nearby and unexpectedly, the best advice is to freeze. You can even make it clear that you are retreating. The bird will fare better if it is not forced to fly when it would prefer to save its energy, and you may have a few moments to savour the incredible presence of this unsurpassed survivor.

*Roseroot*

*Bluebells*

Through the boulder field of Coire an t-Sneachda a winter watercourse struggles between the obstructions, too small to move or wear them away. If you look carefully in summer you can find mountain everlasting, roseroot, milkwort, tormentil and bluebell (campanula), making this quite a garden in August.

The path, too, threads uncertainly between the boulders, drawing ever closer to the steep back slope of the corrie. For a while you would be excused for thinking that two people were standing high on one of the rocky ridges above, until the truth dawns. Those are pinnacles, the fingers of Fingers Ridge. Disappointingly, I don't know of any legend of their creation. This suggests that they were not known or spoken about by the local population in days gone by, or that they were obscured by other rock which has now fallen away. Due to the general lack of story and legend about features like this, though, I would favour the first explanation.

On right and left are two small lochans, unless your visit is at a dry time of year, when only the left-hand one survives. At really wet times, the moraine ridge which divides them can be submerged; you must wade or go round the long way.

This is a good place to stop, though, because continuing on up the narrow path ahead is definitely for the adventurous. It is the Goat Track, fancifully named by Victorian visitors, but innocent of goats then and now. Deer probably formed it, and walkers eroded it. Now it is the all-pervading influence of running water that is ripping the Goat Track up and spreading it down the slope. There has been an attempt to fix it (in the early 1990s), but inspiration, determination and a lot of money will be needed to tidy it up.

# The narrow path ahead is definitely for the adventurous

Occasionally, I considered it, and invariably shelved it. This is an actively eroding slope; the path leads to a difficult area of high ground. It should but it doesn't stop slippers – I have seen trainers used to climb this path. It would be an expensive job to tidy up and in doing so, the path would provide a sense of security on a slope which is prone to be crossed at speed by falling rocks, as the dents in the turf all down this slope testify. Keeping the path work team safe in this environment would be just another nightmare.

The three main rock masses of the headwall of Coire an t-Sneachda stand around the central hollow, separated by rough and craggy slopes. The hollow itself is oriented North-East, but then bends round North-North-West. This is quite unusual in Scottish corries, which mostly spill straight down to the glen from their origin.

On the outside of this bend there is a remarkable feature more easily noticed in descent. A small ridge of gravel and rock lies on the eastern slopes of the corrie, creating a hollow along the side of Fiacaill a' Choire Chais.

The hollow is also unusual, in that walking through it gives a feeling of enclosure not normally experienced in this large-scale landscape.

The ridge is probably a lateral moraine, a ridge of gravel on the outside edge of a glacier. There was an attractive idea that the ridge represented something more complicated. A pro-talus rampart is a pile of stones that is steadily built up by avalanches from a higher slope landing on a persistent snow patch and sliding down to rest some distance from the base of the slope. Although there has been some doubt thrown on this explanation, I still like to call the ridge "the rampart", because it sounds quite dramatic.

The rampart provides a very satisfactory route back towards Coire Cas,

involving only a little rough walking across the rocky slope beyond. When the snow fences were located here, it was the most popular way to and from the corrie, leading to extensive damage to the ground here and in Coire Cas. This use has declined now, as the Sneachda path is so much easier and is so well-graded.

Opposite the rampart, on the other side of Coire an t-Sneachda is the ridge which leads to Fiacaill Coire an t-Sneachda. This is a real glacial arête, the fin of rock left between two adjacent glacier headwalls, sharpened from both sides as the headwalls gradually migrate towards each other. Generally these ridges are rather blunt in the Cairngorms, but this is one of the sharpest. The traverse of this ridge is quite an adventurous route, and one to explore another day.

One last thought about Coire an t-Sneachda might inspire or amuse you. It's a great location for playing an alphorn. According to an elderly visitor who tried out his instrument in this corrie one day the crags reflect the tone of the horn back to the player. He tried in Coire an Lochain the next day, but Coire an t-Sneachda won his vote.

## Coire an Lochain, corrie of the lochs

For many people, Coire an Lochain is a perfect corrie. Dramatic and craggy, it has a beautiful pair of lochans and the classic dimensions of a mountain corrie. I suspect its popularity surpassed all other Cairngorms corries except Coire Cas, for a while, though it is now much quieter than Coire an t-Sneachda. It takes a little longer to reach than its neighbour, but is really worth the extra effort.

Starting along the Northern Corries path, shortly after it crosses the Allt Coire an t-Sneachda on big stepping stones, a narrow path climbs up to the left,

constructed of pitched stone, but soon levelling out to gravel. This is the start of the path to Coire an Lochain which we noticed before.

The corrie was the second location for Jean's Hut, and became a magnet for summer walkers and winter climbers, many of whom stayed the night in the hut. This popularity was reflected in the breadth and erosion of the path to it, which was equal to and possibly greater than the one to Coire an t-Sneachda.

The present path follows a little ridge for a short while. The burn falls noisily to the left, and there is a heathery hollow to the right. The ridge probably represents a pile of gravel dropped by the Allt Coire an t-Sneachda when it was constrained under a glacier – an esker, in other words.

Eskers are very large and continuous in the Spey basin, but these mountain streams were not so large, and had fewer opportunities to drop gravel in their headlong rush down the mountainside.

The path soon drifts off to the hillside on the right and climbs by some beautifully-constructed pony-pitched sections. The path-builder, Colin Delap, assured me it was "The best in the business". He had a rather disquieting habit of working alone, shifting big boulders around and producing a good job. Any path works now require a minimum of two workers together on site.

At a crest, the remains of a braid is visible on the right of the path. This was another case of us choosing for the walker which of two options was to be promoted and which rehabilitated. Grass seed was used to close over the bare ground, but it has been almost entirely replaced by moss, bear-berry and heather.

A little further on, a path leads off left towards the bulky ridge of Fiacaill Coire an t-Sneachda. If you were going this way, you would have a long pull up to the skyline but we will come back to the exciting traverse later.

Our constructed path towards Coire an Lochain climbs gently then falls in a curiously neat and tidy section. An early comment on this path work from a passing climber was that it was a bit like a "garden path", and the name has stuck. The next section, however, is in stark contrast, and gives a taste of what these paths were like before repairs were carried out. The garden path is as far as the work on this path was done before 2002.

Now the climbing path braids (splits and joins) around huge boulders interspersed with heather and bare peat. It climbs to a slight flattening and climbs again to a skyline. It is clear that this spot is quite unlike anything we have crossed to date. The moraines here present steep front faces and broad flattish tops, there are hollows between them drained by hidden rivers, and the ground is much more difficult than on either of the two paths we have already explored.

At last this section passes, and the path fades to faint braids over the heather, sedge and bare ground. A slight rise and we reach a small lochan. Depending on which braid you followed you may have a short and wet paddle to the right across saturated grass to rejoin the main path, or a slightly wet thread of a path past the lochan. If you are with me, we will head for the right-hand braid. Most people seem to miss it and have to paddle.

After this we settle down to a very gentle climb on a naturally-evolved path across lots of stones and boulders towards the corrie. Someone with a taste for seeing cairns marking the route occasionally builds a pile of stones on the way.

In poor visibility, the cairns may help a little, but I don't want to encourage new cairns. We had a bit of a dispute about a cairn on the summit of Cairn Gorm, and I don't want to see any new ones appearing. The surface they are built on becomes shaded and dead, and the holes the stones are pulled from are left as sockets in the gravel which blows away, promoting erosion. Cairns represent a small sign of the intrusion of humans into a wild area. Most people don't need them anyway.

After a little while of very level walking we approach the former site of Jean's Hut. The hut isn't there now, and its arrival and short history here were quite eventful.

When the ski developments arrived, there was no need for Jean's Hut to be in Coire Cas, so a group of skiers and mountaineers

*Jean's Hut in Coire an Lochain*

77

had it transported to Coire an Lochain, where it was reassembled at the spot we have just reached .

With hindsight, this location was a mistake, though it must have seemed perfect at the time. The hut was on level ground, it was easily located in most conditions, and it was beyond the reach of any of the avalanches for which the corrie is notorious. The hut was near enough to the car park to be a useful advanced base for climbers heading for winter climbs. It was for many climbers a standard doss and was often overfull and always under-maintained and under-resourced.

I made a couple of visits to Jean's Hut in the 1970s, and was repulsed by the damp, smelly insanitary structure. My last visit was with Jo Porter, the first Ranger for Cairngorm. He and his successors spent an inordinate amount of time removing rubbish and burying excrement at the Hut. It was no longer an asset to the area nor a fitting memorial to Jean Smith.

The ease of access to Jean's Hut was its downfall. It became a place one could nip out to, expecting shelter and a sleep. Two decades after one fatal accident was brought about by the expectation of shelter in a mountain hut, a similar disaster befell three students. They expected a quick walk out to Jean's Hut, but cut too many corners, and didn't find it, in the dark of a snowstorm. Then – much worse – they didn't find their way back to the car park either and perished in the snow.

There was anguish, of course. Two of them were brothers. A family was cut down at a stroke. There was determination that such a thing would not happen again. Jean's Hut was removed in summer 1986.

The site of Jean's Hut is still visible, but it's a soft grassy place with no more than the ground anchors for the wires that held it down. The other feature of the site is more visible from up on the ridge opposite: A distinct green sward runs from the bothy site down towards the watercourse. I did say insanitary.

Our path into the corrie splinters into the boulderfields soon after the hut site. In snowmelt times the water from the lochans runs through between the boulders in impressive rivers that disappear completely at most times of year, and run underground.

The boulder fields are another remnant of the last glaciation. The last glacier pushed out to here, dropping these boulders. As they too did not fill in with gravel, they were left as you see them, large and angular, lichen covered and infertile.

There is a pleasant surprise for you as you struggle over the boulders past the first little lochan. Gradually the walking becomes easy as the boulders give way to a smooth grass-covered corrie floor. Ahead lies a good-sized stretch of water and beyond is the awesome spectacle of the Great Slab and headwall of Coire an Lochain.

The Great Slab is such a large and distinctive sloping area of granite that you can see it from Aviemore. When the evening sunshine comes round on to it, it glows slightly pink, as it is almost devoid of lichen, or other vegetation, or even a layer of rock debris. This is a classic avalanche slab, the only one of its kind in Britain, though not unique in Europe.

Snow accumulates to a depth of up to four metres in winter, compressing lower layers and often freezing solid to the rock. In a thaw period, though, water trickles down under the snow pack and lubricates the sliding of the whole mass.

Only one person I know has seen it go. The whole surface cracked up like crazy paving and the whole slope thundered off down into the lochan.

From my own observation, what happens then is just as astonishing. The snow mass breaks through the ice with such force that, on occasions, a pressure wave is sent through the lochan which bursts out at the opposite side and continues for another two hundred metres, carrying rocks, loch ice, gravel and turf. An onlooker could be four

*Avalanche debris on the lochan ice below the Great Slab.*

hundred metres horizontally from the site of the avalanche and still not be able to get out of the way in time to avoid the moving debris.

I have not actually seen this happen myself, but I was once present within 24 hours of it taking place, and I could see by the water line on the snow and the size and position of the debris what had happened. I was glad I had missed it at the time, because there was a gale and thick mist, and had the avalanche been coming down at me, I would not have known which way to run until too late.

Later on we will look down on Coire an Lochain from the plateau, and you will see what the long-term effect has been. I mentioned before that there are two lochans here. From above, it is clear they occupy parts of the same oval-shaped hollow, over-deepened by the rotational slipping of the corrie glacier here.

The bouldery and then smooth area between them represents the debris pile from thousands of avalanches, building up so deeply that the loch has been partly filled in. It is this part of the corrie that receives most of the debris from the avalanches, and where fresh granite boulders can still be found in most years.

People like to camp here. It is a wonderful spot, and there can be no danger from avalanches in the summer. For some reason campers bring boulders from near and far to ring their tents, possibly to keep the tent pegs from ripping out in strong winds. If the boulders are not cleared, this kills the grass and makes the place less attractive for subsequent visitors. Litter and worse are regularly squashed under the boulders.

The Rangers decided that as these boulders had clearly been moved from their natural positions, they were fair game for us when we needed rock to use in the construction of nearby paths. We gathered them into a helicopter bag for lifting, but the winter came on and our bag of rocks was frozen in. The weathering of the bag made it unfit for use and, the following year we de-bagged the rock and removed the helicopter sack. These things are quite cumbersome to carry empty, so it was a disappointment to have to bring it back down without having cleared the rock.

Campers then redistributed the rock around the grass and we made a second attempt. The rock that was waiting in the second bag was actually removed from the bag by campers again to put round their tents and had to be bagged up a third time before it could be lifted by helicopter up to the pathworks.

Birdwatchers often come up to Coire an Lochain to see ptarmigan. There are several birdwatching holiday companies in the area, and many of their clients are not as fit as they would like to be, so the well-built path out to the stream that issues from the corrie is a great help for them to gain height and approach ptarmigan territory. From the stepping stones, they follow the gently rising, but rough path towards the corrie, climbing higher and higher across the slope bounding the corrie on the West.

This is a good place for us to look for ptarmigan; this slope is often slightly sheltered from the wind. There are plenty of blaeberry and crowberry food plants here, and the birds can feel quite confident that they can get away quickly without feeling threatened. The path which runs across it is quite narrow and rocky in places. It can be closed by snow until July in some years, and is not a place for those who are nervous on steep side-slopes.

Going back to the stream crossing, this is one of the few places where I can reliably find Scots Asphodel, the most un-flamboyant flowering plant graced with the name Scots, or Scottish. It is a tiny greenish-white group of flowers resembling a grape hyacinth, quarter the size, and with grass-like colour and dimensions to the stalk. It's not an easy one to find! Considering its beautiful name, it's quite a disappointment.

There is plenty of the more showy Bog Asphodel here, too. This is one of the places in autumn to find swathes of wonderful peachy-pink leaves, it's a treat.

*Scots asphodel*

## Lurcher's Gully

Cross one more ridge and the last place in this review of hollows on the north side of Cairn Gorm is Lurcher's Gully.

Before we get there, though, the ridge we cross is familiar as you have already been up here on the approach to the plateau. We'll go this way one day to Ben Macdui, but just now our tour of the hollows is taking us round the contour.

Over the ridge we come onto the realm of periglacial features that we saw as we climbed past them on the ridge path. On the near side of the gully we are walking on gently shelving terraces sloping into the gully, separated by slightly steeper risers, with a few boulders showing. This is what happens when the surface creeps slowly downhill on a frozen layer of permafrost.

*Terraces and meadow at the top of Lurcher's Gully*

Across on the other side of the gully, the slope is steeper and rockier, and the waves have been marked out by rocks which have moved faster and slipped down to the front edge of the terrace, leaving smaller stones and gravel behind on which plants have been able to grow.

The waves are shorter and more lobe-like because in any place where a bigger obstacle stops the flow, this is overtaken by the other material in the wave. The wave continues on with a break in it. There are innumerable places where the waves break on underground obstructions, the overall effect being to create this chain mail effect, likened to necklaces of boulders on the slope.

There are periglacial features in all the corries and on the plateau. They are destroyed if they are overridden by a glacier, so it is clear that no glaciation occurred here in the long period when these necklaces were forming. They are relics of bygone ages when permafrost existed in the ground, and are not active now.

Lurcher's Gully is slightly similar to Coire na Ciste. It has gentle upper reaches, no sign of rotational slipping of glacier ice, no deep U-shape section and it has a water-cut valley running down the northwest side.

Glacier ice may have coursed down Lurcher's Gully in a previous glaciation, but it did not originate here, it overflowed from the Lairig Ghru, when that glen was too full to take all that was being forced through it. In the long period after that episode, the gully settled down to freeze, thaw and creep without interruption from glacier ice.

The only further modification may have come as a result of glacial meltwater flowing down the gully in early part of the deglaciation, but this was by no means as dramatic as in the Chalamain Gap, so probably lasted for only a short period.

Lurcher's Gully probably acted as an overflow channel for both ice and water, but only when the build-up in the Lairig Ghru was deep enough to allow the leakage to cross the high threshold. These conditions did not last long in either case.

Not many people come here in the summer. It is a gentle green place in which to disappear for a while and feel the pleasure of natural effects on your senses. It's one of the best places for juniper on the North side of Cairn Gorm.

In winter, Lurcher's Gully is a draw for ski-tourers, walking out from the car parks in Coire Cas, and fitting skins to their skis to make the long gentle ascent to the flat ground at the top.

In my first week's ski touring my friends and I gradually worked our way up to being able to ski Lurcher's Gully. It was a test of our new-found skills, and one which found mine severely lacking. Now I can look forward to the descent as a good, reliable way down from high ground to low that puts off the inevitable walk back to Base for the longest possible time.

The gully starts very gently, and even when it narrows, it is nowhere as steep or confined as the gully in Coire na Ciste. It is always possible to steer a course onto gentler ground out to the right (descending), eventually to reach the Allt Coire an Lochain and the path back to the car park. Occasionally, when my nerve holds, I might take one of the two much lower routes back home, but they need good snow-cover to ski. I should say again that the snow builds up to several feet deep, and is not usually just deep unconsolidated powder, but forms a hard surface that can be readily skied, or even walked on. What I need is for this to build up sufficiently to cover all the obstacles that lie on the hillsides, giving a beautiful white slope as tempting as a new canvas to an artist.

The gully usually holds this aplenty, but the snow overlying the stream lower down can break through, sometimes with ominous cracks and caved-in sections to avoid. This can be quite a challenge for the skier, but as the ground flattens out, it is possible to traverse far round the hillside, even to the course of the stream coming down from Coire an t-Sneachda, saving seemingly miles of walking.

The lowest exit from Lurcher's Gully is now only possible as a rare treat, and I have only been able to do this once. I descended right to the gully of the Allt Mor and followed the flat ground beside the stream to the Allt a' Choire Chais. Then, putting skins on the skis again, climbed back up to the Ranger Base on snow-fields overlying the peat bog below the Fiacaill a' Choire Chais.

Lurcher's Gully was famously eyed up by snowsports developers. I'll tell you about that later.

The top of Lurcher's Gully, in common again with Coire na Ciste, is more like part of the Cairn Gorm plateau and ends abruptly to the West as the ground drops into the Lairig Ghru. To the north of this lies the outlying peak of Creag an Leth-choin.

This place is the origin of the name of the gully, and peak and crag beyond. According to an old story, a hunting party lost one of their dogs over the cliffs here. It was a leth-choin, meaning half-dog, of the sort still popular today and called – lurcher.

Creag an Leth-choin, or Lurcher's Crag, is a superb viewpoint for the Northern Cairngorms, the Lairig Ghru and Rothiemurchus below. Its bouldery ridge supports a small summit at the West end and spreads out into a broad plateau towards the East, complete with granite tors which appear like a cockscomb of rock along the spine.

Indeed, it is so inspiring a viewpoint that the Aetherius Society has declared it one of the world's 19 Holy Mountains. All I can say is contact them to find out more!

My uplifting here was one windy day. It is one of the few places I have been lifted bodily by the wind and dumped – painfully.

# 6. Cairn Gorm itself

*Okay. We've been all round the base of this mountain. Are we going to climb to the top?*

Yes, of course. I hope the prominence given to the low-level walks has shown how fascinating they can be, and that a mountain is not all about the summit.

The commonest question Rangers are asked in the Ranger Base all summer long is– where is the route up Cairn Gorm? Variations include asking about a recommendation as to which of the two most obvious routes to choose.

The two choices are the vehicle track up Coire Cas and the steep Windy Ridge route. I mentioned already that I always recommended Windy Ridge for ascent, but if variety is important, the Coire Cas track can be taken throughout or can be used to reach the Fiacaill Path, which is the third most popular route.

*"You go out of the Ranger Base and turn left, up the steep slope between the two big buildings and under the railway once. Opposite the red telephone kiosk, turn left up the steep path, signposted Windy Ridge Path. The first 20 minutes are quite steep, so take your time and enjoy the views. You can soon see the roof of the Ptarmigan building ahead, and your route passes close by on the left of it. You are welcome to go into the Ptarmigan building, use facilities, have refreshments, even take the train down. When you are ready, carry on to the summit, again by a choice of routes".*

I could almost say it in my sleep.

# Windy Ridge

The Windy Ridge is another path which did not exist before the car park. It soon became a deep erosion scar. There is a picture of Adam Watson standing in the gully that used to exist here, the depth at least the height of his shoulders.

At that stage, I wasn't really very keen on Cameron MacNeish's Munro Almanac recommendation of this as the way to Cairn Gorm, but since it has been repaired, it is a much better quick route than up the Coire Cas track.

It's incomparably better than the route recommended by Lonely Planet walking guide, which said that the summit aspirant, having driven to the car park, should turn his steps down hill for ten minutes' road walking (anathema!) and then try to find the old Victorian path near Clach Bharraig, which is being steadily lost in the heather. Lonely Planet sold readers a 'sandbag' which added 30 to 60 minutes to their journey. It didn't stop there, because a German guidebook took up the same route in its guide to Schottland, and I have given lifts back up to the car park to lots of puzzled visitors from the Continent I found wandering around looking for the start of the path.

In view of the alternatives and recent improvements to the Windy Ridge, Cameron's recommendation looks to be far the best idea.

The name "Windy Ridge" has been applied to this path since before the ski development, and refers only to the steep area connecting the car park to the main spur of the mountain. This has the name An t-Aonach (the ridge) below and Sron an Aonach (nose of the ridge) above where the Windy Ridge joins.

Some commentators have disparaged the name Windy Ridge, but the main problem they identify is that it becomes applied to Sron an Aonach. I agree. Let's not dilute the Gaelic any further.

The Windy Ridge Path passes the white weather box near the start of the path, and then there are few landmarks until the main Aonach path is reached. A wind-blasted larch tree makes a bid for an altitude record alongside the path at one point. I haven't had the heart to destroy it as a non-native interloper.

The view over Glenmore opens magnificently from up here, and looking into Coire Cas becomes spectacular too. Over the ridge appears the Pass of Ryvoan, with the northern outliers of Cairn Gorm and, in front, the kidney-shaped Lochan na Beinne. In the distance, on a clear day two windfarms can be seen on the lower hills of Moray.

The Windy Ridge route bears right to climb the ridge on the line of the old route from Glenmore. Before going this way, let me point out a lesser-known path that branches off here.

If instead of continuing on the main path, you go straight ahead, through some fencing and pass the hump where once stood the concrete base that used to support the Aonach tow. The land drops away to the left and the narrow path climbs gently across the top of the area known as the Aonach Bowl. I often brought groups of walkers up here when we were leading summit walks from the Base Station, and we often saw ptarmigan in this quiet area.

This lesser-used route curves up to the buildings at Base Four. The strange name arose when the radio sets were being distributed, Base One being the chairlift station, Bases Two and Three at the middle and top stations, and this was Base Four. From here the track onwards leads towards the Ptarmigan building.

Another reason for this little-used path falling further into disuse is the recent improvements to the main path up the Aonach. The path is so obvious, people are not looking for an alternative.

The broad boulder-strewn shambles that disfigured this slope until repairs in 2010 is recovering. Steady uphill progress on gravel and pink granite setts leads directly up Sron an Aonach. The only drawback for the walker was to be accompanied by a ragged fence of chestnut paling marking the edge of one of the popular ski runs down from the top. It too is much better for renewal.

The purpose of these fences is to help the drifting snow to settle in the space between them, so concentrating it here for snowsports. The snow lasts much longer here as a result, and although the fences are faintly visible from afar, the snow streaks they preserve in the spring are very prominent.

Adam Watson pointed out that the native heather, which grew on this spot before the development of skiing, died out on the ski pistes where snow is artificially encouraged to stay longer. A snow-mould affects the heather, and kills it, to be replaced primarily by sedges and grasses.

The ski run is known as the M2, a strange codename, paired with the M1 ski run across on the slope to the right, as both these are motorways for piste skiers. After a while the path crosses the M2 and breaks out onto the hillside to the left of the fences.

*Tor on the Aonach*

Now a small tower of granite appears on the left, on the top of the ridge. This is a modest little tor, but clearly marks the upper part of this ridge as "old" ground.

Near the tor there is an Alice-in-Wonderland little door into a box under a rock. In the early days of skiing, it is reputed to have been the storage space for explosives for use in case of needing to bring down avalanches. It seems improbable now, considering the safety risks.

# An Alice-in-Wonderland little door

The tor is well worth a detour, either for the view, or to seek out the little door, or to think about one of the strangest true stories about these hills.

## The tor story

A tor is a wart-like feature which occurs on many of the mountains in the north and east of the Cairngorms. The celebrated granite tors of Dartmoor may surpass the Cairngorms tors for their towering height, but the English tors are far outnumbered by those on the Cairngorms.

Tors occur in massive rock with irregular jointing in many parts of the world. This story really relates only to the Cairngorms granite tors, but parts of the story apply to the others as well.

When the deep mass of granite started to be uncovered by erosion, the pressures in the brittle rock were released as layers split at the surface. Plywood will do the same if wet and stressed, but the difference is that granite has no natural bedding. The cracks appeared parallel to the original ground surface when the pressure was released. Other cracks, perpendicular to the surface occurred because of the release of tensions set up by cooling. The resultant cracks were sometimes close together, which made the rock disintegrate into small pieces, or far apart, which left massive core stones.

At some stage in the life of all tors they were subject to deep weathering, usually by liquid water, otherwise by frost. This had the effect of reducing all the resulting lumps by a little on their outer corners, edges and surfaces. Because the corners were under attack from several sides at once, they were rounded away the most, though some of the flat edges took only a little weathering. The small rocks disintegrated further into gravel, the medium-sized ones into stones and the massive core stones were almost unchanged. The longer the surfaces were exposed to the atmosphere, the deeper the weathering, the deeper the pits and grooves etched in the upper surfaces and down spillways.

As these tors are now standing out of the landscape, we realise that something must have taken the weathered material away. Much of this was achieved by gentle slope processes, aided by frost heave at the time of the glaciers. This couldn't have happened underneath the glaciers, so it must have happened in places near and around the glaciers that were not covered by ice. We have already met periglacial weathering, and this is some more.

A further complication arises, however, because the tors were all, at some time, subject to the movement of ice sheets. In the case of Cairn Gorm, this was almost entirely from West to East. The glaciers would have removed all the tors if they had been travelling as glaciers usually do, by scraping on the bedrock below.

Study of the movement of ice, and the likely thickness and temperature, has revealed that the Cairngorms ice sheets were frozen to their beds. There was insufficient thickness and pressure to make the ice at the base of the ice sheet melt and provide a slip-plane. In deep valleys, the great thickness and pressure caused the basal ice to melt and slip. In these places, the overall pressure to move would have been most easily released. In between these more mobile

**89**

streams of ice would have existed stagnant or slow-moving ice where the upper layers were moving faster than the lower layers by stretching and by plastic deformation, leaving the ground not eroded but protected by the ice.

The ground that we see nowadays has been subject to not one episode of ice movement, but many, perhaps as many as two dozen, lasting 40,000 to 100,000 years each, and still the tors have survived. The ice must have done the same thing every time it came past. First it built up, and froze to its bed, then accommodated any pressure to move firstly through the deeper sections in the valleys, which got eroded deeper and deeper, and then by the ice shearing and deforming.

# Not eroded but protected by the ice

The height of the tors represents the lowest level to which movement penetrated. In the case of the tor on the way to Cairn Gorm, it is about four metres above the ground surface. There is clear evidence that upper stones were moved off the top of the tor and dropped a few metres away.

The tor is a great viewpoint. I sat and watched the sunrise at around midsummer once, as part of one of Adam Watson's ptarmigan counts. In the windless dawn, it was easy to hear the waking calls of the various male ptarmigan as they stated their occupation of an exclusive territory of ground. I heard three different birds on the far side of the gully marking Coire na Ciste, and another on the nearby plateau. The sun rose from behind Ben Rinnes in the North-east, a memorable morning.

## Old ground

From here to the top of Cairn Gorm is guaranteed old ground.

It has seen many glaciations and represents part of the land surface that existed before the ice ages. The ice ages have lasted two million years, but on old ground much of the upper surfaces follow shapes that are older still. The surface material is deep-weathered, another indication of its great age, and the preserving power of the ice. Had it been as erosive as the wet-bottomed glaciers of the West, there would be bare slabs of granite over much of its surface.

Now from the sublime to the ridiculous. The next section of plateau up towards Cairn Gorm is very level, rising gently towards the snow fences. Racomitrium moss grows luxuriantly here. It is one of the most easily damaged habitats, as in Coire an t-Sneachda, so I recommend walkers avoid it. I found out one day why it grows so luxuriantly here, and I recently came across a picture of the tank they used. I was not imagining it.

In the old days, when the chairlift was in full swing and the Ptarmigan had a rudimentary bio-disc sewage system, the residue was occasionally pumped out into a bowser and taken down the hill to this area where it was spread on the surface. I saw this happening once, and was

*Sludge truck*

nearly knocked over by the stench as I descended past the Ptarmigan down the Sron an Aonach. That's why the moss grew so well!

The pull up to the Ptarmigan building ahead always seems to take longer than it should, especially if lunchtime is approaching. The path was rebuilt in 2011 having developed into a broad stony swathe. At the last it winds round the left hand side of the building, under the gaze of the curious, envious or indolent on the terrace.

# The Ptarmigan

This is an experience not to miss. Sometimes, when crowded, I would rather miss it, and some people regard it as such an affront to their idea of what should be on a mountain they make a point of missing it, but just for a moment, let's have a look round.

If snowsports are in season, you will be met by dozens of people, not all skiing or snowboarding, standing around and slithering around outside. You will already have walked all the way up and might be feeling a little superior because you can keep your feet. You are welcome to go in by the main entrance, and regular crowds of people will be surging out of the doors.

During one such mass exodus, I once saw a young man blithely pushing his way in while still wearing crampons. I let him know how dangerous he was being and asked him to go back outside until he had taken them off.

If snowsports are not happening, the doors will be closed, you will need to ring a doorbell and be admitted. At present you are required to sign in so that you can claim your right to be let out again, but there may one day be a simpler way of achieving the same level of control without someone having to wade through hundreds of scrawled sheets every year. There is no intention to restrict incoming walkers' access, but the railway operator has agreed to keep train passengers in the building. Why? I'll come to that later.

Once through this process you may use any of the facilities, and even buy a ticket to ride down the train. The top platform is a big echoing space designed in concrete-chic with exposed piping and electrics. The train slides up comfortably to stop just short of the buffers on a surprisingly steep track. Once it has gone down the tunnel the point of light at the far end seems very distant, but soon the other carriage comes into view, bringing its own lights up with it. The cold draught that comes up here in the winter explains why there is no heating in this part of the building.

Through the double doors, another cold area gives access to the main entrance, restaurant and stairs. Down the stairs are toilets, the Shop at the Top (down?, oh, well), and then you go down some more to the Exhibition.

I could go on at length about the efforts that went into the exhibition, the disappointing outcome and the difficulty of effecting subsequent changes, but they are not really part of my story. I'll confine myself to a few salient points:

The original installation was irrelevant (peat, archaeology, shooting costumes?), dull (some is no more than a book on the wall), not interactive (automatic moving parts that go too fast for the model to be appreciated), insulting the intelligence of visitors and the genuine qualities of the natural world being described, error ridden (photographs reversed, and other mistakes), plagiarised (you'll have seen that before, somewhere), over-complicated and ultimately confusing. The job was given to a big firm of outside consultants who charged a fortune and are responsible for this kind of installation all over the place.

My own direct effort was very small. I carried the tripod for making the film and am rewarded with a huge credit at the end which is hardly justified. Nevertheless, the film is, in my opinion, the one bit not to be missed.

Most train riding visitors to the Ptarmigan are keen to see the view, and the viewing terrace is also their only opportunity to go outside into the mountain weather. An information panel points out the wind farms visible. Soon, I fear, it will be well out of date. The photographic panels are very fine. Andy Gray's digitally-enhanced long-lens photography of the mountains on the skyline achieves superb clarity but on close inspection resembles a painting as much as a photograph.

Many people break their climb here with a drink, snack or meal at the restaurant. If there is no pressing reason to linger, we will carry on to the last stage of the walk up the mountain.

# The Summit Path

From the Ptarmigan to the summit of Cairn Gorm there is a choice of routes. When the chairlift delivered 40,000 visitors a year to this fragile high ground, many of them made a bee-line for the summit, ignoring the long-established but less direct path round the east side. The direct path, known as the Summit Path, became a cause of great concern, a prime example of an eroded path developed on a deep-weathered mineral sub-base.

In the 1970s an attempt was made to create a crazy-paving effect, using labour from a nearby penal institution. The first section still exists, with big rock slabs cemented into the ground. The cement construction did not continue up the slope, and the stones were often in a state of disarray, avoided by walkers, who preferred the deep, mobile gravel alongside. This became heavily gullied during rainstorms in the summer and snowmelt after the winter, and land owners Highlands and Islands Development Board had a series of posts erected alongside the path, linked by chains, to keep walkers on it.

*Old summit path and chairlift buildings*

The effect was of chaotic dereliction, totally unfitting as the approach to what was then claimed to be the country's fifth highest summit. It was easy to associate the development of the buildings at the Ptarmigan, skiing and dereliction and, as a visiting sightseer, dissociate one's self from responsibility for the mess. If it hadn't been for the ski development, one could argue, this mess wouldn't be here and by visiting, I'm not adding to it.

# Chaotic dereliction

With the continued summer operation of the chairlift and open access onto the hill, there was no prospect of reducing the number of people seeking to climb. Interestingly, the numbers using the chairlift – and also the Summit Path – were declining of their own accord, but that is part of a different story.

HIE, as successors to HIDB took action on the Summit Path over the course of four years, finishing in 1997. The path was completely rebuilt by footpath professionals using only natural stone. The original works had denuded the surrounding area of stone, so tonnes more were airlifted up from the ski area. The works were often interrupted by adverse weather, and many young people had their first experience of path work on this path. The turnover rate was understandably high.

*New summit path. The author is sweeping gravel off the pitched construction*

The technique contrasted completely with the borstal boys' path. For a start, no cement was used. The stones were placed perpendicular to the slope, so that you walk on the ends, like walking on the spines of books set into the slope like a wall.

The upper surface of the stones follows the slope, in pony-pitching style. This style is less comfortable to walk on and succumbs readily to being overlain by snow or even by gravel washed from the surrounding surface. People often prefer not to walk on it, but walk alongside, widening the path and preventing the vegetation from recovering.

We decided to renew the posts, and replace the chain by polypropylene rope. This guides walkers, discourages them from straying onto the surrounding vegetation and provides a handrail and something to haul on to ease the climb, if needed.

The rope makes quite a job for the Rangers, twice a year. When the snow is melting, the posts, being permanent fixtures, emerge and guide walkers up the route, but as soon as the ground is bare, the ropes need to be attached. They are stored all winter on old wooden cable drums, and run out and threaded through each post. Two 300m lengths of rope on each side reach almost to the top of the posts. When walking up, the halfway knot always seems a long way up the path, and it is usually a good point for a breather.

At the other end of the season, judging the correct time to bring in the ropes is always a challenge. Leaving them too long is an invitation to getting them frozen in, covered with rime ice and ultimately – it happened one year – having them covered by snow and stuck till next spring. Taking them down too early loses the value of having the posts. October is quite a busy time of year for walkers, so Rangers try to leave it to November or, at risk of ice, December.

Some people say that the robustness of this path, combined with the access restrictions for rail passengers, represents a waste of the money spent in constructing it, and that with such a well-built path to the summit, there is no need to minimise the numbers of people climbing it.

I will answer the points about the access restrictions later, but just to say that before they were in place, 20,000 people a summer used the path. Now 16,000 do so. This still represents a huge number of people to be accommodated on a high mountain, and the 16,000 may dispute the detail of the construction, but are infinitely more sustainable on it than on the previous amateur job, or worse still, none at all.

There are a few interesting things to look at on this first climb. One is the white rocks, some of which have been built into the path surface. These are quartzite, a dense crystalline mineral which condensed out of the granite while it was still liquid and floated up to near the top of the underground chamber, there to solidify in lumps, like bubbles, or like fruit in a heavy cake, all rising to the top. From this, geologists deduce, the present ground surface is probably close to the upper limit of the original granite mass.

Quartzite is called this because it is the relatively impure form of quartz, and we will find some pure quartz just up the path a short distance.

If you can keep going, then all climbs must eventually come to an end, and the top of the pitched footpath on Cairn Gorm always feels like a welcome point on the way up the mountain. From here on, the route is on the summit plateau, an inclined slope which passes the 4000 foot contour, and a rare place in Britain.

# If you can keep going, then all climbs must eventually come to an end

The path is one of the earliest examples of the "light touch" approach of the recent era of path building. Similar technique from much earlier times can be seen at the top of the Lairig Ghru and on the summit of Ben Nevis. Rocks have been cleared aside, tilted, flattened, switched round slightly and an obvious walking route has been created with the minimum intrusion. This is the pattern for high ground for the future.

Shortly beyond the last post, a large granite boulder contains one of the few publicly-visible, wild, Cairngorm quartz crystals. The guides on the regular summit walks point it out, and lots of people know about it, but it has never been collected and removed, unlike all the others. The reason is – the boulder it is in is far too big.

Like most wild crystal, it looks rough and unconvincing, but a skilled lapidarist will see the optimum cleavage to show the crystal in its best form, and a jeweller will set it in a silver brooch or in the handle of a *skian dubh* and the stone will live forever in our admiration.

The natural colour of Cairngorm crystal is usually smoky brown, the best are clear and translucent. They form proper hexagon crystals with a pointed end, and are just what a crystal should look like.

The fashion for collecting was well under way by the time Queen Victoria fell in love with the Highlands. In 1833 she stoked the cottage industry to a new pitch by paying one fortunate James Grant of Ryvoan £50 for a crystal, a pound for a pound. Had he wished, he could have retired on this enormous sum, an unheard-of luxury. His upbringing wouldn't allow him to do such a lazy thing, though.

# Cairngorm crystal

The fervour for collecting brought people up from the straths to the well-known sites of previous finds with their shovels, pickaxes and heavy hammers. Their story is well worth reading. They were the first denizens of these hills since the Stone Age.

A line of cairns accompanies the path. This is unusual on Cairn Gorm, and it is intended to direct those for whom a default option is needed (in the absence of independent thought) to get them back towards safety.

Until 2002, the cairns, which were erected by my predecessors in the Ranger Service, were each marked by a wooden pole, secured by cross-pieces at the base, with the cairn built round them. In severely icy conditions, these posts would support rime ice which built out in the manner of a flag for two metres or more. In the mist, summer or winter, the posts actually stood out more than the cairns, and many times I followed them from post to post, unable to see further than the next one.

One day in 2002, however I came across the line of cairns with the posts all lying on the ground, the cross-pieces sticking up in the air, the cairns in ruins around them. Who did this I have no idea. Presumably they took exception to what they considered to be an intrusion on the top of the mountain.

I contacted lots of people that I could think of to gauge their reaction. Should we go to the effort of replacing the posts? It would be a major job. All but one respondent said they didn't mind if the posts disappeared. The sole objector had been involved in putting them up in the first place and was outraged.

Over the next year or so, as the Rangers were coming down off the summit, we would carry one of these big, heavy, sodden posts, and gradually they were cleared. The cairns were rebuilt as part of the light-touch pathworks, and remain, as they were originally intended, the only line of cairns on the summit.

# The summit cairn

At last the summit cairn comes into view. And what a cairn! Pyramidal, robust, with a pointed top, it commands a superb view, which I'll describe in a minute, and is a fitting crown to top our mountain.

# A fitting crown

A cairn very like it appears in Walter Poucher's book A Camera In the Cairngorms, of 1947. In the meantime, and when I first knew it, the cairn had disintegrated to a very different structure. The original cairn had not been built for climbing, but of course, people climbed on it, and gradually demolished it. They indulged in the very common habit of adding a stone to the cairn, as they still do. The terrain for a long way around was denuded of loose stone, and slabs were even pulled out of the ground to build on the pile.

As it had no structure, it continued to spread out sideways and resembled a fried egg in profile. It completely covered the tor plinth on which it had been built. I heard tales of walkers walking right over it and on to the building beyond, there to inquire where the summit cairn was.

The old cairn was no fit way to mark the summit of one of our four thousand footers. It had succumbed to the same degradation that characterised the whole route up, especially the Summit Path.

During the last of the Summit Path works, my boss in HIE decided to have the summit cairn rebuilt with a small proportion of the stone and have the rest removed to lower ground for further path works. This took place during my first few months in the job, and, enthusiastic and excited, I arranged for a press photographer to come and record the event.

Well! If I had known the furore this would unleash I would have sat on my hands. My effort to show the work of HIE in a good light backfired spectacularly.

My boss in Cairngorm Chairlift Company was so worried when the photographer arrived that he might see some of the other things that she preferred not to have publicised, that she took personal control of him, having him in her office and feeding him chocolates while he waited for his chairlift ride with me.

# The furore this would unleash

She hauled me in after his picture appeared in the local newspaper to voice her intense displeasure about the occasion, for which she blamed me, and to show me his excellent picture in the newspaper. In the background, among other things, were buildings managed by the Chairlift Company. Who knew where this might lead? People could see our buildings in the newspaper! I didn't see the significance of this, but didn't argue.

The more serious backwash was the vociferous campaign orchestrated by a predecessor of mine who felt we had made a serious error in removing the cairn on the summit. For weeks my HIE contact and I were bombarded by angry letters, letters in the press, letters in the climbing press and dozens of e-mails accusing us of wasting the mountain and removing the cairn, so that no-one could tell where the top was any more.

The famously polemic Angry Corrie magazine had a cover cartoon of Cairn Gorm with a helicopter removing the last bag and various mountaineers being totally perplexed, navigating over cliffs and the caption to the effect: "It's True. It really is the Gorms, now!", The Gorms being the common slang for the Cairngorms, but without the cairn, it would be true.

One correspondent to the local paper, from Nethy Bridge or Boat of Garten, I forget which, claimed to have been able to see the summit cairn from her house for as long as she could remember, and now, as we had removed it, had completely spoiled her view. We must put it back, she said.

This was based on a presumption, not an observation. The new cairn was much more visible with 10 tons of rock in a pyramid than it had been with 100 tons in a low spreading hump. Part of that total had been provided by another correspondent from her own garden, and she was outraged that her rock had been removed.

Some really important people joined in. The MP for Moray wrote to HIE to pass on the displeasure of her constituents, as the summit of Cairn Gorm is on the boundary, of her constituency. The local planning committee were disappointed to find out from senior planning officers that the demolition or erection of a cairn was not a planning matter, or they would have had more to say about it.

The whole valley seemed to have lost their heads about the cairn on Cairn Gorm, and it was not until many of them visited the new one to see what Cairn Gorm looked like "without a cairn" that they were mollified by the new cairn we had supposedly been forced to build. The Chief Executive of HIE made a public undertaking that HIE were not going to remove any further summit cairns, an undertaking I was more than ready to ignore, as we had not removed any in any case.

So that's enough about the cairn.

# The view from Cairn Gorm

The top of Cairn Gorm is 1245 metres above sea level, or 4084 feet, according to old Ordnance Survey maps. Until 1997 it was the fifth highest mountain in Britain, but then with the addition of Sgor an Lochan Uaine to the list, and revision of Cairn Gorm to 1244m (4081 feet), it was demoted to sixth. There was an exasperated comment from a Journal of the Scottish Mountaineering Club (SMC) "The things bob up and down like yo-yos", referring to the habit of surveyors to revise the heights of the mountains. However, the SMC were themselves responsible for the latest change in the status of Cairn Gorm as it is the SMC that updated and revised the Tables of Munros.

The whole of the select band of four-thousand foot mountains can be seen from the cairn. Three are in distant Lochaber, five are in the Cairngorms, and I'll introduce you briefly:

First is bulky Ben Macdui, at 1309 metres or 4295 feet. It is 5.37 kilometres away on a bearing of 196 degrees, or South-southwest. The cairn on the highest point appears directly in line with a slightly smaller hump on this mountain known as the North top. I promise we will get round to going there later if you like. There are often patches of snow on Ben Macdui late into July, but it generally looks like a big hump in the view from Cairn Gorm.

Much shapelier are the two to its right: Cairn Toul (*Carn an t-Sabhail*), 1291m, 4236 feet and fourth in height, with a trapezoid summit; and Sgor an Lochan Uaine, 1258m or 4127 feet. Poor Sgor an Lochan Uaine had its beautiful name substituted by the superstitious Victorians for "Angel's Peak" to balance the Devil's Point nearby, and it still struggles to shake clear of this nonsense.

*From Cairn Gorm to Cairn Toul, Sgor an Lochan Uaine, Braeriach, and then, beyond Sgor Gaoithe and Sgoran Dubh Mor, faintly in the distance are mountains in Lochaber*

The ground rises steadily to the right to culminate in the highest point of a fairly level plateau, the third highest mountain in these islands at 1296m or 4252 feet, Braeriach.

There is the hint of the cliffs of Braeriach in its profile from here, but nothing to prepare you for the grand architecture of its corries which fall in most directions from the plateau.

# Which one is Ben Nevis?

To the right the near mountains fall slightly, with a mountain face seamed by gullies, above which two smaller peaks, Sgor Gaoithe and Sgoran Dubh Mor grace the ridge line. On a clear day, you can see that it is not a skyline, however, and unless it is very clear indeed, binoculars will be needed to pick out and name the peaks of Lochaber far beyond.

Which one is Ben Nevis? It is 89.7 kilometres away on a bearing of 246 degrees, just left of Sgoran Dubh Mor. It peeps over the great ridge of Aonach Mor, which lies across the line of view, but Aonach Mor doesn't get in the way as it is 'only' 1221 metres or 4006 feet high. Aonach Mor holds snow very late into the summer and is the site of the Nevis Range ski development. At its left (South) end, the ridge dips and rises to Aonach Beag, the seventh in the canon, at 1234 metres, 4049 feet.

The litany of distant mountains continues, of course. Right of the Lochaber giants is a deep glen, Glen Spean, by which the main road to the west passes. The land rises again first to Creag Meagaidh, which is a high plateau at 1128 metres, then dips in a distinctive notch, called The Window, before rising to another high plateau which seems to persist without a break or distinctive feature from there right round to the Northwest, and merges into hills further round still. Above this plateau appear much more distant hills: Knoydart and Kintail (104 km away), then Carn Eige and Mam Sodhail above Glen Affric, the Fannichs (105 km away) and Ben Wyvis north of Inverness.

It might be a bit of a shock to realise that at this inland peak, you can see clear over the Moray Firth to mountains on the border of Sutherland and Caithness. The furthest mountains – and this needs exceptionally clear weather all over the north – are seen between these and Ben Wyvis. In line with the middle one of the low hills overlooking Glenmore can be made out the most Northerly mountain of over 3000 feet. This is the isolated peak of Ben Hope, a staggering 155 km or 96 miles away on 338 degrees, just West of North. Other peaks, Ben Loyal and Ben Klibreck nearby can be recognised if you are patient.

Now let's look at the view round the other way from Ben Macdui. The best place to stand is around the other side of the building, so I'll tell you about the building after we've looked at the view.

Left of Ben Macdui the skyline is rather rumpled and unremarkable, being composed of the outlines of Perthshire hills west and east of Glen Shee, where there is another important ski centre.

In front of these hills is a shapely peak also known as Cairn Gorm. It's in an area known as Derry, so it gets called Derry Cairngorm. At 1155m high, this Cairn Gorm is proof that the Cairngorms is not only about the Spey side of the hills.

The far skyline rises to Carn of Claise then again to the White Mounth, of which the peak now known as Lochnagar is the highest. This has a small pointed peak to the left end, Cac Carn Beag, which overlooks Balmoral Castle in Deeside.

I vividly remember one fine snowy day on Cairn Gorm when the only point of this distant range visible was the summit of Cac Carn Beag, appearing like an isolated rock island above a sea of cloud. What a view there must have been from it on that day. I noticed later the cloud must have lifted a fraction and the rock was submerged in the cloud sea.

# This noble skyline

In front of this noble skyline is the warty outline of Beinn Mheadhoin. This has retained a Gaelic name to puzzle English speakers, with no easy alternative. Try Ben Vee-an and you won't be far wrong, and, more importantly, other people will know what you are talking about. Mheadhoin translates as middle, but I hope you won't call it middle hill, for down that road lie the dull and unimaginative mountain names that grace so many American peaks.

The tors on the summit ridge of Beinn Mheadhoin are worth a visit in their own right. We will go over there if we have time later. No small amount of time will be needed, however, despite Cameron MacNeish twinning this mountain with Cairn Gorm. There's an enormous deep glen between them, a crossing of which is not to be undertaken lightly.

Further left the nearer mountains start to take precedence over those behind. First is the amazingly level summit plateau of Beinn a' Bhuird. This is Scotland's Table Mountain, and that's also the meaning of its name, at 1197m, only just outside the elite few of the highest.

Merging with this great plateau is another, the tor-pocked undulations of Ben Avon (Ben A'an to all locals). This mountain breaks into so many tors, I am sure they are uncounted. Some reach forty metres in height, and so are the most massive tors in the country. A few show no serious modification by the passage of glaciers, though the remains of others are spread out in a train of boulders clearly indicating the direction of ice movement and transport of their upper parts.

The river of the same name flows from the loch also called A'an. The river and loch are best seen from down the slope south of Cairn Gorm, but I think that will have to wait for another visit.

Peeping out from behind Ben Avon is the mountain of Morven, which overlooks Logie Coldstone on the extreme East of the National Park. The next hills are on the plain of Aberdeenshire, including Bennachie, another tor-topped granite mountain much beloved of many Aberdonians.

After a few smaller hills, including The Buck above the road from Dufftown to Rhynie, the remaining distinctive hills are nearer home, in Ben Rinnes, which overlooks the lower Spey, and the Cromdale hills, which overlook Grantown.

## Weather stations

Now what about this small square building on the top of Cairn Gorm, with its lattice work mast and strange cylindrical tower? This is variously known as the igloo and Summit building, or weather station.

There are actually two weather recording stations here. At the top of the tower are several pieces of solid-state equipment that can measure wind speed, temperature and humidity operated by the Met Office. It is a Severe Icing Environment Synoptic Automatic Weather Station, or SIESAWS. (I would like to see a justification for all those adjectives in the name, but it makes for a fun acronym).

*Cairn Gorm summit building*

*Opening time on Cairn Gorm*

Cairn Gorm is one of a series of SIESAWS which feature on the Met office website, so you can check out the wind speed and temperature from home before setting out, if you like. It's amazing what you can find on the internet.

The black cylinder on the roof of the building is an older weather station installed by Heriot-Watt University, with its own website at http://

cairngormweather.eps.hw.ac.uk/ . There have been long periods recently when this piece of kit has been on fault, but with the continuing enthusiasm of Physics Department staff at Heriot-Watt, repairs are made, and it whooshes into action twice per hour. This can give you quite a shock if it suddenly happens in the silence of a whiteout.

The inside of the building – which is not open to the public – is taken up with rather prosaic shelves of radio and electrical equipment to support the operation of the weather station and the radio repeater station also attached to the mast.

There is a user group which looks after the building, principally the Police, Met Office, Heriot-Watt University and Cairngorm Mountain Rescue Team. The building was erected in days gone by without reference to planning permission or the landowner (Glen Avon Estate). The present land owner is the one organisation that gains no direct benefit, but pays the business rates: The Royal Society for the Protection of Birds (RSPB). You may well ask what the RSPB is doing here. They own the Avon basin as part of their Abernethy Forest Reserve.

The building is the highest in the country with electricity. The underground mains cable can be seen entering the building through the stone cladding on the West side. A critical look at the building will reveal a cheap breeze-block built box with a (new) wooden roof surrounded by rough dry stone cladding, some of which has been removed to accommodate the mast.

I remember being present when the Executive Committee of the Mountaineering Council of Scotland (now Mountaineering Scotland) considered a proposal to replicate SIESAWS on many more Scottish mountain tops to promote mountain weather awareness and therefore safety. The reply was "No thank you". While the four we have are interesting, proliferating development on mountains to make it less hazardous is not what M. S. is about.

Wildlife at the top of the mountain is scarce. Ptarmigan and dotterel may occasionally be seen. If breeding locally, snow bunting will bring juveniles up to the vicinity of the cairn to feed. Wheatear, meadow pipit and mountain hare are the other animals at home here. I have photographed a pygmy shrew in the summit cairn, and the weather building is infested with mice.

Plants are very scarce, of course, but include dwarf willow and various lichens. The only plant apparently comfortable in this wind-blasted zone is the three-leafed rush, *juncus trifidus,* which can be found growing sparsely but very commonly all over the plateau. I have even found it as low as 750 metres, growing where the wind regularly hits the ground, and the other plants find it too hard going.

# Visitors to the summit

When the Cairngorm Chairlift Company ran the open chairlift to the Ptarmigan and hundreds of people took this route as a way to climb the summit, the Company felt obliged to make sure its customers made it back down the mountain at the end of the day. Clearing the summit of chairlift passengers was a daily task for the Rangers when I started, and continued till the blessed demise of the chairlift in 1999.

At around half past three in the afternoon, the Ranger would take the chairlift to the top and walk up via the Marquis' Well path. We would approach anyone at the summit and inquire politely if they intended to take the chairlift down, as it would be closing soon.

Sometimes we had to descend to the West to see whether anyone was coming up from the plateau. This made me realise just how convex that slope is.

On several occasions families who had clearly travelled up by the chairlift declined the invitation to travel down, remaining unmoved by the onset of the klaxon at the Top Station indicating the impending closure. Many times I walked down the pitched Summit Path with my hands over my ears, for, even at several hundred yards' distance, the little blaster at the black building down there gave out a piercing noise that was audible for miles over the plateau.

Now, with planning permission for the building of the railway secured by the promise that it would not be used to allow visitors to access the European sites, and funding from Europe dependant on the Closed system around the railway, the traffic on the Summit Path is presumed to be negligible. It is not so small if the counts we have carried out and the automatic tally of the people counter is to be believed, but at least they walked up, and could presumably manage to walk down again.

The Walk at the Top is a guided walk which was intended as a response to the continuing demand for access to the top of the mountain for visitors. It is based on the principle that the railway development was obliged not to damage the environment or disturb the wildlife, but with inspiring leadership and interpretation, visitors do not wander off the paths and can experience and learn something about the highest tops and feel included in their conservation, rather than excluded.

In 2010 Cairngorm Mountain Limited asked for permission to run guided walks for train passengers to the top of the mountain, expecting to be refused.

To everyone's astonishment, two weeks later, in June, we were told we had been given permission, subject to agreeing an acceptable operating procedure, and we would start as soon as we liked. CML took the view that mid-July would suit, and after a flurry of preparation, which seemed to have immense ramifications for several departments in the company, we were ready to start.

I will be accused of hiding guilty secrets if I don't tell you about my walk with several very important guests intended to demonstrate to them what a good idea it was. If I do tell this story, will you take it as a cautionary tale, not as a stick to beat me?

I was in illustrious company indeed. Several CML Board members, including the chairman, the Company Chief Executive and a BBC radio journalist making an Outdoor programme walked up the Summit Path and met a similarly august party in the guidance of Jim Cornfoot at the weather station, where the BBC man did a few recordings. It was a day of dense cloud and light wind, and I said to my group as I led them off from the Summit "Now I'm going to do something I don't want the other guides to do. I'm going to try and find the Marquis Well Path from the Summit Weather Station in thick fog".

I must have been aware that we could have missed the path, but that didn't stop me from missing it anyway. All the vegetation is short and interspersed with a lot of bare ground, there is no path to see at first. Then there was no path to see at second, and then – still no path to see. We wandered along, hands in pockets, chatting, but I was beginning to get worried. I thought it must be over to the right and trended rightward, but no luck, then over to the left. Nothing. Where were we? The ground started dipping away to the right, surely that was the path down to the right. No luck.

Then the cloud parted momentarily and I could see the path well off to the left, I had been guiding the party down the middle of the Marquis Well basin, instead of on the path as promised. I had made exactly the mistake I had not wanted the others to make.

Oh, well. If the Head Ranger can do it, it can't be hard. The group was a little amused, but not concerned. No mention was made of it on the radio, but I got a chorus of catcalls every time I put my face in the company offices for a month.

This story reminds me that the Marquis Well path is used as part of the circuit at the top. It's a pleasant path curving round the east side of the summit dome, taking in the top of the highest tow on the hill, a stony spring and the Marquis Well itself, the highest water on the hill.

The guided Walk at the Top climbs by either the Summit Path or the Marquis

Well, and returns by the other. Some guides prefer one, some the other. They lead no more than two walks per day; with travelling back to the Base Station between, this is as much as they have time for, and quite often do each route once, for variety.

The Well which gives the area its name is attributed to a Marquis, probably the Marquis of Huntly, a title that first appeared in 1599. The title probably fell into less popular use after 1686 when the Gordon family who held it became Dukes of Gordon. The dukedom itself fell into disuse in 1836 and the Marquissate continued and still exists today.

*Marquis Well*

Disappointingly, we don't know which one is commemorated by the name of the Well, but the fourth Marquis is reputed to have pursued enemies from the Battle of Cromdale up here in 1690.

# Dotterel

The intense caution with which the walks are conducted is to preserve the integrity of the visitor management system and to avoid disturbance to the wildlife around the summit. The most highly prized of all is dotterel, a Schedule One species of bird that nests only in the Arctic, and in small numbers in Britain. You may be fortunate enough to see dotterel on a walk to the summit of Cairn Gorm.

They have even been spotted from the Ptarmigan building, and I well remember a chairlift trip with some visitors in 1990 when we saw them from the Summit Path. The best prospect is from the Marquis Well path shortly after the birds have arrived on an improbable migration from Africa in late April and early May.

Dotterel are wading birds, similar to plovers. They are much shorter than curlew and larger than sandpipers and dunlin.

To understand dotterel, you have to know the unusual adaptation they have made to nesting in a niche habitat with the worst weather in Britain.

Rather than wasting her time sitting on eggs when she could be laying a further clutch, the female dotterel gets the male to do it. This leaves her free to go off to another area, mate with a second male and have a second clutch of eggs in case the first one fails due to

*The female dotterel has developed the bright plumage*

poor weather. This second clutch could be far across the sea in Scandinavia. It is a story which often finds favour with the ladies, perhaps who fancy the same arrangement themselves.

The female dotterel does not need the dull cryptic colouration of egg-brooding, so has developed the bright plumage, and the male is the dowdy one who remains close to the ground, trying not to be noticed.

Before egg-laying, the birds are delightfully unconcerned about humans, trotting around the heath on a blur of legs, rushing up to a spot where there may be food, stopping momentarily to peck, standing upright to look at the surroundings with a bright black eye, and moving on again.

Chicks start to appear any time from mid May to mid July, depending on how badly the weather has treated the incubation process. It is commonplace for the sitting bird to tolerate snow fall in May and June, when the incubating birds cannot leave the nest even for a moment to feed, and the female will sometimes assist by taking a turn. If snow persists for too long, the birds will abandon the task and move to lower ground, leaving the eggs for the ravens.

Another cause of failure can be heavy rain which chills the birds and especially the chicks, again causing abandonment. One year, in 2005, the birds were unfortunate enough to suffer snowfall at one critical time and prolonged heavy rain at another, the upshot of which was no chicks were found that year.

For many years during the chairlift's open access regime, no dotterel were found nesting on Cairn Gorm itself, despite careful searches. They have now returned in small numbers to the summit area, but we must be extremely careful not to disturb them.

Even a close approach with a camera is considered an offence, and the Rangers have to apply biennially for a licence to allow then to disturb dotterel, although they have no intention of doing so. The main reason for this is in case they accidentally disturb them or in case they have to intervene with someone else disturbing them, whether accidentally or otherwise. The licence answers the counter-accusation that Rangers are themselves the problem. All the Rangers and Walk at the Top guides are included on the licence.

Seeing the father with his one or two chicks quartering the ground for insects and other food is always a real pleasure. The adult birds know how vulnerable the chicks are and will try to distract attention away from them if anyone approaches too close. The bird will run along in an area away from the chick, dragging a wing, tripping and falling and making a great show of injury, sometimes with a trilling call, but always just out of reach of the observer.

The intention is to lead the predator away from the helpless ball of fluff and then, when the distance between them is enough for safety, to flit off leaving the observer enthralled but none the wiser about the reason for the performance.

If you see a bird doing this, it is a good idea to stop in your tracks and look off to the left or right of where the distraction display is being performed, and you could be rewarded with a glimpse of a ball of fluff running quickly away from you. It is more difficult to avoid disturbance in a big group, or with a dog, of course, but it is really important that these birds are left alone if we want them to carry on coming back.

## Tragedy in the Marquis Well

The crash of a light aircraft into the Marquis' Well area in a snowstorm in April 2008 has been better told elsewhere. The Mountain Rescue Team put a huge effort into locating the wreckage and evacuating the pilot's body. There is no question that they should have had any interest in the bag of money that came down with it. But someone did.

In the intense blizzard that followed the recovery of the pilot, all activity on the hill was suspended, but someone, and this has never been proven, did go back to the wreck and illegally removed a suitcase containing, among other things, banknotes of Sterling and US currency.

There were other valuables, too, but as the CML team gradually dug them out of the snow in the bright warm days that followed, they were without exception returned to the rightful owner, via the Police. Most of the tiny pieces that remained, however, had to be removed by the Rangers.

There were millions of shards of plastic packing boxes, decorated crockery, Christmas decorations and – worst of all – personal belongings of a young girl. The quantity of these items appearing in the first days gave me cause to suggest that there might, in that blizzard-ridden shell of an aircraft, have been a second casualty. Thankfully there was not. Her school certificates, artwork and clothing surfaced, but she herself was safely back with mum at home in England.

# A sickening sight

In mid-April, a passing walker on the plateau told me that there was a lot of aircraft paperwork in the pools and springs on the south side of Cairn Gorm. This is a relatively unfrequented area where the summit dome tails off to a lower plateau then drops abruptly over cliffs to Loch Avon. Down there I found dozens of papers relating to the plane and the pilot's business and – money.

It was a sickening sight. It had to be cleared, as litter, but there was no doubt where it had come from. It had blown nearly a mile along the ground from the crash site and become mired in the wet springs and pools appearing among the last remnants of the snow.

It was with very mixed feelings I paddled barefoot in these icy waters to retrieve what I could of the grieving family's possessions. Coming after the painstaking trawl of the crash site for shards of glass and slivers of foil decorations, this was much easier in some ways, but harder in another. The money went straight to the Police, I didn't want it because I knew whose it was.

Imagine my astonishment, then, eighteen months later, to be recalled by the Police to give it back to me. The owners had not wanted it.

# Fiacaill a' Choire Chais

We climbed Cairn Gorm from the North, but there are far more ways to approach the peak. The Summit Path and Marquis Well are the two most popular choices, of course, but there is a third popular choice, and any number of less popular possibilities.

A lot of people climb Cairn Gorm via the Fiacaill a' Choire Chais, the blunt tooth on the West of Coire Cas, the right hand side as you look up. This is the mountain path we left to another day as we took the Coire Cas Mountain trail while walking in Coire Cas. The path has given path builders years of work, and only in 2011 was completed to the cairn at the top, though the maintenance and improvement of the lower sections is not over yet.

The path passes the end of a snow fence which guides skiers across from the Coire Cas tow, by the route followed by the Mountain Trail in summer. As the trail walkers turn downhill, those continuing uphill are clearly heading for high ground and a hidden people counter enumerates them. After a section on unpopular pony-pitch construction (some people find it difficult to walk on), the path crests the ridge and the big view of Coire an t-Sneachda opens up. A remarkable boulder staircase eases the ascent.

Higher up, a series of boulders all exhibit a similar line scratched across them, starting on a big rock with a curved mark, then proceeding across several boulders towards the cliff edge, where it is lost. These marks provided me with another puzzle to figure out, and three solutions have been proposed, the last being far the best.

Firstly I thought a steel cable had been used to raise or lower a stretcher and casualty on the steep slope nearby. It would have scratched the rock as it ran out and was being reeled back in. But why the curved section?

My second idea was a lightning mark. But again why curved? The only sort of lightning that could do this is ball lightning.

The third idea was Boyd Henderson's. He was supervising the 2011 path contract and agreed not to move the rocks on

*Another puzzle*

which the marks were made. He had also been an agent for a safe rock-splitting substance and knew a bit about explosive fuses. He said it was like the mark of a fuse that would have been used to bring down a cornice with a controlled explosion.

Not many people will notice this scratch on their way up, but if you remember that everything here is old and natural and must have an explanation, it might puzzle you as it did me.

Most people climbing Cairn Gorm this way intended to climb that way anyway, but a significant number were toiling up Coire Cas and got dissatisfied with the vehicle track through the corrie and decided to try something else. The top of Fiacaill a' Choire Chais looks like an attainable mountain peak, so some people cross the top of Coire Cas to the ridge and climb from there. When they reach the cairn at the top, another peak, this time the real summit of Cairn Gorm, appears, and up they go.

On one occasion, on a cloudy day in October, I met a group of people in Western and Asian clothing near the top of the path. The wind was flapping one lady's shawl distractingly and one of the ladies had on strappy sandals to show off her painted toenails. The leather jackets and jeans of the young men were not designed to give them any protection. I took pity on them and advised them that it was time to turn and go back down. They did not argue, but I looked back ten minutes later and saw that they had progressed only a few dozen yards down the path.

I shouldn't give the impression that it is all uphill traffic. Quite the opposite. This path is one of the few asymmetric-use routes. More people go down than up, especially in winter.

It makes a good finish to the return from Ben Macdui, when the ascent of the Western flank of Cairn Gorm is not appealing. It is also the most obvious descent route from climbs – especially winter climbs – in Coire an t-Sneachda. Mountaineers starting down the ridge in the late afternoon have a heroic, triumphal appearance, returning back to known country after a day out on business in inhospitable places.

That Western flank of Cairn Gorm is the last part of the ascent from Fiacaill a' Choire Chais to the summit. It is permanently wind-scarred and foot-trodden. There is no adequate baseline to determine the degree of recovery from having fewer feet on it since the closure of the chairlift. Some light touch path works in 2011 managed to define the path for a while before the general creep of gravel obliterated them again.

# The Rim of the Northern Corries

The walk along the crest of the crags forming the steep back walls of Coire an Lochain and Coire an t-Sneachda is dramatic at any time of year, passing over a high point at the head of each corrie. It is, in my opinion, one of the best walks on the mainland of Britain.

I have to dispute the Internet assertion that it is "a good easy walk for a short winter day", if only to object to the use of the word easy. It is potentially a hazardous undertaking, and not to be sniffed at in winter or summer.

The undulating walk could be taken east-to-west or in reverse. I am often asked to recommend one or the other, and I usually refer to the wind direction and how likely the walker will fail to navigate successfully.

When the wind is in the West, let it help you along the – er – crest I was going to say, but that sounds too much like country lore. I mean: Start at the plateau above Coire an Lochain, climb by the broad eroded slope onto Cairn Lochan and carry on towards Cairn Gorm.

*The Rim of the Northern Corries: Cairn Gorm and point 1141*

If the wind is in the South, you might be wanting to make sure it won't blow you off the cliffs. It has happened. If the North, it will be a cold walk whichever direction you take.

Neither of the peaks along the way is a Munro, but both are listed by virtue of being subsidiary summits ('tops') of mountains with full Munro status.

The one at the head of Coire an t-Sneachda was listed by Irvine Butterfield in his High Mountains of Britain and Ireland as Stob Coire an t-Sneachda, the name adopted by the SMC when revising the tables in 1997. This infamous revision added many overlooked peaks to the list. Lots of happy people who believed they had finished their Munros were confronted with additional mountains to climb. It also demoted Cairn Gorm from 5$^{th}$ to 6$^{th}$, but back to Coire an t-Sneachda.

Stob Coire is a very common hill name in Lochaber. There is everything from Stob Coire Altruim to Stob Coire Sgriodain. Screeds of them. In the Cairngorms there are three. We have better local names for our mountains, including Cnap Coire and Creag Coire.

So why did we get the Lochaber variant introduced? Suspicion for Stob Coire Etchachan and Stob Coire Sputan Dearg falls on Bob Scott, stalker of Luibeg, who would have known Lochaber names and probably had his own reason for suggesting them when asked by surveyors.

Stob Coire nan Lochain on Braeriach was actually abandoned in 1991 in favour of "Braeriach, top above Coire an Lochain". Fairly trips off the tongue, doesn't it?

Irvine Butterfield cannot answer for his source of inspiration, though I think he tried to find a Gaelic alternative to "Top of Coire an t-Sneachda" and hit on a Lochaber name instead of one of the fine local ones.

Without knowing of its adoption by the SMC for Munro's tables 1997 revision, I wrote to Harvey maps pointing out that this name was wrong, and should be Creag Coire an t-Sneachda, to which they responded by removing the name altogether. My satisfaction at one correction was wiped out by the Ordnance Survey by the adoption of the Stob name on their maps. They have a very strict naming protocol, but have let us down here.

What is a Stob? You may well ask. It's a fence post. It's quite appropriate for the steep-sided pointy peaks of Lochaber. But the Cairngorms? What's wrong with Creag?

Suppose our traverse of this delightful high-level walk starts in the West. We will take the familiar Northern Corries path and the ridge route up to the plateau. Shortly after this, the route dips slightly onto level ground and then we take on the last big climb to Cairn Lochan.

This slope is marked by a large gravel scar alongside which the path climbs. It is possible that the origin of the scar was walkers going up and down this slope, but it seems very wide and shallow. The outcrop here of this pink gravel is a reminder of the widespread overburden of deep-weathered loose material on these mountains which has not been scraped away by glacier ice.

# A dire warning about the perils of traversing this mountain

Cairn Lochan is the Western of the two tops on the Rim route. Nearly 4000 feet high but never listed as a Munro, it is not considered to be a separate summit. It is, in fact, a subsidiary of Ben Macdui, not Cairn Gorm, as the dip at the top of the Goat Track (1111 metres above sea level) is lower than the dip at Lochan Buidhe (1123m).

I was given a dire warning about the perils of traversing this mountain when I was already quite an experienced mountaineer and working in Fife. There was, I was assured, a chasm dividing the two equal summits, and it was the easiest thing to walk over the cornice here in the mist. I now recognise this as a description of the wide gully known as the Vent, but I have never been tempted to drop into it. It is quite easy to follow the plateau edge round the top of the gully under all but the most dire conditions.

I might have dismissed the warning out of hand had I not heard that the leader of the Kinloss Mountain Rescue Team had, when there on his own one thick whiteout day spent a good while terrified to move in any direction as he was not sure he could avoid falling into the Vent.

*Cairn Lochan cornices and two walkers*

The cliffs of Cairn Lochan are very well seen from our approach to its summit. A narrow ridge called Ewan Buttress climbs up at one point, with a huge vertical face on one side, which we can see clearly from the cliff edge.

This was the scene of an adventurous event known as a Raid. After much careful preparation, the organisers commissioned a team of French guides to set up the abseil down this huge vertical face on Cairn Lochan. Applying the ethics of their homeland, the guides drilled the granite and set steel bolts from which the abseil was to take place. This is anathema to British climbers and represents a serious lapse in the standards of the natural aspect of the cliffs and operation of the event.

The event itself was curtailed by snowfall, and the abseil did not take place. Climbers complained about finding bolts after the event and chopped the protruding parts of them to make them unusable. They promised to return with suitable material to fill the holes to naturalise the site of the damage, making it undetectable over time. Such is the strength of feeling about the natural qualities and standards of their mountains.

The Rangers have to reflect those standards too, and pre-empt any possible complaint by insisting on high – perhaps impossibly high – standards from anyone wanting to make any changes to these mountains.

The most dramatic view of the cliffs from Cairn Lochan is from the Eastern of the two summit cairns. Here the cliffs drop away hundreds of feet below a sudden edge, and the vertical corners of the cliffs opposite can be seen in full height. Quite frequently a party of climbers can be seen on the most popular of these climbs.

*Savage slit*

Moving from Cairn Lochan down to the top of the Goat Track there is one possible navigational pitfall from following the cliff tops religiously. The sharp, rock ridge of Fiacaill Coire an t-Sneachda comes up to the plateau, and if we adhere too closely to the left hand slope we will be scrambling fairly difficult ground, with a big drop on one side to Coire an Lochain and an even bigger one on the other side to Coire an t-Sneachda.

So, leaving the top of the Fiacaill Coire an t-Sneachda with its wonderful views of both corries and heading to the right, our route now descends to eroded ground at the top of an open gully. The next section of the descent to the top of the Goat Track has developed on more of the pink gravel layer which lies at the surface. Unfortunately this wore into a gully a metre deep before recent light-touch path works stabilised it.

The crags of Coire an t-Sneachda are just as dramatic as those of Coire an Lochain. We climb from the top of the Goat Track up leftwards towards the clifftops and a strange anvil-shaped stone appears. On closer approach, this is seen to be on the edge of the crags.

From beside it an even more impressive view opens of Fingers Ridge. If we are lucky, a team of climbers might be traversing them, making a tremendously dramatic scene.

*Fingers Ridge*

Further up the clifftop several steep gullies open out onto the plateau. Another rocky profile rises from the corrie, that of Pygmy Ridge. The top of this the ridge is higher than the plateau edge, and descends to join our route just as another ridge, bounding Aladdin's Couloir, also joins. The ground at the top of the Couloir is so trodden about with crampons that no vegetation grows, the mountain is just bare and pink.

Our route follows the top all the way over the high point at 1176 metres with its disputed name, and descends to the top of Jacob's Ladder. This is usually worth a peep down, unless it is corniced in winter. It is another broad gully, of the sort that crops up on the granite here, and on Lochnagar, and Arran. No-one would consider climbing here in summer, but in winter it's a different prospect, as we shall see.

The next landmark on the way round is the Windy Col, the low point between here and Cairn Gorm.

The path forks, the right hand path going to Cairn Gorm summit. For many people this last reascent will be one too many, and they will take the left one to the top of Fiacaill a' Choire Chais and descend to Coire Cas that way.

Recently, the Mountaineering Council of Scotland was contacted by a correspondent who disliked the cairns which mark this route, considering them to detract from the wildness of the area, and the need for self-reliance in navigation. He had last seen them round here 50 years previously but believed them to have been removed. He was disappointed on a recent visit to find that they appeared to have been reinstated by "a well-meaning agency". He wanted to canvass support for their removal.

While agreeing with him about the loss of wildness these cairns represent, I had to correct him on two points. They had never been removed, and no agency had been responsible for building them. They had indeed been built by well-meaning mountaineers. If removed now, we would have to take into account the impact on the ecology, where we would put the stone and the cost of helicopters. Nothing is straightforward.

If we had been starting the Rim of the Northern Corries by taking in the summit of Cairn Gorm first, it is straightforward to descend the eroded Western slope onto the plateau and then follow the paths round the cliff tops. In poor weather the only significant navigational challenge is to make sure you descend in a Westerly direction from Cairn Gorm and, if cornices are present, to avoid walking over them.

We would ignore any alternative route leading away from the edge of the cliffs – or down them –until we had passed both summits and the cliffs of Cairn Lochan. Then our route would lead gently down the slope until it reached the gravel scar and turned directly down to the Miadan Creag an Leth-choin, the flat area overlooking Coire an Lochain.

Even on a misty day, this can be a tremendous walk.

During one event connected with the Aviemore Walking Festival, I had a group on Cairn Lochan in thick mist. The event always seemed to coincide with a wintry week in May, and although we were walking on snow, there were landmarks all along the route: cairns, stones and other people's tracks. It was a summer walk with snow, rather than a winter walk.

One lady wanted to know what whiteout was. To answer, I took her by the arm and led her away from the group and away from the edge of the cliffs only a few yards, to be confronted by a complete blank. No matter how the eyes strained to distinguish the end of the snow and the start of the sky, it was impossible. Whiteout disturbs some people. I can see why.

We went back to the group and continued our walk, the more aware of the narrow ribbon of land we trod between the abyss on the left and the terrors of milky blindness on the right.

That particular walk was well rewarded, for, after navigating our way all along the rim of the crags, we reached the cairn at the head of Fiacaill a' Choire Chais and the cloud was suddenly dragged away and we were standing on bright sunlit snow. It was a transformation. Everyone wanted to finish the walk with an ascent of the summit dome of Cairn Gorm, so we did.

In summer time, the vegetation cover on the plateau will be looking very sparse, partly because there never will be a lot of vegetation in this environment, but also because it cannot cope with the inevitable trampling this plateau edge receives. This is not something to make a conservation agency leap into action, it's just a natural consequence of lots of people wanting to walk here.

I was shown a frontispiece to the volume by Mary Wheeler Walker of the Flora of Inverness-shire, featuring the author sitting on a distinctive rock overlooking Coire an t-Sneachda. All around the vegetation cover was nearly complete. If you go there now, it is ragged and patchy. Could this all be due to trampling and disturbance?

Certainly, if you look closely at the plants, they are all growing in places where it is difficult to trample on them while walking past. They are clustered between rocks, round the edges of rocks and in the spaces by cairns where people have diverged round the obstruction. This is good evidence for trampling being a cause of bare ground. There will be some other minor advantages to the plants in terms of the way the rock or the cairn retains a little moisture when the rest of the desert around is being baked by an unrelenting sun, as sometimes can happen. In these conditions, rock surfaces can reach 40 Celsius, which the plants find too hot.

You may be forgiven for thinking that some of the stones standing on the plateau are erected by ancient people. They stand, looking for all the world like small standing stones. Would you be surprised to know that these, too, are a natural phenomenon? No? Good, you're getting the message.

# A natural phenomenon?

The cause of these standing stones is the same as the shattered crags in Coire Cas and the boulder necklaces of Lurcher's Gully: Periglacial action.

During the permafrost period the ground slid downslope imperceptibly slowly. In Lurcher's Gully, the rock shapes are predominantly round, but in some places on the plateau, the granite is more slabby. It doesn't take much imagination to envisage some of these slabs becoming undermined as gravel under the lower edge is washed away.

As they are creeping downslope themselves, they sometimes come to an obstruction which stops the front edge of the slab from moving any further. Material is still edging down behind, though, and gradually tips the slab into a more and more upright position. For a given angle of slope there must be a limit on the size of the largest slab that can be stood upright, but I suspect, from examining the specimens on the Western flank of Cairn Gorm, that there is quite a bit of the rock buried in the ground.

## Other good ways to climb Cairn Gorm

How about a route to Cairn Gorm where we won't meet anyone else?

A really good one is to climb from the North by following the long ridge over Sron a' Cha-no and Cnap Coire na Spreidhe. The route starts at the car park in lower Coire na Ciste and heads North along the crest of a ridge of gravel deposits, an esker.

The path here is considerably recovering, having been much more popular in times past, and climbs to Lochan na Beinne. This water appears abruptly, as it is hidden and held back by a ridge of ground. It might be a kettle hole on an old meltwater channel, or held back by a moraine.

Beinne is very like the word for mountain, but it is a *beanie* that is celebrated here. A beanie is a small sprite or fairy that comes into your house and helps with the housework when you are not looking.

There is a good view into the Laogh corries, and we get to see the remains of the trial plantation from above.

Small paths lead up to the ridge of high ground ahead. There are some dramatic water-cut notches through the ridge where melting glacier water was prevented from running directly down the hill by the mass of ice remaining in Strathspey. The water formed a long-lasting lake against this slope, but it is not possible to determine how far out from the slope it stretched.

I don't feel too bad about calling these glacial features lakes. There was no-one around at the time and the adage *a loch is a Scottish lake* didn't apply before there was a Scot.

The shoreline of this lake can be traced around the slopes of Coire Laogh Beag and appears as a sloping bench, representing a beach formation, with frost-shattered boulders above and smoother slopes of fine water-borne deposits below.

The outflow from this water body was over the ridge to the east, through a steep-sided, sinuous channel and down the big slope into Strath Nethy. As the ice dam receded slightly, a lower overflow became available which took another torrent through the gap near the top edge of the plantation, allowing the water to escape across the head of a small valley and then pour in enormous cataracts down the side of Creag na h-Iolaire into Strath Nethy. It over-steepened the slopes, producing crags which have since decomposed into steep scree slopes, but remain craggy at the top. Creag na h-Iolaire is ahead of you all the way down the ridge if descending by this route.

The channel and the ridges and terraces of gravel in Strath Nethy are a remarkable feature, even requiring their own contours, and are well studied by geomorphologists (those who study the formation of the shape of the world) and landscape photographers.

*Strath Nethy*

As Strath Nethy appears, so does Bynack Mor, another fine mountain for another fine day. Beyond and to the left the hills above Strath Nethy stretch towards Dorback and yet another notch formed by melting glacial water appears, the Eag Mhor between Abernethy and Dorback.

The path towards Cairn Gorm makes steeper progress, and suffers from some water erosion, but it levels out before long. On the left, above the steep slope to Strath Nethy, part of the land has split away from the main ridge, probably as a result of the release of pressure of the glacier ice. Though not common in the Cairngorms, this type of land slip (rock slope failure) is often seen across the Highlands.

Before long we get our first view of the summit of Cairn Gorm, seemingly far ahead. The ridge becomes very broad for a while, an outlier of the Cairn Gorm plateau, home to dotterel and, surprisingly, thrift.

The most interesting route is to visit all the tops and stick as close as reasonably possible to the edge of the cliffs. Some of the tops still have the remains of tors.

One group of boulders on the edge of one of the cliffs is held in place with a capstone, which is gradually being edged outwards. When it goes, they all go and tons more boulders will crash down into Strath Nethy.

The names are intriguing: Sron a' Cha-no, the Nose of the fresh ridge. The freshness of the vegetation on this ridge may have inspired this name.

Cnap Coire na Spreidhe is a name I like. Adam Watson advises the pronunciation is Crap Cor na spray. I think most people will prefer Nap to Crap, but I will not argue the point. Cnap is analogous to cnoc, or knobbly hill, and Coire na Spreidhe is on the Strath Nethy side. The Spreidhe is a herd of cattle, probably stolen and hidden here in this out-of-the-way place.

Coire na Spreidhe is also the location of one of the isolated mountain huts built by the 51st Highland division (of the Army) as an advanced training shelter. Its location is curious to us now, lying on a slight spur among the boulders, missed by avalanches but not an easy spot to find. It took me at least four attempts, though my information was not very clear, and the remains of the hut are difficult to see from a distance.

Cnap Coire na Spreidhe is where the Rangers decided to bring people to watch the annular eclipse of the sun on May 31st, 2002. We knew the eclipse would be a popular spectacle, but realised that our railway would not take people to a point from which they could watch it. It was due to be taking place at sunrise, and by the time the sun had risen above the ridge of Cnap Coire na Spreidhe, and visible from the Ptarmigan building – the limit of railway passengers access – it would be over.

The only option was to walk, and this was going to take some organising. We asked people to give us a ring to say they were coming and gave up keeping a tally at seventy. This was in spite of uncertainty about the weather.

Our preparation was thorough. We placed two casualty bags and first aid kits on the hill in case people had to stop and wait to be rescued. The commercial opportunity was not lost on the Cairngorm Mountain people and they offered cooked breakfast at the Ptarmigan at 7am.

Over 100 people gathered in the darkness at the Ranger Base at some unearthly hour, and a trail of tiny lights nearly a mile long threaded its way up the Windy Ridge path, passing the Ptarmigan at about 4am. I was at the head, Jim Cornfoot near the middle and Ruari Macdonald at the back.

There was cloud on the summit of Cairn Gorm and to the west, but Cnap Coire na Spreidhe was clear, and the view to the east a somnolent brightness, not yet ready to wake up.

*A strange sun rising*

# The satisfaction of a pre-dawn mountain walk and sunrise

In the event, we waited for nearly an hour for the brightness to grow. Some participants were getting a bit impatient. One demanded to know when it was going to happen, the answer to which was "When the sun comes up". One person presented a cut and bleeding finger to be patched up, our only casualty.

Finally the show started, an hour later than I expected, as I realised that my information was GMT, and I had been working on BST. Fortunate it was that way round, not the other, though if we had been planning a 6am start, I think we would have suspected an error and investigated it.

The sun that came up that day was a strange shape. It emerged from a very low band of cloud as a spike, which we later saw to be like the top horn of a crescent. Gradually the disc of shadow in front of the sun moved across its face until there was an almost complete ring of bright orange fire.

It was definitely a spectacle not to be missed, and a very contented band wandered back across the rocky heath towards the Ptarmigan where a different kind of phenomenon – the production of 100 cooked breakfasts in a few minutes – was much appreciated. This was a welcome piece of opportunism by Cairngorm Mountain, as they closed down after everyone left to walk back to their cars, and reopened, with a different team, at the normal time.

*A very contented band wandered back*

It was only later we discovered that the eclipse had been well seen from most of Strathspey, but on Cairn Gorm had we had the satisfaction of a pre-dawn mountain walk and sunrise. We had been lucky in several ways. Had we nominated Cairn Gorm summit as our viewpoint we would have been in cloud.

The rest of the day was a bit of an anticlimax. I climbed back to the Summit of Cairn Gorm and descended by Fiacaill a' Choire Chais, completing an eight-hour day around one o'clock.

There was a bit of a trend for night-time events for a while. In the year of the Outsider Festival, a one-off mudfest in fields at Rothiemurchus, we arranged a midsummer sunrise walk, with a bivouac at Ciste Mhearad. This is the corrie on the east side of Cairn Gorm, easily accessed from the top of the chairlift in bygone days. It was so easily accessed, in fact, that skiers and snowboarders regularly went over there for their sport after the end of the ski season, finding a huge patch of snow.

I was taken there for my first taste of snowholing, a gale-ridden adventure when the overnight 120 mph moderated by the morning to a more reasonable

60 mph, and we made our descent from the deserted summit back to Glenmore right down the Sron a' Cha-no.

In summer, the gravel left behind by the melting snow was historically heavily trampled by visitors curious to touch midsummer snow and oblivious to the damage they were doing. A species of lichen, already very rare in the world, became even rarer when the only British location among the gravel at Ciste Mhearad was lost sometime in the 1970s or 1980s, and trampling was the likely cause.

By 2006, our event was a small-scale wander up from the Ranger Base in late evening. Eight people had come to join in, but, despite going as slowly as we could, two well-equipped ladies decided it was too difficult for them and turned back. Around Sron an Aonach, we broke through the upper edge of the bank of cloud and had a fine evening looking down on it.

We found a soft mossy terrace overlooking the Ciste Mhearad snows and set up tent or bivouac for a few hours. I was amazed that two of the participants had a festival tent, a single-skin plastic affair with a floral print. Fortunately there was no wind, they had a good night's sleep before going on to the Outsider the next day.

Dawn was very clear, the sun warm and the sky blue. This was the only sunshine that we experienced that weekend. As soon as the sun-facing slopes of the mountains warmed up, we saw puffs of cloud like steam rising from them, and cloud also started to form higher. We had a simple breakfast and wandered over the summit of Cnap Coire na Spreidhe and then up to Cairn Gorm.

This last bit of the ascent is further than it looks. The natural tendency is to gravitate towards the constructed footpath in the Marquis Well basin, but I prefer to hang left and aim for the prominent tor on the east side of the summit.

Before we arrived, we threaded through huge boulders which have clearly been heaved off the main part of the tor by the only available force – glacier action. At the tor itself is the last peek we would have of Loch Avon, the deep ribbon-loch at the bottom of the great trench south east of Cairn Gorm. The little puffs of cloud that had been rising from the sun-warmed slopes were by now towering piles, extending up hundreds of feet and gradually merging into the high cloud level above. Before we had finished our walk round the Rim of the Northern Corries, it had started raining, and continued for most of the week.

The Outsider Festival, as I said, became very muddy, though is still fondly remembered as one of the friendliest festivals many regulars had been to.

The tor brings us to the top of the long ridge up Cairn Gorm from the North. It is a good descent route, too. I have even been able to ski it once or twice, though it requires very good snow cover and light winds.

127

# 7. Something a bit sterner – climbing on Cairn Gorm

## Climbing on Cairn Gorm

You may think that by climbing *up* Cairn Gorm, we have climbed *on* Cairn Gorm, but there is much sterner stuff to draw climbers to this area, apart from walking up to the highest point.

Climbers are interested in the steep rough bits walkers keep away from. Although Cairn Gorm is a big baldy-headed mountain with gentle slopes all around its summit, there is a surprising array of steep ground that is some of the most popular in Britain for climbing activity, especially in winter.

# "Obviously" risky

I'm going to assume that you are interested to know about this, but it's not the sort of thing you are going to try for yourself. This might be the sort of thing you wouldn't dream of doing, or it might be just tantalisingly close, if you could only find out how to get started.

The traditional way to get started is to trust someone you know to show you what to do. This might be risky, because you can't judge whether this person really knows what they are doing or whether they, too, are almost as inexperienced as you are.

*Final Selection above Loch Avon*

Another tactic is to join a club, as many young students do, and take advantage of the wealth of experience there. Clubs are located in every big town in Scotland, and most will accept members from anywhere.

# Not the sort of thing you are going to try for yourself

Experienced climbers are always pleased to offer advice about technique and equipment. There is plenty of need for it, because without it, many people have been rescued from risky situations with only the most inadequate equipment and no idea how to use it.

Climbing has become so notorious as an "obviously" risky undertaking that many people are very aware of the perils of setting out on such a course without properly preparing. The climber, as opposed to the walker, is now much less likely to come to an avoidable accident.

Many people who arrive daily at Cairngorm have a woeful lack of mountain awareness and equipment and are not wanting to rock or ice climb, they are wanting to walk, and by-and-large they get away with their unpreparedness.

The easy part of the preparation is collecting the gear. You just go into a shop and buy it. Or look in your granddad's trunk and find it. The hard part is knowing when it is fit for use or if it's just worn-out junk, and then when and how to use it.

One of the early shocks for the aspirant climber is just how much gear is needed, the cost and the variety on offer. The next shock is how much it all adds to the weight of the rucksack, even with the most lightweight kit.

Another approach, which is complementary to everything else, is to do a training course. The ideal training opportunity is just down there at the foot of Cairn Gorm, at Glenmore Lodge, the National Outdoor Training Centre.

So I'm not going to tell you how to get ready and do this activity, there are better ways for you to find out. This is more of a sightseer's guide to the steep bits of Cairn Gorm and what people get up to on them.

# Coire na Ciste

In the lower part of Coire na Ciste is a small crag interrupting the smooth north-eastern side of the corrie. It's a curious little area of eroded rock and scree. There are a few named routes on it, but it is hardly in the same league as the other crags. I mentioned it before because of the remarkable through-route on its extreme right-hand side.

I have a low opinion of this crag apart from this. Years ago, on a training exercise in moving roped on steep rocky ground, I found myself at the top end of a rope and boulders were coming down at me dislodged by the other party on the course. I could do no more than watch them come and miss me on each side.

## Coire Cas

Another little crag lies above the lower part of Coire Cas, skirted by the enormous boulderfield. These boulders could not all have come from the little crag, but some have. Most of the slope here has been burst up by frost. The crag is only about two metres in height, hardly a challenge for a prospecting climber.

Generally Coire Cas holds little for the climber, unless you count the winter techniques carried out on the headwall and the steep side of Fiacaill a' Choire Chais. Step cutting, ice axe braking and steep ground rope techniques are all learnt here.

## Coire an t-Sneachda

By far the most popular of Cairn Gorm's climbing is in the two large Northern Corries, Coire an t-Sneachda and Coire an Lochain, and the great ridge that separates them, Fiacaill Coire an t-Sneachda.

Coire an t-Sneachda is magnificent in any terms, and has three distinct areas of interest to climbers: Fiacaill Buttress on the right which provides the sense of exposure to those scrambling up the main Fiacaill ridge; the main buttresses on both sides of the central 'Trident' gullies, and then after a slightly disappointing break, the Mess of Pottage.

The name of the Mess of Pottage gives a hint of the derision with which the crags in the Coire were regarded for many years. Granite rock climbing is a bit of an acquired taste, and it was a visit by Tom Patey that established a reputation for the climbing, and even then, it was regarded as inferior to neighbouring Coire an Lochain.

If there is one party rock climbing in the coire it is likely that they will be on Fingers Ridge, the one with the pinnacles we noticed before. Steep slabby walls lead up to an airy traverse along the pinnacles. The other popular rock route they may be onto is Pygmy Ridge, first climbed as a winter route in Easter 1901, and now regarded as little more than a scramble. The crest of Pygmy Ridge looks from a distance like an old-fashioned lamp, giving rise to the names of the routes referencing Aladdin, the Genie and even Ali Baba.

In winter, the Coire is no longer out of fashion; it is the place to be. Next to Ben Nevis, this is the most reliable winter climbing area in the country. When the winters are lean and everywhere else fails to produce good climbing conditions, this is where climbers can rely on getting a challenging climb, and it is only just over an hour from the car. This gives it massive appeal, and makes it such a good place to cut your winter climbing teeth that it is not surprising that it vies with the North Face of Ben Nevis as the nation's most popular winter climbing venue, despite Ben Nevis being unchallenged for quality.

Local guides have a saying that if a training corrie was being designed from scratch, it would end up something like Coire an t-Sneachda, it has a bit of everything they are looking for.

The Mess of Pottage has many routes which crowd up through the steep rocky ground. Some have names which are variations on Mess and Pot: Honeypot, Pot of Gold, Message and then the reference to the doyenne of 1970s Scottish climbing, Dougal Haston who found the Haston Line.

Jacob's Ladder is the straight, open chute of snow which forms the right-hand boundary of Mess of Pottage. We peered down this from the plateau earlier.

There is a stretch of scrappy crags and scree before we come to Aladdin's Couloir. This is a broad dog-legged gully, steeper near the bottom. It forms an icy pitch in early season before the snow has built up to bank it out. The gully is often used as a descent route from the top of other climbs, enhancing its popularity. It is also descended on ski or snowboard in late winter.

Aladdin's Buttress is next right: steep and bulky. This is where Tom Patey tried the place out first.

*Trident Gullies all rise from the large patch of snow where four climbers can be seen*

Next Right are the Trident gullies: The left-hand one is perversely named Central Gully, the middle one is Runnel, after the groove near the top which leads to the cornice. Despite the highlight being so short, Runnel is still one of the most heavily-visited routes, rarely missing a party, and often overcrowded. The right-hand gully is Crotched Gully, the most complex of the three.

Right of the Trident gullies the buttresses are very steep and rocky. It seems unlikely that any routes would exist on them, but that is to underestimate the taste and ability of the winter climbers seen on mixed routes like Wavelength and Broken Gully.

Moving on beyond the crag the next shallow groove is called – surely ironically – Point Five gully, referencing the iconic standard-setting climb on Ben Nevis. I prefer to give it its other name, Easy Gully. Under favourable conditions it is little more than a steep walk.

Last is the steep Fiacaill Buttress. The central route here, Fiacaill Couloir is largely hidden from view in the corrie, it goes up the left hand side of an embayment in the buttress. Facing it is a steep little crag split by the Seam, a route rarely giving ice pitches, but a classic of modern Scottish mixed climbing. This means climbing cold rocks in crampons and hooking with ice axes.

The only other climbing in Coire an t-Sneachda is mixed ground (snow and rock) on the halfway buttress overlooking the lower part of the Coire known as Twin Ribs. There is also the Flat Ice area in the back of the corrie. Both are used for training rather than serious roped climbing.

# Fiacaill Coire an t-Sneachda

Fiacaill Coire an t-Sneachda is the pre-eminent scramble of the Cairngorms. It is the longest and most famous. It is not necessarily the best, nor hardest, but it is a must-see for anyone adventurous enough. So, if you are up for a summer-time scramble, I'll take you up to the plateau this way with no more specialised equipment than you use for hillwalking. However, I will remind you that if you or your companions are inexperienced, this is probably not the place to be trying your first scrambling adventure without a suitable guide. This book is no substitute!

The ridge starts in rather a dull manner as a long boulder-strewn slope reaching up to a peaked skyline. To make the approach a bit more interesting, I could take you up the Sneachda path and cross the moor to the foot of the slope.

Either way, we climb by bouldery slopes with a little blaeberry poking through and come out on the exposed slopes above. The effects of trampling are intermittent as people thread their way up between and sometimes over the boulders on the crest.

A granite buttress drops down to the left, towards Coire an t-Sneachda, and from here there is a grandstand view of the crags. With binoculars you can pick out all the climbers on the routes I described before, and get a realistic perspective on their upward progression.

There is a rocky high point to scramble over, but nothing yet compares with the exposure or steepness to come. The way ahead appears all but closed off by crags falling to left and right, and concentrated on a single knife-edge rising up in front.

Some massive rocks lead down to the main col on the ridge. In windy conditions, we could hide on either side of the ridge here and find a good

measure of shelter. This is quite unusual in the Cairngorms. Narrow ridges like this are much more common further West.

The low point on this ridge is where the glaciers of both corries have ground most intensely down, their areas of influence overlapping. In one direction, steep bouldery slopes fall to the head of Coire an t-Sneachda. In the opposite direction, the lochs and crags of Coire an Lochain dominate the view.

The delight of this route is that it is nothing like as difficult as it looks, and yet provides a whole variety of situations, on ridge-top rocks with gaping drops on both sides, on ledges skirting round difficult bits where the climber is kept out of balance, there are slabs, chimneys, cracks and big flat ledges.

After scrambling up the left side of the first buttress, it becomes obvious that you could have avoided it on the right. The same applies to every difficulty you come across, but what's the point? We came here to scramble on a granite ridge, there is much to be lost by shuffling round the side on loose gravel to the detriment of the sides of the ridge.

On up a narrowing groove goes the route, onto a flat-topped rock ridge with tremendous exposure on both sides, and then the first of the little step-downs that are just part of the fun of this scramble.

Another fun moment comes with a traverse round a big blank wall on ample footholds, but disconcertingly out of balance.

# Within the capabilities of any aspirant mountaineer

Shortly afterwards is the most serious piece of scrambling, but first look across to the right at the desperately badly-eroded hillside alongside the rocks. This is the way many more cautious walkers will work their way up. Decomposing, unstable and steep, it is a classic eroded path of the Cairngorms, and because of where it is there is almost no chance of it being repaired.

The problem is caused because some people are intimidated by the scramble on solid rock and prefer to follow the unstable path. Perhaps it looks easier, or perhaps they are not confident to scramble on the steep rocks without ropes and experienced leadership.

It would be a pity to say that Fiacaill Coire an t-Sneachda is not the place to take these people, because it is a wonderful experience. But it is true that they are making an unsustainable mess of this area, and their presence here is a problem for conservation of the mountain.

The ascent of Fiacaill Coire an t-Sneachda in summer should be within the capabilities of any aspirant mountaineer. They will want to carry through what they have started and scramble the whole crest to the top.

So, up the rocky corner we go. There are ledges on the left and holds on the right. Anything worth using as a foothold is so heavily crampon scratched, that it shows bright and fresh, in contrast to the dark rocks around.

Don't get too close in to the crack or it will get more awkward to get out again. Don't worry about falling off and you won't. Your feet will be on great big ledges and you will end up on a large sloping shelf with a smooth step up that is quite easy to make. Beyond that it all eases off and on we go!

The final obstacle is a buttress which drops away very steeply on the left. By trending towards the drop on more rough slabs, the way up becomes obvious and soon the fun slackens and a short level crest leads to the top.

In winter of course it is a different prospect. The crest becomes a graded route, and the eroded ground, frozen and covered by snow, is the natural route for anyone needing a straightforward ascent or descent. The erosion doesn't get worse in winter.

From the top we can look down on the next challenge – Coire an Lochain.

# Coire an Lochain

Around in Coire an Lochain, the cliffs are far more compact and steeper. No-one climbs seriously on the Great Slab. It is too low-angled, and in winter is famous for enormous avalanches.

The rocks are recognised as standing in four buttresses, unimaginatively named One, Two, Three and Four. Summertime interest is concentrated on the right hand, or Number Four buttress. Here a remarkable series of walls alternates with steep corners or steep ridges, reminiscent of the corners of a building. Most celebrated is the Savage Slit which we saw from above, but others such as Fallout Corner deserve and get occasional attention. This is a high mountain crag, north facing and not quick to dry after rain.

I had two attempts to climb Savage Slit. My second attempt was on midsummer's day in about 1980. I remember having to stop several times, wedge myself bodily into the crack where I was unable to fall out and put on my Dachstein mitts to warm my hands up for a minute or two before I could continue. It was snowing at times on the route, but we gritted our teeth and climbed it anyway.

As with Coire an t-Sneachda, winter is the main season in Coire an Lochain. The location of Jean's Hut in the Coire gave it a tremendous boost in popularity. The buttresses are divided from each other by deep gullies which become much more evident when appearing white against the dark buttresses in winter.

First from the left, Number One Buttress is steep and rocky. On my last visit, a team was making good work of an impossible looking route on it, quite distracting me from my own progress on Milky Way, just to the right of the Vent.

The Vent itself is a huge gash, climbed only when the snow is deep enough to permit the climber to surmount the main obstacle, a step in the lower third. After that a huge funnel-shaped slope leads up to the cornice.

Buttress Two is split by Central Crack, a varied route which goes at a surprisingly modest grade considering its spectacular location.

The next big gully is just called The Couloir. It is a big ramp of snow through dramatic craggy scenery that could be used as a descent route, except that to complete the descent, a traverse of very steep ground above the Great Slab is no easy option.

Ewen Buttress is next, a pleasant ridge connected to the plateau by a narrow neck reminiscent of routes on Ben Nevis.

*Near the top of Central Crack*

Then comes a pair of gullies connected at the foot and named Y-Gully. I came round the top of this one day just as two of my friends were topping out of a route. We were called over to a party near the top of Y-Gully. An unfortunate leader had fallen and broken an ankle. My friends threw down a rope for his climbing partner and she made a good job of coming up the steep snow, while her leader shivered on a belay. A rescue helicopter arrived and they were all sorted out soon after.

The last buttress is the one containing Savage Slit. There are several major routes here, all climbed in winter as well. To be perfectly honest, the style of climbing that requires ice axes and crampons to climb what is substantially bare rock doesn't appeal to me at all. The crampon scratches are a permanent disfigurement which the summer climbers have to climb over. In some places the inadvertent chipping away of the rock is making the summer route harder

The other change which is altering routes and depleting the conservation interest is placing ice picks in turf, especially when it is not frozen. As the turf harbours many plants which are living here in refuges away from grazing animals, the conservation outlook is not good.

The best solution is only to climb when the turf is frozen, but enthusiasm for early routes at the first appearance of winter pulls young men up to the crags before they are ready. It happens every year.

Coire an Lochain is the last of the climbing areas on Cairngorm Estate, but there are several more wonderful opportunities that can be reached from Coire Cas.

# The Loch Avon basin

The crags overlooking Loch Avon form one of the premier climbing areas in the country. There are few comparable glens with so many good quality mountain crags in such a small area, and few, indeed, where so little has been done to make access easy. Here there is no bulldozed land rover track, no climber's hut, no abseil posts nor even a Mountain Rescue box.

Crossing from the Glenmore side to the Loch Avon basin is an act of commitment. For every step down into this dramatic landscape there will be at least one back out again – uphill.

Add to this the possibility of a change in the weather while committed to a route, the climber could be taking on a real tussle to get back to the car. This situation has caught several people out, the saddest resulting in fatalities, and was very much in my mind at New Year recently.

At first light we had a gentle Easterly wind, backing round to the North and broken cloud, with the forecast of a rapid change to a 100 mph North-Westerly and heavy snow. Anyone going over to the Loch Avon basin could find themselves trapped there until the weather abated. I made the point of hanging around the trail head and showing climbers the weather forecast and telling them as they went out "Big change coming in the weather". Most of them knew already, I didn't press the point.

Fortunately, before ten in the morning, the cold front arrived and the air was full of big snowflakes on a strong, gusty wind. The climbers came back, speaking of impossible conditions in the corrie. It was not a day to be crossing to the Loch Avon basin.

So – what's the attraction? The basin has been greatly over-deepened by glacial erosion and crags line both sides and the head of the glen, and cataracts cascade down from all directions towards the loch.

On the far side of the loch from Cairn Gorm are the impressive cliffs of Creag Dearg – the red crag – but they are a bit disappointing on inspection, being quite discontinuous and wet. Then there are the immense crags of Carn Etchachan.

The Etchachan cliffs are split by a huge gully, Castlegates Gully; those on the left are tremendous but those on the right awe-inspiring indeed, and go by the name of The Sticil, pronounced *steecyil*.

Right of Castlegates, the climbs on the Sticil are unremittingly steep and hard, requiring the best technique, and regularly alarming first time visitors with their boldness and exposure.

To gaze on them is all we mere pedestrians are permitted. Should there be a climbing party on one of the routes we will struggle to spot them, and then gasp in amazement at how small they look in such a vertical world. There are few crags in this country in the same class as the Sticil. To see it is to be inspired, or terrorised, or both.

*Forefinger Pinnacle*

The right-hand side of the buttress is defined by a broad gully with a pinnacle in it near its top which provides the obvious inspiration for its name – Forefinger Pinnacle.

To our horror, a mass-circulation magazine recently ran an article about what a good wheeze it would be to trot round of an evening after work, solo climb the pinnacle and trot back again, giving some good bragging rights in the office next day. This casual approach to a risky enterprise, depending on unbroken good weather and in totally remote country has not led to a rash of accidents, perhaps because readers had more sense.

To the right again is the cataract of the Garbh Uisge – the rough burn – and immediately beside it is a slabby buttress which provides an interesting and fairly easy route, little more than a scramble, indeed.

There is another small crag at the head of the valley, which provides a bit of interest in the winter, but the next major feature is beyond the Feith Buidhe, which cascades down pink granite slabs.

Hell's Lum is a classic glaciated granite crag, with rough slabs rising steeply to beetling overhangs and near-vertical crags above. In most summer conditions when I have seen this crag, the slabs are glistening, or running with water.

The eponymous Hell's Lum (chimney) is a huge cleft at the left end of the crag. At the opposite extreme of the crag the superb direct winter climb Escalator goes up the flat face of the cliff. It forms as a sheet of crinkly grey water-ice with no apparent stopping or resting places. Amazingly, it's not all that hard. These are the only two routes I have managed to find the organisation and partnership to climb both in winter, and both with my wife Judith on different visits.

Between them the great steep mass of rock remains unexplored for me. I would love to get the dry conditions to climb Clean Sweep, a plum route up clean slabs in the middle, but the long-lasting water weep and generally dreadful weather have always said no.

Moving on, the next crag round the head of Loch Avon is called Stag rocks, probably from Stac, which means a pile. This is one of the most accessible of the Loch Avon cliffs and has two of my favourite granite routes, Afterthought Arête and Final Selection. They are both at the left hand end of the crag, close to the curiously-named Quartz-diggers' Cave Route.

*The author on Afterthought Arete*

People really did come over to this side of the mountain to dig for smoky quartz to sell for costume jewellery. You can still see their cavern excavated with hand tools in the massive granite. It is all of two metres deep. Such is the hardness of this rock and meagre the reward. This is certainly no gold mine.

Yet another crag towers over Loch Avon, separated from the last by the stream falling from Coire Raibert. This is another Stac, this time Stac an Fharaidh (Crag of the Ladder, pronounced stacanarri). It is another array of granite slabs and walls, one to visit if for no other reason than to enjoy the wonderful view of the whole basin from the top.

Stac an Fharaidh continues on right round into Strath Nethy, crossed by the county boundary. Some people looking at the map mistake the boundary marking for a footpath and ask me whether the route is waymarked. I have followed the boundary closely once, in an uphill direction. It was not too difficult, though I would be less confident launching off downhill, with the cliffs below out of sight until I was at the top of them. A recently published guidebook recommends this route as the main way of climbing Cairn Gorm, after slogging up Strath Nethy!

One more crag needs to be mentioned, and we will come almost full circle back to where we started. Overlooking the middle of Strath Nethy, the rocks have recently been recognised as providing some good sport in winter. The crag has been named Creag a' Cha-no, and the guys who pioneered the routes reckoned that the crag was the most accessible in the Cairngorms, as it could be reached in an hour (at their speed) from the Car Park in Coire na Ciste via Coire Laogh Mor.

*Creag a'Cha-no*

# 8.          Winter walking

What is it about winter in the mountains? It's the hardest season, the shortest days, the storms, the snow and ice. There are no flowers to dally over, no dotterel or chicks, just snow sculptures, ice formations, snow bridges and smooth whiteness.

## The Cairngorms are the headquarters of winter

Yet many people I speak to say that it is their favourite season, and I have to agree with them. It's not just the skiing; it's the elemental battle and the keen cold air. The winters rarely disappoint.

The Cairngorms are the headquarters of winter. If there is any winter anywhere, it will be present in the Cairngorms as our wintriest mountains.

We've been for a summer walk; there were so many plants and things to look at it took us ages to get anywhere. In winter it's a different world. There will be even more preparation but at least we'll not need to take the flower book with us.

There are always a few people, summer and winter, who skip the preparation, either because they can't see the point, or because they haven't heard the scary stories. We can have some scary stories later, perhaps.

In summer, I can appreciate the casual approach. In practice, people get away with it. So, what's different about the winter, and what about the other seasons?

Firstly let me explain that there are really only two seasons here, summer and winter. Spring might be snowy to start with and show no signs of spring until it's summer. There may be a need for winter kit until the snow has shrunk to tiny amounts, so treat it as winter.

Autumn is almost imperceptible from summer, save the sedge and asphodel turning colour. We may see some new snow on the tops later, but unless it's really heavy snow, I would treat autumn the same as summer.

## Let's get ready for a winter walk

Where are we going? If our route involves anything steeper than the gentlest slopes, we will need to make sure we don't slip. Nearly all the possibilities out of the Coire Cas car park will demand care in ascent or descent or both.

The best summertime walks are still excellent wintertime ones, provided there is enough time and energy to carry them out. We should always keep in mind options for shortening the day. Deep snow can change everything, making a straightforward walk into Coire an t-Sneachda into two hours of exhausting slog, instead of an hour's easy going.

How long are we going to be out? In winter, the days being so short, we will need to shorten our plans and be ready to walk and navigate back in the dark.

An early start is essential. It's no good waiting till after lunch, unless you are intending to stay out overnight. The big time-waster in winter is faffing around; doing things while stopped that are not helping to progress the expedition. This could include making a packed lunch, fastening on gaiters, fiddling with crampons and searching for the headtorch in the pack. A sense of urgency is needed in everything. This is not summer. This is no picnic.

Always consider the conditions overhead (the weather) and underfoot (the terrain). The best weather combined with the best underfoot conditions might mean we wouldn't need warm and windproof clothes all the time, but even in the best underfoot conditions, we will have to pay attention to our footwear.

The weather can be very changeable at any time of year, and the day can start out as the best and end up as the worst of all conditions, so it is always advisable to hope for the best and prepare for the worst.

A major consideration is the equipment to wear and carry. This is why people usually start hill walking in summer, before they have had a chance to collect all these things.

Most of this kit is more expensive than the normal stuff you wear, and invariably, the cheap versions of things break and wear out too quickly and don't work as well. So scrimping is not a good plan.

# This is no picnic

Getting ready starts with getting dressed in the morning. What used to be called foundation garments are essential. They go on and stay on.

It's worth making the point again: Cotton might be ideal for hot dry places; it is best avoided for this cold, wet climate. Various man-made materials have been developed that dry quicker than cotton but are just as warm and comfortable. Some people like wool and silk. I agree with wool for socks and silk for thin gloves, but it is too warm for anything else.

I also find long johns much too warm as well. A (male) friend – a good climber – used to wear thick tights under everything. I didn't try this, expecting it to be too warm.

The foundation layer stays in place, other layers can come and go. Some people like an all-in-one fleece and windproof next to the skin. This is an all-or-nothing approach, I prefer layers; but sometimes layers are a pain.

The problem with layers arises when, through overheating, the mid-layer has to come off, but to remove it, the wind/waterproof outer layer has to come off first. While they are both off, the base layer is exposed to the elements, and could get wet or snowy, and even when the waterproof goes back on, the mid-layer garment is out in the weather until it is stuffed in the sack.

Base layer – mid layer – waterproof layer, it's just like in summer, but the waterproof layer usually stays on in winter. Conditions usually demand it.

A hooded jacket with an integral hood (that doesn't detach and blow away) can be a very expensive item. Choosing one is a critical decision. How adjustable is the hood? Are the pockets closable? Can snow blow in through the zips?

Legwear for many climbers is a variation on the bib-and-braces or salopettes. Having a well-covered midriff in winter is essential if you value your kidneys. If your waist band doesn't have to support the weight of your snow-crusted trousers, it's less likely to slip down your hips, dragging the under layers with it. I've nothing against a good pair of over-trousers, but the shoulder straps are a big help in winter.

Gaiters perplex many people. A lot of people struggle so much to fasten this piece of shaped material around their lower leg and ankle, with a strap under the instep, that they do it before setting out. Then, even in summer, they will enjoy a walk to Ben Macdui and back and never need them.

For years I thought I was saving money by removing the neoprene strap under my gaiter and replacing it with garden wire. Every time I replaced the wire I told myself how much longer it lasted than the strap would have done. Then I took a reality check, used the strap as supplied and found that they last as long as the gaiter, or longer.

The main reason for wearing gaiters is to stop things getting in your boots, especially snow. Once snow packs down into your boots it can freeze your skin tissue unless you clear it out. That way lies frostbite.

Once, on a day of sunshine and deep snow, I met three well-equipped guys and a young lad. The youngster had no gaiters. The three guys were completely oblivious to the problems this was causing him. They might have thought it expensive to kit out a growing lad, but they would have been well annoyed if he had not been able to carry on and the plans of all four had been spoiled.

Gaiters provide another puzzle. Do they go under or over the waterproof overtrousers? There is a similar overlap at the waist, but people never seem to have the same difficulty deciding which to put on top there. (Do they? If you see someone with his overtrousers up over his jacket on a wet day, give him a wide berth!) So why do people put gaiters over overtrousers? Any rain or melted snow will run down inside the gaiters and into the boots.

So far, the kit could be summer kit as well, but the extremities need special care in winter. Everyone is different, and females withdraw heat into their core quicker than males, so they feel cold hands and feet sooner. The downside for men is that their body core cools and they die quicker of hypothermia.

Even people who 'never' wear a hat will keep one handy in winter. Winter hats grip your head, usually because they are stretchy, such as a nylon fleece. They come in a bewildering array of shapes and sizes. Some amazingly high proportion of your body heat escapes through your head, and having a hat on or off gives a great deal of control over how you feel.

I must admit to years of preference for woolly balaclavas worn folded-up like a peaked hat or pulled down in an instant to give great protection in changing conditions. Having worn out or lost more of these than I care to remember, I have retreated to the plain thin fleece cap.

Hands are very vulnerable extremities, too. I have experimented with fingerless mitts, woollen, nylon and silken gloves, big woollen Dachstein mitts and the multi-layer fleece-lined mitts and gloves that can cost upwards of £60.

Even though my hands are more often too hot than too cold (I'm a man) gloves are essential. A matching pair, mind.

It must be pretty long odds against finding an identical odd glove to pair with one you already have. Not only does the size and colour have to match, but you need a left and a right. I found a neat North Face glove on the ski area one winter. As usual, I kept it in the Ranger Base, hoping someone would claim it. It didn't match any of the odd ones we had, nor any of the ones at home. A couple of years later, on the track from Inverie to Inverguseran in Knoydart I found another neat black North Face glove and kept it. Back at Cairngorm, I was delighted that it not only paired with the one I already had, but it was a left to the Cairngorm one's right! They were too small for me so I gave them away.

The lower extremities are much more expensive to cover because they do so much work in such difficult conditions. There is no compromise on boots, especially in winter.

The boots are so important to stability and forward movement that you can tell instantly if they are not good for the planned day. If they don't fit they can be so uncomfortable your day becomes a misery. The success of your day depends on you and all your kit, but especially the boots, working together as a team.

Winter boots give insulation and shock protection through stiffened soles, support the ankle with the high cuff and are fairly waterproof. They fit crampons because the sole is almost flat. There is sufficient protection at the toe for kicking steps. Summer boots will not do this.

The sort of equipment I've described is a minimum for a winter day out. You can carry the bits you're not wearing in the same rucksack you use in summer if you like, but it's going to have a lot more demands on it.

The rucksack will also need attachment points for ice axe and crampons on the outside, so it might need to be a completely different sack from the summertime one after all.

Now we come to the accessories, and this is where we really know winter is upon us.

Will we bother with goggles? No harm, they might make the difference between being able to see and not being able to see. Ski goggles will do. I once had some folding goggles that fitted in my pocket for warm weather in the Alps, but they steamed up terribly in winter.

The real essentials are ice axe and crampons.

The ice axe is the most iconic piece of mountain kit, even more than boots or rope. For walking, the ice axe is useful as a prop, so it needs to be long enough to reach the ground to be leaned upon. As the ground on mountains is usually sloping, this doesn't mean that your ice axe needs to be as long as a walking-stick would be. Fifty cm suits me (I'm 1.85 m), a different length will suit others.

Your ice axe can be carried on your pack until the ground is steep enough to need it as a prop or more crucially as a brake should you start to slide. In these circumstances it needs to be to hand, not on the pack.

When I was younger, the axe was invariably fastened to the back of the pack, head down and ferrule up. Now it is more often carried in the compression straps on the side, head up with the pick pointing backwards. Really cool operators thread it down their back between the wearer and the pack where it sometimes finds an unexplained hollow to occupy comfortably.

Crampons strike terror into faint hearts, convinced that life-threatening antics are planned. True, they are a bit of a handful. You can buy expensive nylon bags for them that hide away all the sharp points and strap to the lid of your sack, or you can buy fiddly crampon point protectors, like rubber bungs all connected together, or do without and wish you hadn't. It's up to you.

If you are taking crampons, they need to be fitted the night before. You need to practise putting them on and taking them off quickly. In the event it might not be necessary all day until after dark in a cold wind with numb fingers. Then you need to be slick.

I think crampons are often overrated. Some people treat them as a magic walking mechanism completely removing the need for an ice axe. I see crampon marks on snowless footpaths and even in the car park. They are responsible for a lot of damage to the mountain when the wearers should be nipping them off and walking along comfortably on rubber soles. It might be possible to go all day without needing them, but I would be reluctant to set off without.

Walking in crampons takes a bit of practice, too. They are the devil for tripping you up on rocky ground, and unless they have anti-balling plates, the points can pick up a huge ball of snow, making the effect of walking on platform soles with a strongly converse heel.

# Crampons are often overrated

I came down Number Four gully on Ben Nevis once, nearly one thousand feet of steep soft snow, and had to tap each crampon in turn with my ice axe at every step, to dislodge the huge ball of snow that had built up. It became an extremely tedious descent.

Crampons should fit the boot and not come off by shaking even when the straps are not fastened. Once the straps are fastened, they should not come off even if you try to prise them off. You will need to be ruthless when fitting them. If they can come off, they will do so, and they won't wait for a convenient moment.

There are several types of crampons available, as you might expect. You have to consider what you are going to do with them. Twelve point crampons will probably be adequate. Leave the devices designed to help people get around on snowy pavements to the pavements. You will need a mountain pair with no brittle plastic bits to break.

On a different foray on Ben Nevis, I was staying in the mountain hut there (the CIC hut) and paired up with an older climber as all my other friends had made other plans. We set out in crampons, heading for Slingsby's Chimney, a serious ice route, but not one of the hardest. On the approach, one of his crampons fell off. He picked it up easily and inspected it and announced that it had broken. A structural section of the crampon was made of nylon, and it had failed.

While relieved that we had been spared a nerve-racking descent from our route, I was mightily disappointed that after all the effort of carrying up supplies and equipment to the hut, my two days' climbing had been cut short by a design fault.

My companion regaled me with all the superb routes these crampons had done. Later in the month he rang to say he had bought some new ones and had been back and done our route with another party, so it all ended well (for him).

I realise I'm committing the sin I warned against, of not getting on with the short winter day, but telling stories and delaying our departure. Let's get a move on!

All kitted up and ready to go – where? What's the weather forecast? How much snow is there, and is it likely to slow us down? What is the avalanche risk? There are rather a lot of imponderables in winter.

The best winter plan is quite a short one, until you are confident that you can move quickly and cope with whatever challenges you face. Something like the round of the Rim of the Northern Corries could be an excellent challenge, or you might be content to visit one of the Northern Corries for a closer view. The summit of Cairn Gorm is another good idea.

Nevertheless, deep snow underfoot or strong head winds can make even a short route a huge challenge. You might consider shortening it part-way round.

Unplanned route changes, short cuts and retreats can pose great problems in route-finding. Moving over difficult terrain can call into play skills that were not anticipated at the start of the day. It's as well to consider them as possibilities while you're still fresh.

# The best winter plan is quite a short one

An internal narrative might go like this: "Pretty windy on top. We'll be slightly sheltered until the plateau, then we'll really get hit by the wind. Maybe have a rest and refuel before we go over the top. Get the kit sorted, mittens on, that sort of thing. We can keep the cliffs on our right but there's no easy way down them until after the second summit. If we must use one of the difficult ways down, it will be crampons for sure, perhaps the rope, too. Can all the party do crampons quickly? Will they panic?" And so on.

## On the hill

The first thing to notice, apart from the cold, is the way the snow takes over from all the familiar landmarks. The path might be visible at first, but somewhere on the way, it starts to get lost, marked only by larger stones, and then not distinguishable at all.

On a popular path, the broken trail takes over. This has been trodden out by all the people who went before, for which you are very grateful. Try walking off the beaten trail for a moment! You soon come back to it, don't you?

The snow is too soft to support your weight, and you sink into whatever is under the surface. Snow, vegetation, more snow, liquid peat, a stream, more snow,…

Pity the first person who came along this morning. Notice how the wind has drifted new snow over the trail since the last person walked on it. If we were to stop here for a few minutes, it wouldn't take long before the trail was drifted over completely, and we couldn't rely on it any more to show us the way. Then we would have the same lovely job as the first person had, sinking in to the depth of our knees in snow, streams, puddles,…

Come to think of it, that snow wasn't drifting so fiercely when we set out. Is the weather changing, or are we just climbing into the stronger winds higher up? Let's consider what the sky is doing. Has the cloud cover increased dramatically? Are the skylines still visible, or are they obscured by cloud, or snow falling or drifting?

Falling snow is not of itself an obstacle. It's much more pleasant than rain, even if it brings additional hazards with it. Many a day will start in rain, progress up into the colder air where it's snowing, and return back down to the rain at the end. If so, the middle part is usually far the most pleasant.

The snow whipping against our faces might not be the soft fluffy sort. It might be hard pellety snow or eroded ice being blasted off the ground higher up and re-deposited around us. Either way, the effect is of a stinging numbness, if you can have such a thing. It's like a gnawing ache at your bare skin.

# Wind is the greatest enemy

This is time to deploy some accessories. You probably have your hat on already. Pull your hood over it. Still uncomfortable? If your hat pulls down to form a balaclava hood, now is the time to do it, otherwise your hood will need to be fastened right up, or you could use a neck-warmer or scarf.

This still leaves your eyes unprotected. Out come the goggles. They need to fit well round your face. You can put them on over everything else. Once they are on, though, try to leave them on. If you take them off for a minute you will steam up the lens. A way round this is to smear them with a thin layer of detergent before you set out.

As the wind rises, more problems come about. At forty miles per hour – a strong breeze in mountain terms but gale force 8 on the Beaufort Scale – it will make a strong adult stagger occasionally.

Steady wind is the exception rather than the rule, and the familiar term "buffeting" describes many winds commonly experienced in the mountains. I have to explain this term to visitors who are not native English speakers – and some who are – as "strong gusts", "rafales fortes" and so on.

If the wind rises, movement against it will become interrupted, then opportunistic, and finally impossible. We will have to crouch and duck to avoid its pressure, brace our legs and feet against it and keep in touch with the ground with ice axe or gloved hand.

I have heard of tales of people crawling to the summit cairn. Such progress is so slow, they will have had to have made a decision about whether they could sustain the activity long enough to reach their destination, and the chances of being whipped up by the wind and rolled along.

My great heroes, the Cairngorm Mountain Rescue Team, were called on to help a strong, fit, well-equipped walker on the return leg of his expedition into the mountains on a day when the summit weather station was recording gusts of 136 mph. He was sheltering, uninjured, in the lee of the summit weather station building and spoke to them on his mobile phone. He had lost the plot, being too scared to move out of his shelter because he was being blown around, despite his heavy pack.

The three rescuers went up from the Ptarmigan building with a blistering cross-wind all the way up the Summit Path. One of them was blown over and along five metres but was uninjured and was able to recover and continue. From the summit cairn they could only just see the top of the tower at the summit building above the plume of cloud and drift. They crossed that ferocious desert and arrived safely, but not before the man had made a further telephone call to find out what was keeping them.

The four of them, with the walker on a confidence rope, made a quick dash back down the path without incident, pulling off a very simple rescue in the most inhospitable conditions imaginable, and at material risk to themselves.

Only days before, another very fit and experienced climber had been blown off the path in Coire an t-Sneachda and broken an ankle. There have been worse injuries and even fatalities caused by the wind blowing people over cliffs, so we will watch out for this possibility.

All these horrors can happen on the path, as I mentioned in the chapter about Coire an t-Sneachda, but I wouldn't like to exaggerate the chances of it happening to someone who has planned their route and kit, and has a companion to offer mutual support.

The summit rescue was on a day well-expected to have hurricane-force winds. The rescued man didn't have prior warning, but could have drawn a valid conclusion from his observation of the weather on the day. He probably didn't think: "The wind is nearly lifting me off my feet here on the plateau, so I'll go up to the summit to see whether it manages to do it up there". He didn't decide to take the shortest route down, either.

The people surviving being blown over the cliffs probably wish they had stayed further back from the edge. Even on low ground, you can't always choose your landing spot.

I think I have made the point: Wind is the greatest natural enemy, and winter is the time when it displays its most ferocious strength.

Snow and cousin ice are the playthings of winter. At best, snow is a free toy, a modelling and building medium, a broadloom carpet to smooth your footsteps and speed your skis, a reliable, uniform climbing medium, a daylight-lengthener, a distant clarion to the mountain, a protecting layer for plants and burrowing animals, a magical whirligig of myriad uniqueness and a ladder of steps to help you securely up the slopes.

At worst it is a blinding, frightening maelstrom of cold, stinging particles, sapping all your efforts to see, to step or to walk, rearing up in unseen obstacles to impede your progress, letting you sink in to your knees, to your waist, covering trip hazards and water features, melting into slush swamps and uncrossable torrents, demanding complete conformity to wear and use unfamiliar equipment, and bring woe to anyone whose equipment or clothing is lost as it falls off or blows away.

# A magical whirligig of myriad uniqueness

Snow may be unpopular with many lowlanders, but it is a boon in the Highlands. Much better winter snow than rain. Snow announces its presence. You are not left guessing with snow as you are with frost and ice. The white crystals are their own warning.

Frost and ice are much more insidious. They appear out of the air and the ground without warning. The wet road of the previous evening can be like a bottle in the morning, glassy and slippery, as black ice spreads under clear skies. The seeping drain on the path can produce a smear of ice that no-one anticipates, many slip on and some fall.

As the freeze progresses, the mountain paths can become the worst place to walk. These are the only conditions in which I have seen the pavement-crampons demonstrated satisfactorily, once fastened to a young man's Wellington boots.

My advice is to persevere with the path until it is plain that the conditions are intolerable, and no relief is in prospect. Then take to the hillside, which is what the mountaineer is well-equipped to do in any case. The usual reaction is to walk along the edge of the path, causing the phenomenon of winter damage that we try to avoid.

I would say, at any time of the year, but particularly in winter: If you don't like the path, walk on a parallel route some tens of metres away.

There is, in all aspiring mountaineer's career, a point when the question arises "When are we going to put on the crampons?"

On my first winter climbing expedition to the Lake District, I followed several more experienced friends up from Ruthwaite Lodge into Nethermost Cove on Helvellyn in snowy conditions. We were heading for a snow gully which led up through the cliffs like a ramp, clear from bottom to top. The snow was beginning to be a nuisance, making us trip over stones and slide around. I soon learned that the least effort was to put my step in the mark left by the people ahead. We used our ice axes as supports and eventually came to a place where we could hack a shelf in the snow big enough for us all to stand on and put on our crampons.

Despite the blue sky and sunshine, it was cold work fiddling with the jaggy steel frames and trying to squash our boots onto the small platform securely, then fastening them up with the neoprene straps.

I failed at the first hurdle, and found that the crampons would not adjust for my boots. Somehow I managed to fasten them on back-to-front, I can't remember how. The straps were the wrong lengths and the instep part of the crampon came under the ball of my foot. This all demonstrates the need to fit the crampons the night before. I learned the hard way.

However, they didn't fall off, we climbed our gully and were rewarded with fine views all over the Lake District from the top of the gully, and again all along the promenade that is the summit of Helvellyn.

Many of my early winter mountaineering experiences were on Helvellyn, including my first ice gully. One day we went swimming in deep snow on a steep face on Saint Sunday Crag. This was after a huge fall of snow while we were staying in Ruthwaite Lodge. We decided to climb a gully and found the snow soft and head-high. The avalanche gods were sleeping. I'll let them sleep a little longer but we will have to wake them sometime.

So we were wondering when to put on our crampons. It's quite a late decision. On the way up to steeper ground, there may be a point while the ground is still low-angle that makes it easy to put them on. There may be long icy stretches to cross, making crampons essential. Another time the good footing may lead right up the steep slopes to near the top. Every day will be different.

I like to have a flat surface to step on to put on my crampons, a rock will do, or a snow ledge I have cut in the slope.

Putting on the crampons is a fairly significant moment for all your kit. Will you need overtrousers or salopettes while your crampons are on? If so – better put them on first, because although it might be possible to get trousers on over crampons, it's not easy, so why bother?

Walking in crampons changes your gait. For a start you are up on points, like little platforms. You can fall off them, twisting an ankle or falling sideways. A friend stood mistakenly on the side of her boot instead of on the crampon points and slid 1500 feet down a gully on Bidean nam Bian once, pulling her companion with her. They got up to walk off, but it was a serious warning.

The idea with crampons is to get as many points to bite into the snow and ice as possible. On the flat, this means adopting a flat-footed walking style, placing all the points simultaneously.

On a slope, you will need to flex your ankle round to present all points to the snow. On steeper ground this becomes difficult, and the heel may tend to lift, but the boots should be stiff and all the points facing the same way, so the pressure on the front points will bite securely. You can start to angle your foot round diagonally or along the slope if it gets a bit steep.

It's a good idea to have a bit of a practice with the crampons on low-angle ground before taking them anywhere steep. As I mentioned before, Coire an t-Sneachda is an ideal place to do this, on the "Flat Ice" at the back of the corrie. Parties of trainees can often be seen clambering up and down, jumping on their points, hopping, getting thoroughly used to the unfamiliar sensation.

On most types of terrain, the ice axe is more useful than the crampons, and should certainly be in play whenever the crampons are deployed. Most ice axes have a wrist loop, but I have never dropped one when walking and have given up using it. The wrist loop tends to make you use the same hand all the time, and when zig-zagging up a slope, there is always a need to swap hands, keeping the axe on the upper side.

*An ice axe is more useful than crampons*

# The most iconic of mountain kit

For years I carried my axe pick-forward with my palm resting on the adze. I was told this was wrong and took a while to adjust to the opposite pattern. If you slip and need to use the ice axe as a brake, it is much quicker to get the pick in the snow if it is carried with the pick facing backwards.

If I am quite nervous of a descent, and I am not sure whether I will suddenly slip and need to brake, I carry my axe in two hands across my chest, one hand on the head, pick down, and the other on the shaft.

Should the slip happen, the priority is to get on your front and get the pick into the snow, but not so suddenly that the axe is jerked out of your grip, hence the two-handed style I mentioned.

It's a good idea to practise every season on a snow slope with a gentle run-out and no rocks (and wearing your old waterproofs and no crampons) sliding down the slope feet-first, on your back, then head-first, head-first on your back and, scariest of all, rolling over wand over. You can't predict which way you will fall.

The slide is controlled by a series of actions, some of which might not be necessary, depending on what's happening. You have to control the roll – throw a star-shape. You have to get head-up – dig the pick in on one side and swing round it as you slide. You need to get on your front and you need to force the pick in using your weight if it's not slowing you down much.

My first real arrest was on a glassy stream in the Peak District. I actually slipped over one small waterfall before forcing the pick into the steely ice on the next flat section, saving myself from going down over the next ten-foot waterfall. "Well held!" was all my companion said, though later I had my leg pulled for carrying a walking stick, and my companion was able to say that I had saved injury with it.

Most slips are controlled in the first one or two seconds. It's only on the snow slopes of Cairn Gorm you regularly see people trying to build up as much speed as possible before applying the brakes. They are in training or being assessed. It's an essential skill.

I once helped to load a young chap into a helicopter on Ben Nevis. He had been trying to slide in crampons and had broken an ankle. Slides in crampons are really dangerous. The points can easily bite into the snow and throw the sliding person right over, changing a straight on-the-front head-up slide into an on-the-back head down one or a barrel roll in a second.

The points of the crampons are obvious hazards for the person wearing them and everyone else, too. Many an injury has been caused by one going into a leg, especially in a slide or fall.

Crampons, ice axes, goggles, all the kit. We're armed to the teeth! We've faced the wind, coped with slippery and snowy slopes. What else is there?

There are still some more big scary hazards out there, we haven't finished yet!

# Avalanche!

I've already mentioned the avalanche gods. Excuse me for adopting a superstitious introduction. Avalanches are a product of physical forces, not supernatural ones, and they can be well-understood and studied.

*Slab avalanche on an open slope in Coire an Lochain*

Until 2010, I would have confidently said there would be no danger from avalanche if you stayed on the flat ground and didn't go poking around in steep places, but a couple of situations that winter made me change my mind. In that year there was a huge build-up of snow, and avalanches were recorded on the approach to Creag Meagaidh and again in Coire an t-Sneachda which crossed flat ground at the base of the slopes where they had originated.

In many years, the Coire an Lochain slab avalanche has covered great areas of the base of that corrie, and in one year, the open slope opposite the Slab collapsed and blocks of snow the size of grand pianos landed on the flat ground. While no-one was caught in any of these avalanches, it was only a matter of luck, as they are all popular places.

Studying the avalanche report and forecast is as much part of planning for a day out in winter as studying the weather forecast. The next stage in the defence is looking out for previous activity, especially recent falls. Then you could dig a neat pit in the snow slope down to the hard layer (or the ground) and try to make layers slide on each other. If the snow above your pit is stable even with you jumping on it, the inference is that the slope is not likely to avalanche while you are on it.

Another tactic is to follow the people ahead, keeping your distance. In extreme conditions, we might climb one at a time. Snow stability can be variable over the slope. I have seen a film of skiers descending a slope safely, each on a different track, until one crossed a fresh area between the previous tracks and brought the whole slope down – and was killed.

If the slope did avalanche, the others should keep a look out for the victim and spot where they might be to dig them out.

That reminds me – did you bring a shovel? No? Another piece of kit! Fortunately snow shovels are very lightweight, but not cheap. Some come with avalanche probes hidden in the handle.

If you were well-equipped and concerned about the possibility of avalanche, you would have an avalanche transceiver as well, switched to "send", so that everyone else with a transceiver on the same wavelength could switch to "receive" and locate you quickly.

Speed is of the essence, as a buried avalanche victim's chances dwindle rapidly with time.

# The avalanche forecast is as much part of planning for a day out in winter as the weather forecast

I've never been buried in an avalanche and in need of being dug out, but my one avalanche experience was terrifying enough in any case.

I had arrived at the CIC Hut on Ben Nevis in the morning of a reasonable day and my friends had already gone off to climb. So I decided to climb Tower Gully, thinking that the class 2 avalanche risk was low enough to be reasonable. I followed three other guys who were unknown to me up Observatory Gully and decided that because of the snow that was falling I would need to go back down. They, however, decided to go on to Gardyloo Gully. I was intrigued and took off my pack to get out the camera to photograph them.

I moved to a position to see the leader slowly working his way up towards the gully. At one moment, independently of anything we were doing, the sides of the gully all sloughed off at once. They were suddenly decorated with a delightful filigree of gently falling curtains of snow – all adding to the deep snow in the main gully where I was standing. It was ineffably beautiful, and I was totally distracted.

Then I saw the leader founder slightly, as if his foot had punched deeper into the snow, and the surface around him all cracked up and started streaming towards me. In my panic, I tried to step over the stream to return to the side where my ice axe and rucksack were sitting, but I was carried down, camera in hand.

In the minute that followed, I was piled on by some pretty heavy powder snow and wiped along the harder snow below. For a while I was on my front and felt my knees being scraped on rocks, then freefall for a moment before a soft landing and continuing down. I felt my mittens being scraped off one by one as I battled to throw the snow off my head. My camera was long gone.

# Recklessness is unpunished and distraction is made to pay

And then I was on the surface, sitting up, riding a roller-coaster snow slide down the gully, slowing and eventually stopping. I stood up and saw one of my mittens in the snow. I thought I had injured a knee. I calculated later I had gone 250 metres.

I shouted up "I'm all right", but there was no reply. Later, the party started coming down from above. The leader had gone about 50 metres, and was uninjured. He had my ice axe. There was no sign of my rucksack – a sore loss. The other two guys had been at the edge of the gully and their block of snow had remained unmoved. They had watched, petrified as their leader had caused the catastrophe and disappeared down the gully. None of them knew I had been involved till later.

I plodded back to the CIC Hut with my sole mitten and ice axe. I was particularly grateful not to lose the latter as it was on loan from Judith.

Once there, my friends returned and I cleaned myself up. My nemesis agreed to phone my home number and say I had been caught in a snow slide, but I would walk down to the Youth Hostel in Glen Nevis. A friend would drive my car home.

The walk down took ages. The staff at Belford hospital made a great job of cleaning out the round hole that had appeared in my knee. Most of what came out was fat. I have no idea to this day how a neat round hole was made in my knee. I couldn't reach it with a crampon point, and have no recollection of being screwed up by the snow in that way.

I was off work for two weeks, and much the wiser. Insurance paid me the value of my lost property, but my lovely little Olympus 1 N camera and my excellent Aiguille sack full of everything, even my lunch, was never handed in.

How we evaded the avalanche gods that day on St. Sunday Crag, I've no idea. Perhaps we were lucky, but when recklessness is unpunished and distraction is made to pay, it's a strange world.

# Hypothermia

There are three further winter hazards to guard against. One is the obvious – getting too cold. I've already said enough about gearing up and keeping warm. There are several other defences against hypothermia. Keep cheerful and keep self-aware. If the rest of the party is going too fast, call a halt.

I tagged along behind a fit party of my friends one time, and the wind-driven snow was making my head hurt. I was tripping and swearing – not usual for me – and realised I was becoming hypothermic. We stopped, I sorted out my headgear, had some chocolate and continued much more comfortably.

The other defence is to keep in touch with your ideas about what you are doing. It has been shown that fear can bring on hypothermia. Keep talking. If someone else looks done-in, keep them cheerful and positive. Let them explain what's wrong, and change plans if you can. There is no advantage in having a hypothermic member of the party.

# The hazard of drink – not enough of it!

Dehydration is not a hazard you might expect in cold, snowy times, but even with all the adjustable clothing and a good pace and rests, dehydration is a real problem. The defence is – drink plenty! It's not rocket science. In winter my hot flask is a source of comfort, but I find I'm sipping liquid that is too hot, when I should be swilling it down. I could always add some clean snow to it.

How do you know if you are dehydrated? Look at the colour of your pee. If it's browner than weak tea, have a drink and top up!

Alcohol is a definite no-no on the hill, but it is surprising how many people have a hip flask for celebrating their arrival at the top. It's one of those remedies that has been totally debunked. The St. Bernard dog with the cask of brandy round its neck is delivering a rush of blood to the outer skin of the rescued person, depleting the heat in their inner core. A swift and possibly pleasant end, then.

# Benightment

The iron discipline of winter cannot be dropped even in good weather, good snow conditions, high states of fitness and competence, good health, warmth, high spirits and a good state of hydration. Why not?

That perfect sunset that comes on in late afternoon is the precursor to a subtle chill that comes over the landscape as the sun drops below the horizon, or the mountain, or cloud bank. It's as if the music has changed from major to minor in the last few bars of the piece. Other people have seen it as the angel of death breathing over the winter landscape.

The oranges and yellows drop out of the scene, leaving only the blues, fading slowly.

Actually I enjoy living in these Northern climes. The long twilight is something I relish, from the long pre-dawn *crescendo* to the long post-sunset *morendo*. In summer I enjoy the longer daylight in the North and miss no opportunity to gloat at the way the sun is still splitting the skies while someone in England on the other end of the phone is seeing the streetlights coming on.

This long twilight is a perfect opportunity to prepare for the darkness to follow, and to defy it as long as possible. By all means root out the headtorch and have it in a pocket, but I always try to avoid using it for as long as possible. Once you turn the headtorch on, it desensitises your eyes and you find it too dark to turn off again.

There will be a point, though when it becomes mandatory to use the headtorch, to read a map or negotiate a tricky section or signal to others. It can't be helped, but I prefer to leave it as late as possible, if only to prolong battery life.

Walking back in the dark always gives me time to think back over the time I wasted during the daylight, and to wish I hadn't. I have to fight down a feeling of distress. I'm a real home bird, unless the situation is a planned one for a night-time stint. A glance at the time helps. Only seven o'clock? That's not late.

Keep up the energy levels and plod on. While your light is still working, it's not sore. It's when it gives out or stops you have to worry!

# 9. Further afield

*Now we have explored Cairn Gorm, what else is there?*
The list is endless. After Cairn Gorm, the most obvious mountain summit accessible from the car park at Cairngorm is Ben Macdui.

## Ben Macdui

The highest point in the Cairngorms was long considered to be the highest mountain in Britain. This shows how difficult it is to distinguish heights from observation. Imagine the disappointment that must have been felt in Deeside and Aberdeenshire when the government's Ordnance Survey came along in the middle of the nineteenth century to depose it.

Ben Macdui's loss of status has been its saving, in my opinion. Consider for a moment the injustice heaped on our highest mountain by those whose idea of climbing a mountain is to dominate it, to display their prowess and disdain for difficulty. Or those whose approach to climbing a mountain is no different from going for a daunder anywhere.

No model T Ford has been driven up Ben Macdui, no piano discovered dumped in a cairn, no summit observatory turned hotel now used as a toilet, no incessant summertime procession of the ill-equipped, misguided, and insane, clad in bicycle capes, kaftans and flip-flops.

For those who arrive in Aviemore intent on knocking off their second mountain in two days, having climbed Ben Nevis only yesterday, the contrast must be startling. The high starting point, at 635m, must give the impression that half the job is already done.

The preamble is not a business-like incline climbing from a deep forested glen, but a well-made gravel path which seems reluctant at first to get on with any serious uphill at all. This is the Northern Corries Path we explored earlier. At last some real uphill action brings the walker, as I described, up a broad ridge to arrive at the first plateau, Miadan Creag an Leth-choin.

Again, the path up this high mountain seems to become more of a tour around the mountains than a climb up one of them. The path is fairly narrow and slides along one hillside and then another without any inclination to get to the top of anything.

After a while the walker will be aware of a great declivity – a cleft through the mountains – on the right. It is, in fact, so deep, that a significant detour down the slope would be needed to see the bottom of it. This is the Lairig Ghru, the glen through the heart of the Cairngorms.

On a clear day, the mountains across the Lairig are some of the most attractive in the country – a similarity to the Ben, looking across Glen Nevis. On Sgor an Lochan Uaine the eponymous water body is one of the most dramatic in the Cairngorms, draining by a sliver of water down naked granite to join the River Dee below.

The peaks to the west demand attention all along here: The gullies of Sron na Lairig, the broad flat top of Braeriach, Sgor an Lochan Uaine, Cairn Toul and the sliced half loaf of the Devil's Point. Further along the walk the undying snow patches of Braeriach become visible, even late in the summer. This is a rich accompaniment to the climb, provided, of course, you can see it.

Nearly two hours into the walk, the aspirant is confronted with a distant view of the objective, a double-headed dome in the middle distance. Through binoculars, tiny figures may be seen, giving the whole mountain an immense scale. Now the walker realises, just when the views across the Lairig are really tremendous, that miles and miles of barren stony landscape lie between this point and the summit. Worse – the first section is downhill. There is nothing like this on the Ben.

At the base of the slope, a gentle ascent is resumed, with one steeper section, which continues directly to the summit. No tiresome zig-zagging across an endless steep stony slope here. The path goes straight across the open plateau between Lochan Buidhe, the highest named lochan in Scotland – therefore the world – and the head waters of the stream falling into the Lairig Ghru known as the March Burn.

It is worth remembering that this is the easiest and most direct route to the country's second highest mountain, therefore it is a very popular route and one traversed by expert and tyro, fell runner and family outing. Despite this, the combined wear and tear from all these feet is insufficient to sustain a path in the next section, as it crosses a stony desert that is like nothing so much as a dry lake bed, except it is on a slope. The occasional cairn guides the walker, and eventually, after several hundred yards of stumbling along, a path appears heading in the correct direction.

The lesson of this section is that this is a big, confusing place, especially in a mist, which can arrive in minutes if weather is changing. There are no cliffs or crevasses to fall down, but the hazards are still serious. Again, they are un-dramatic. If there were more dramatic hazards, some of the inexperienced and ill-equipped people that have come to grief here might have been more cautious, but steep dramatic hazards also claim victims, there is no simple formula.

In the direction towards Ben Macdui, the natural tendency is to follow the cairns across the stony slope and pick up a good path going in the correct

*The cairn nearest to the junction of Inverness-shire, Aberdeenshire and Morayshire.*
*Ben Macdui beyond.*

165

direction, no problem. Coming the other way, virtually everyone fails to transfer from the good path across the stony slope to the path we have just come up. Those that are determined to turn their steps to the West side of Cairn Lochan usually make their course adjustment near Lochan Buidhe.

The bulk of the top of Ben Macdui now looms up to the South. It is utterly desolate, without a scrap of cover or shelter. I said earlier I have seen families setting out across this area in the face of an approaching thunderstorm. Should you be enjoying the propulsion of a stiff Northerly breeze on the way out you will need all your energy to fight it all the way back.

The last big uphill section is, at the time of writing, one of the most eroded sections of path in the country. It has spread to occupy a shallow gully, down which snowmelt and summertime rainstorms tear their course, bringing huge quantities of gravel to bury rocks and vegetation.

At the top of the eroded slope, the path enters a unique landscape of wind-eroded hillside where the wind has removed the vegetation and soil over very large areas, and the path threads faintly through it, marked by occasional cairns.

I found a dead redwing here once. It had probably been on migration. It was a bleak place for a woodland bird to die.

*The approach to Ben Macdui is utterly desolate*

One more spring hollow to cross and the final ascent to the summit is in a different direction at last. Some strange stone shelters litter the route, and then, great celebration, the summit cairn topped by the trig point is reached.

We have been walking three hours, possibly four. It is a long-winded ascent, free from the repetitive back-and-forth across a convex slope but much less dramatic than the climb to Ben Nevis.

Unlike the Ben, too, the return is going to take quite a bit of effort. It's not just a case of brakes off and let gravity do the work. We'll think about that in a while when we've enjoyed being here.

I described the panorama from Cairn Gorm earlier on. The view from Ben

Macdui on a clear day is, if anything, even more impressive. The observer gets a real sense of the layout of Scotland from up here, more so even than from Ben Nevis.

In addition to all the peaks visible from Cairn Gorm, the slightly more southerly and higher position of Ben Macdui brings more southern hills into view. The first ones I look for are the Lomond Hills: West Lomond and Bishop Hill in Kinross-shire, where I used to live. They peep out 97km away on 166 degrees, between the peaks of Carn an Righ and Glas Tulaichean in the hills West of Glen Shee. East Lomond is obscured, directly behind Glas Tulaichean.

The dim and misty hills beyond these are the Pentland Hills beyond Edinburgh. Atmospheric haze probably accounts for any slight lack of clarity, but binoculars will be needed for the next hill to the right, which I have seen, but is not on the viewpoint indicator. Tinto Hill, at 164km South of Ben Macdui is one of the longest views in the UK. I have had this feat disputed, but not by someone who was there on the day.

In the opposite direction, Ben Hope is visible 159 km away, giving a range of over 300km in the view.

The whole of the Highlands of Scotland, and a good bit of the Lowlands are laid out around you. The mountains of the Highlands can be seen to be arranged in a shape reminiscent of a hand, the fingers together stretching North, and the Grampians representing an outstretched thumb. Lower ground between them, from the Great Glen to Strathspey, is largely hidden from view and does not confuse the image.

Somewhere to the south, the Central Belt represents a wrist, beyond which the hills rise again as with a cuff. It is a vision that glorifies Scotland, not diminishes it.

In this vision of distant greatness, it is surprising that so many nearer places claim the attention. Perhaps the most insistent is the straight-on view of Garbh Choire Mor on Braeriach, home to the summer snows that have only melted seven times in the last century, the last time being in 2017.

To the right of Braeriach, by a quirk of topography, Aviemore in Strathspey can be seen through the gap of the Lairig Ghru. If this was the day's start point, it seems a very long way away.

# Vision of distant greatness

Cairn Gorm is seen to be a distinctive mountain, with the large tor on its eastern side, and two summit features, the building and the smaller cairn. Ben Macdui's smaller Northern top now becomes evident, something that could be completely ignored on the ascent.

As with Cairn Gorm, the most dramatic views from Ben Macdui need a short descent, either to the South where the ruined Sapper's Bothy gives a view down the high shallow valley to the east of the summit. Better still, to the West, where at the top of Coire nan Clach is an unrestricted view of the summertime snows, and the memorial to an aircraft crash, accompanied by some of the wreckage.

Nowadays, any new aircraft wreckage is scrupulously removed from crash sites, but the means and the motivation were not there in wartime and the years immediately after. The sites were regarded as war graves and left to moulder away. The more recent (2001) crash on Ben Macdui has less to show than this one, and I prefer our present approach. To me, the remaining bits and pieces are part of the shame of it all.

As I hinted before, returning from Ben Macdui is not necessarily straightforward, especially in a mist or a wind. I once met an elderly gentleman who believed he was returning from Ben Macdui towards Braemar. He had found his way up with a leaflet describing some good walks around Braemar.

Going up was the easy bit. He just kept going up until he reached the top, and then he stopped. In going down, every direction was downhill, and two at least are marked with lines of cairns. He chose the wrong one, and was not able to check his choice against a map or compass, even if he had thought of it, because he didn't have either.

I met him near Lochan Buidhe about 4pm. He would need an hour to return to the summit and then four to Linn of Dee and another one to Braemar if he was unlucky and didn't get a lift. 9 or 10pm were his likely return times.

# Am Fearlas Mor

I believe it was at this point Professor Norman Collie had the following experience:

> *"I was returning from the cairn on the summit in a mist when I began to think I heard something else than merely the noise of my own footsteps. Every few steps I took I heard a crunch, then another crunch as if someone was walking after me but taking steps three or four times the length of my own. I said to myself 'this is all nonsense'. I listened and heard it again*

*but could see nothing in the mist. As I walked on and the eerie crunch, crunch sounded behind me I was seized with terror and took to my heels, staggering blindly among the boulders for four or five miles nearly down to Rothiemurchus Forest. Whatever you make of it I do not know, but there is something very queer about the top of Ben MacDhui and will not go back there again by myself I know."*

This has given more credence to the legend of Am Fearlas Mor, which had been in general circulation as oral history from time immemorial. There are several theories to explain the phenomenon and spin-off tales, even a film. Am Fearlas Mor, known in English as the Grey Man of Ben Macdui even has his own website, and I expect you can catch up with his social network over the Internet, even though no-one has ever actually seen him.

I don't want to poop too many parties, but on the Cairngorms, I have been in the conditions he described many times, yet I have completely missed feeling the sense of a presence hinted at by Peter Densham, who worked for the RAF in Mountain Rescue during the Second World War:

*"Though your nerves be of steel, and your mind says it cannot be, you will be acquainted with that fear without name, that intense dread of the unknown that has pursued mankind from the very dawn of time."*

The only dread I have felt is of not knowing where the cliff edge was in a whiteout. Perhaps my sensitivity is low, rather than my nerves of steel.

I will admit to another unfathomable feeling, not of dread, but of restfulness. Sitting for long periods observing recreation until the light has started to fade, there is a feeling that, when the last person passes, the remaining wind is completely on its own. I think of it as an empty wind, blowing for its own purposes, acting completely independently. It may be something to do with scent, because scent and sound carry a long way on the wind, but when the wind is empty of both, a great peace descends, and sleep beckons.

## The Curran Shelter

Lochan Buidhe can be a bleak spot, a good place for empty winds. Just on the south shore, east of the Macdui path is an empty piece of ground. It is the site of a high, remote shelter, the Curran Shelter, named after its builder, Jim Curran. It's not there now and led directly to the Cairngorm Tragedy which is well written up elsewhere.

I find disasters difficult to read about. I have no interest in seeing the film Titanic, as I will spend most of the time thinking "Don't do it! Turn back!" This is particularly true of the Cairngorm Tragedy. The narrative includes phrases such as "Making a relatively late start" and "the weather was now taking a serious turn for the worse".

The outcome was that of two parties of children: the one with experienced leadership made it through a November snowstorm to the Curran shelter, and the other, with inexperienced leadership, did not. Five children and an adult leader died, buried in snow somewhere near the stream that flows out of the loch. They were less than a kilometre short of the shelter, but it might have been the width of the Antarctic.

On a solo foray one day, crossing the shallow valley that drains from the lochan, I came across a cairn of weathered stones near the burn. What could possibly have required the building of a cairn in such an unremarkable spot? I wondered. Then I remembered the Tragedy, and the short turf and babbling stream smiled for me, and the place looked so peaceful and sweet, almost.

The bothy plagued its builder with guilt and mouldered away until in 1975

*Gaining entry to the Curran bothy still deep in snow*

it was removed. Most people give no thought to it and turn east beyond the lochan to follow the clear and undulating path along the south side of Cairn Lochan. Jim Curran wasn't the only one who thought isolated high-level shelters were a good idea.

The Army's 51st (Highland) division erected a shelter above Stag Rocks, naming it after St. Valery, the Normandy town where their predecessors had faced the Germans in 1940. They built one in Coire na Spreidhe, East of Cairn Gorm, too. It was named after their more successful defeat of the same German commander (Rommel) at El Alamein. After the Tragedy, the decision was taken to remove both. As I have hinted already, this was only carried out on one of them, also in 1975.

High level shelters may have a romantic appeal, but these were too easy to get to, get stuck in or worse – fail to get to at all. At the time, it was considered that Jean's Hut was not so dangerous and could stay.

The path between Lochan Buidhe and the top of the Goat Track is a regular highway in summer, but soon drifts over with snow and becomes unusable in winter, only re-emerging piecemeal as the last snows melt. Many walkers have returned from sunny springtime walks dazzled by the snow and doubly sunburnt, as the snow reflects the burning rays back up under chins and noses which often get overlooked for protection.

Shortly south of the Goat Track, the path overlooks Coire Domhain. "Duvvan" is a good approximation of the pronunciation, not domain. Snows accumulate particularly deeply here, and it is one of the two most popular spots for people who want to dig a snowhole, or cavern, or build an igloo, and spend the night in an arctic bivouac.

# Snowholing in Coire Domhain

Snowholing is an emergency technique that has become quite popular as a separate adventure in its own right. Walk up with some pals, dig the hole, pile in for the night and spend the hours of darkness in your clothes and sleeping bag on your best sleeping mat, collecting snow from the walls on the inside of the hole until they become contaminated with the smoke from the candles, and boiling endless brews on a little stove. Magic.

Snowholes are fun to go into and spend some time hiding from the bad weather outside. Having spent a total of five nights in snowholes in the course of

*At the snowhole*

my winter mountain leadership training and assessment, I feel no need to repeat the practice.

Sorry to bring this up, but where's the toilet? Er, there isn't one. With the concentration of activity on these two favourite spots – here and at Ciste Mhearad – both in the headwaters of nutrient-poor streams, there has become a bit of a problem with contamination. There are no biological processes in winter acting to break down human waste left in these places, so the problem accumulates and emerges from the snow in spring.

# Not very nice

Natural systems are adapted to cope with a spring flush of nutrients from atmospheric deposits on snow in any case, but this is much stronger, more concentrated and – not very nice either.

My colleague Heather Morning, to her great credit, launched the Poo Project to deal with this problem, encouraging anyone who went out overnight to take biodegradable plastic bags and to carry them in screw-top containers in side-pockets she made for rucksacks. The clever part was that the contents of the screw-top containers could be emptied straight into the sewage system that had been installed at Cairngorm. The screw-top pots could then go in the disinfectant bin nearby to be washed out and reused.

Heather had several years' experience of Antarctica and knew that this was a big problem that wouldn't go away by itself. Working at Glenmore Lodge, where returning human waste had already been piloted, showed her the possibilities. However, the Lodge's waste goes out with the clinical waste collection, an expensive option, and Cairngorm's is just digested on site.

The response has been fantastic. People do their business in the bags, tie the top, pop it into the pots, and screw the lid on, no mess. Only one or two instances of failure to comply appear out of the snow each year and – last touch – the Rangers remove them, also in the biodegradable bags, and the site is cleared.

I was snowholing in Coire Domhain with a party from Glenmore Lodge on one occasion when a man and a teenager stumbled down the slope to meet us, and sparked a full-scale rescue alert. A helicopter was called and the pilot made a tricky approach below the cloud which later saw him highly commended and the two strangers were whisked away. Their story appeared on the front page of the Times.

The man, an experienced climber, had been taking his son for a winter adventure and they had suffered several setbacks and made several poor decisions which had led them to sit for two nights and a day in an emergency shelter with nothing much to eat. In a severely dehydrated condition, they had eventually made a break for a return and happened across our party who summoned the helicopter. They were very lucky not to have severe frostbite requiring amputations, but their attitude bothered me.

Despite having made life-threateningly poor decisions, the older man was dismissive of any suggestion of recklessness, and the younger one obviously accepted unquestioningly anything the older one told him. The responsibility that comes with leadership in that kind of relationship is completely different from that between roughly equal companions. Nobody warms to lack of humility in the face of the game being up.

The walk back from Ben Macdui joins the Rim of the Northern Corries at the top of the Goat Track. This is just another enjoyable stage in this walk, if you don't mind the regular cairns not recently built by a well-meaning agency, which we saw earlier.

# Loch Avon and Beinn Mheadhoin
# (Loch A'an and Ben Vane)

A popular trip from the top of the chairlift was to go over Cairn Gorm and descend to Stac an Faradh on the South side where a spectacular view opens from the cliff tops down to Loch Avon in its deep trench below.

The view includes the ribbon-loch, Loch Avon, and, beyond, the pimply mountain of Beinn Mheadhoin. To the right of this, you can see Loch Etchachan, and right again Creag Carn Etchachan and the Sticil – the Shelter Stone crag.

I mention this again here to introduce the Shelter Stone itself, which is visible from the cliff-tops, a giant among huge boulders. This rock has been known from the first explorations of these mountains, and revered as a shelter in an otherwise inhospitable mountain landscape.

Those deploring the present access arrangements at the top of the Railway would have you believe that with the demise of the chairlift and new access arrangements have made travel to view Loch Avon – let alone visiting the Shelter Stone – too arduous for ordinary mortals.

Certainly, my first experience of this remote mountain area was punctured by the exclamations and cries of a family party with children which floated to me across from the south side of the loch in 1977. It took me years to realise that their presence there was due to the access provided by the chairlift, and they still had to make a long and arduous return back over to Cairngorm. This would probably not happen nowadays.

However, before even the road was built, far less the chairlift, the Shelter Stone was being visited by an average of 525 people per year from 1931 to 1943. This is shown by a count of signatures in the Visitors' book under the stone quoted by Adam Watson in the SMC District guide to the Cairngorms. Furthermore, this is when they had to walk from Glenmore, possibly from Coylumbridge. In 1933 alone, 1018 people visited, compared with an annual total of 173 in 2011.

So the descent to Loch Avon and return must have seen a great decline in popularity in the last 100 years, and this must reflect in the nature of the paths threading their way down the shallow upper slopes of Coire Raibert and Coire Domhain and snaking through the boulders alongside the loch.

I once had a visitor at the Ranger Base, an irate and very wet walker. She complained that the map marked a non-existent bridge across the river flowing

*Approaching the Shelter Stone*

into the loch. I replied that no such bridge had ever existed, but she was right enough about the map. I checked back to some historical editions to find that a crag marking could have been interpreted as a bridge, but the Ordnance Survey had put a bridge on their most recent 1:25,000 scale sheet without checking it on the ground.

The river crossing is quite wet at low water, and in high water, a detour up the slope, possibly back to the plateau, will be needed. This is a completely wild place, so no man-made intrusion making it easier to access is required. Even quite recently, a party of ten had been repulsed here, just two of them making it across to the Stone. Their entry in the log book mentioned they were not looking forward to the return trip to rejoin their patient friends on the other bank.

There was a televised climb near the Shelter Stone in 2009, when several cabins and all the equipment were flown in by helicopter. The routes between the cabins had to be protected by boardwalks and every scrap of waste scrupulously removed. Unfortunately, it rained, and the live climb was not made. However, the lead climber, Dave MacLeod returned soon after and made one of the scariest climbs of his illustrious career, and the film of that was aired on TV.

Crossing the river brings us to the Shelter Stone itself, which sits prominently on the boulder field below the impressively steep crag. It is distinguished by a small cairn built on top of it. The entrance has been built up slightly with stone, but most of the accommodation is entirely natural.

It takes your eyes a while to get used to the low light under the stone. Then the immense rock slab above the space is visible. There is room for four to spread out fully. I might have said "in comfort" but that would not be true. Head room is limited, the floor flat and hard and the resident mice will make any sleep fitful, if entertaining.

I had a night under the Shelter Stone on my first visit, an August backpacking expedition with my brother Alasdair. It was a fine afternoon, and we saw people climbing on the massive crag above. We wondered if there would be time for them to finish their route before nightfall. Not only did they finish but they came down to the Stone, said hello, had a meal, and went back up for another route that evening!

Discussion that night was around how easy it would be to find work in the "Spey Valley" and come here more often. Perhaps there was work as a porter at one of the potteries in the village, they suggested helpfully.

Next day, a splendid sunny one, Alasdair and I continued our journey by climbing Beinn Mheadhoin. We threaded through the boulders and admired the many other howffs, as we didn't call them, because we didn't know that word for a small rough shelter. We climbed the diagonal path heading for Loch Etchachan, but before reaching the loch we shucked off heavy packs and turned East to climb the long stone and turf slopes onto Beinn Mheadhoin.

The summits of this mountain are adorned with six large granite tors, making it one of the most distinctive skylines in the Cairngorms, and we romped across to the highest one before returning to our packs. The rest of our day saw us take in Derry Cairngorm and Ben Macdui before making the long descent to Corrour, where we camped.

I mention this as an illustration of what is possible. The tour from Cairngorm car park (with or without a visit to Cairn Gorm) to Beinn Mheadhoin is a serious day out, involving three large ascents, but if energy is plentiful, Derry Cairngorm and the big bald-headed Macdui can be included as well. The distance is greater but it cuts out one of the re-ascents.

In 2003, Cairngorm Rangers observed recreation around this area, centred on Loch Etchachan. Thinking back to those days, we were thankful for the fine weather that summer, we could not have done it in any of the summers since. We established that three-quarters of the people in that area were coming from Derry, and one quarter had started from Cairngorm.

*Loch Etchachan and Derry Cairngorm*

Loch Etchachan is a big open loch with a small island at the north side on which an isolated colony of common gull nests. This is natural behaviour, and is marked by the Gaelic names of many Highland lochs as Loch na Faolieag. This loch has a good enough name, though rather a jawcracker until it becomes familiar. It's the double "ch" that does it, the usual solution is to pronounce the first as in church, and only the second as in loch.

From the loch, an excellent path leads up to Ben Macdui, passing the turns to Derry Cairngorm, Coire Sputan Dearg and the top of Sron Riach on the left. Hereabouts is another Stob Coire something. It is possible to look down one of the big gullies through the cliffs to the left. Sputan Dearg means red spout, so perhaps this refers to one of the gullies in the cliffs.

Just before Ben Macdui, there is an isolated ruin known as the Sappers bothy. There are several ex-military installations on the top of Ben Macdui, mostly dating from the Second World War; stone built and mouldering away. On the North top are several more shelters built by soldiers in training. They have all naturalised to such an extent that they no longer appear intrusive.

## The Empty quarter

The two ascent routes to Ben Macdui enclose a huge area of high ground drained by Garbh Uisge Mor and Garbh Uisge Beag – the big rough water and small rough water, and by the Feith Buidhe, the yellow burn. And then there is the oddly-named six zeroes.

These water courses, apart from six zeroes, all pour into the trench occupied by Loch Avon in spectacular fashion, coursing down pink granite slabs and foaming over waterfalls. The catchment areas are some of the most bleak and trackless in the country.

Feith Buidhe rises from Lochan Buidhe and passes a snow patch which is so long-lasting it prevents vegetation from growing. When the snow eventually melts, the ground appears as a gullied gravel patch on the gentle slope. The Feith Buidhe then passes the cairn marking the Cairngorm Tragedy and finally drops in spectacular falls to the Loch Avon basin. It was here James Grant of Ryvoan found his prize crystal.

One spring walk I led across here showed that the remaining snow bridges were quite thin, and we were required to cross. One walker chose a picturesque arch of snow on which to make his crossing, falling right through it with both feet into the icy water when it collapsed under his weight. The trick then was to keep moving, avoid chilling, and we all returned in high spirits.

Garbh Uisge Beag rises near the path to Ben Macdui, just before the last big rise to the summit. It has a very quiet valley to flow down. The only real point of note is the persistent snowpatch and the great bank of snow on its left bank as it starts to fall more steeply. This is one of the four most popular snowholing sites on the high ground, and one of the last patches to melt.

Garbh Uisge Mor rises near the Sappers Bothy and flows through a rounded valley known as the snowy corrie. I have a slight problem with this name, not least that is in English, when everything else is Gaelic. Although corrie, or Coire, is a name for any hollow, it usually denotes a glacially-modified one, and the term Lag, or Laggan might be more appropriate. Snow is Sneachda, so I propose this valley be known as Lag an t-Sneachda.

It certainly is a snowy hollow, holding great swathes of snow well into May most years. One fine April day, I crossed on ski from Cairn Lochan and sat down sideways unexpectedly, my knees bent forward slightly so my right leg came into contact with the edge of my left ski. I stood up unconcerned and continued to the foot of the slope that rises to the north-east top of Ben Macdui and stopped to take off the skis.

I was horrified to find my right leg streaming with blood and a big flap of skin hanging off helplessly. I pulled up my sock to support it as well as I could and immediately set off back to the Ranger Base, ski-striding for an hour and walking for another hour. Ski Patrol patched me up slightly and I went straight down to the Health Centre for nine stitches. Not a good injury to have when out alone.

The snowy corrie is where two USAF planes came down in 2001, making the water run with aviation fuel and detectable for years afterwards.

The rocky ground in the lower part of the corrie is where a snowy owl was last seen in the Cairngorms. One year a pair bred, before my time, and I always think of them here, in the hope of seeing one. They are rare migrants – vagrants – and very rare breeders, but the terrain is so similar to the tundra of their homeland, I always hope for them to reappear. There are many isolated white quartz boulders that look like the compact owls and turn out on closer inspection to be – white boulders. They are the perfect foil.

One big obstacle to these birds recolonising Britain is the food supply. We have no lemmings, the notoriously fecund and numerous rodent of Scandinavia. They just didn't make it back to this island in time when the ice melted, or perhaps they died out too soon. When a snowy owl did occupy this territory, in 2014, it decimated the population of young ptarmigan and dotterel, to the extent that dotterel showed hardly any breeding success that year. So I suppose I should be careful what I wish for.

Another stream drains this empty quarter. This falls steeply into a small glacial corrie close to Garbh Uisge Mor and then into Loch Etchachan. The corrie is the fourth most popular snowholing site in the Cairngorms and is referred to as four or six zeroes.

This strange name comes from its position in the grid square NJ0000, a location so remarkable that it deserves special mention. It shares this distinction with only five other places on land in Scotland:

- Hearrabhal (a hill) on Taransay at NB0000,
- Allt a' Mhaingir (a stream) on the south side of Loch Quoich at NH0000,
- A ridge of Beinn Ghlais above Furnace in Argyll at NN0000,
- Pool of Muckhart (a village) in Clackmannanshire at NO0000,
- A slope of Queensberry (hill) above Ae in the Borders at NT0000.

The lochan on Ben Macdui is actually in sub-square NJ000000, as its ten-figure reference is NJ00032 00059, putting it only 67 metres from the intersection of the grid lines. Anyway, enough of this stuff! The corrie is a barren place in the short snow-free season, and empties steeply into the larger Loch Etchachan, making it awkward to approach from below.

# The Heart of the Cairngorms

I have left the best feature of this Empty Quarter till last. It is a place which for me epitomises the heart of the Cairngorms, approached only by arduous walking routes, but giving the most sublime views of the central, untracked part of the Cairngorms. I mean Carn Etchachan.

The bastion of Carn Etchachan is like a cathedral-tower above Loch Avon, instantly recognisable when seen from Bynack Mor or anywhere along the loch shore or cliff tops above. It provides the most dramatic part of the view all along the quiet plateau paths from the Goat Track towards Lochan Buidhe and towers over the Shelter Stone, dominating it completely.

Despite the fearsome cliffs, the summit is easy to approach from the South or West, where the climb is a walk.

The top edge of the Sticil cliff is split by a vertical crevasse, a mouldering mossy impending crash of granite which seems to hang out at an impossible angle.

Slabs by the cairn lead down to a place where I never fail to be aggrieved. A carved square of granite is fastened upright to the natural stone to memorialise a climber who died on the mountains, but not these mountains. He died on Lochnagar.

*Carn Etchachan*

The erection of memorials like this is, in my mind, an act of vandalism that says more about the perpetrators' willingness to desecrate the heart of the mountains more than their regard for the deceased.

All such memorials should, in my view, be removed and, if necessary, be placed in gardens and parks set aside for the purpose in villages, not displayed as an act of insensitivity in wild places.

To my horror, when I referred to it in less than flattering terms, one visitor said to me: "Leave it to me", and I half expected him to appear with it next day, but it's still there.

Carn Etchachan is to me the Heart of the Cairngorms. As far from daily normality one can reach in this other-worldly massif.

# 10. Development

In ecological terms, development at Cairngorm can be seen as a colonisation by a species whose needs were met by suitable conditions at the time. If it had tried today, it would not have got started. The window of opportunity swung open in the 1950s, 60s and 70s and has now closed, but we have a legacy of decisions we were not party to and development we did not plan. That still leaves us with such a lot of work to do.

Arguably, this species had not been keen to colonise this mountain much before the 1940s. The individuals, pathfinders, mavericks and radicals that did explore before this were mostly satisfied by the conditions they inherited. Their modifications were small. The quartz diggers' caves and huts, the anti-aircraft spotters' shelters and the viewpoint indicator on Ben Macdui make up almost the entire list of the archaeology on the high tops. 'Development', whatever that meant, was not an option.

## Skiing

There was interest in skiing long before World War II, but equipment was scarce and expensive. Technological improvements and the contacts forged with Norwegian skier-soldiers, combined with the availability of ex-military equipment in the 1940s and 1950s fuelled a great increase in interest in skiing in Britain.

Cairn Gorm was one of the prime sites. Coire Cas had good snow holding, as it was so high. It was well-seen from Strathspey, and well-known as it was adjacent to the popular trek up to the Summit. The main drawback was remoteness. Glenmore was reached by a difficult single track road through Sluggan Pass, and the long walk in from the railway station at Aviemore was quite a trek carrying skis.

Glenmore Estate, on which Cairn Gorm stands, came into the ownership of the Forestry Commission in 1923. The land was therefore publicly owned. When development of skiing on the North side of the Cairngorms was being proposed, some people considered Braeriach to be a preferable option, despite the opposition of the owner, Grant of Rothiemurchus. Leaving aside this interesting prospect, let's concentrate on Cairn Gorm for now.

Cairngorm Sports Development Trust was formed by local skiers and businesses to guide the development of skiing (and later, other winter sports) on Cairn Gorm. The Trust was and is a non profit-distributing company set up with the highest ideals of the post-war environment, to reinvest profits in skiing on Cairn Gorm. This may come as a surprise to some, who thought that some fat cats were creaming off the profits from ski development, and should have put some money into Aviemore, or other local communities, if only to broaden their portfolio in the event of poor returns from winter sports.

Other ski areas successfully diversified into other leisure facilities in their district, such as hotels and golf courses. Cairngorm could not do this. Perhaps it would have been better if they could have done, but with the level of public funding support for Cairngorm it could have been construed as unfair competition. Strathspey is not short of other interested parties.

The breakthrough for the developers of Cairn Gorm was the anonymous donation which allowed the completion of the access road to the car park in Coire Cas in 1960

*Tea hut*

and the construction of the first chairlift, the White Lady chairlift, on the steep upper slopes of Coire Cas in the following year.

Familiarity with the present arrangements makes the incremental development through the 1960s and 70s seem quaint. An upper chairlift existed for three years without an access chairlift. Instead the tarmac road continued to what we now know as the middle station. There was no Ptarmigan building. Refreshments were dispensed through a window from the tea hut, which was part of the stark black box that was the upper chairlift station. At times a canvas-covered scaffolding frame served the same purpose.

Only later was there a car park and lower chairlift (imaginatively named the Car Park chairlift), although they were separated by a 50ft climb to give the visitors some exercise and provide room to accommodate the queues which formed on winter mornings.

There was no shortage of people willing to queue. Queuing became one of the main features of skiing at Cairngorm, and one which the ski area management strove constantly to reduce. Skiing became big, big business, especially in the context of sleepy Strathspey of the 1960s and 70s. Royalty learned to ski at Cairngorm, it was the IN thing to do, and there were big crowds. There were good snowy winters, a golden age for skiers who didn't have to look too closely at what was being done to Cairn Gorm on their behalf, because it was always covered in snow when they visited.

Other people were looking, though, and their view will be presented later.

Without any shareholders to cream off the profits, this lucrative period funded the expanding infrastructure and possibly (depending on who you listen to) a good time in the bars of Aviemore.

Many of the early workers on the Ski Area had escaped to the hills for the love of it, leaving behind the industry of the Clyde shipyards where many of them had served their apprenticeships. They had the skills, the can-do attitude and the toughness of mind to make this development

*Queuing at Cairngorm, Easter 1981
(and no white stuff)*

happen. They were making machinery work in the most difficult conditions on a windy Scottish mountain, in all seasons.

Some days would start before light, bashing ice from moving parts and continuing in similar vein: fitting replacement parts, greasing, heavy lifting, adapting components to work better, making sure a whole family of tows and chairlifts was ready to work safely at the press of a switch, shift of a gear lever, crank of a handle, kick of a boot. No wonder they worked up a thirst.

In the building phase, which took place in successive summers from 1961 to 1981, the result in terms of facilities available in the subsequent snow seasons was the objective, the touchstone by which skiers and developers judged the success of progress.

Did they need an access track? They brought in a bulldozer. A smoother ski run? Bulldozer again. Did they need to carry a tower up to position on a new tow? You get the idea.

The upshot of this means of working on the mountain, particularly on Coire Cas, was disastrous, and became a byword and cause celebre of the environmental movement. One researcher could even find it credible enough to publish the claim that 100 hectares had been laid bare by the development, though it was probably nearer 4 hectares, which was bad enough.

Bare ground is natural on the mountain, but large areas of bare ground are bad news. Although the rainfall amounts are less than in the western Highlands, the summer rain has a nasty habit of arriving in heavy bursts, and when these follow dry periods, the bare ground surface sheds it very quickly. The effect is a quick rake-over of bare gravelly surfaces, some gullying and erosion. Large volumes of water and gravel end up in the watercourses, and sometimes, deep piles of gravel smother the remaining vegetation. Fixing the problem is something to tell about later on, but a basic change of approach was needed.

In the 1980s, new tows such as the Fiacaill Ridge and Day Lodge tows were installed by helicopter. A very good contrast can be appreciated by looking up the two adjacent tows near the car park.

The piste for the Car Park tow was bulldozed, then had to be revegetated. Fortunately, recovery has proceeded very well, with the native vegetation, heather, sedges, and even willow, now taking over.

To the right, the Fiacaill Ridge tow had little or no modification of the track line. Rank heather still occupies the line and the bare patches on the peat cover are no more than natural. So there was no need to repeat the expensive business of ground repair all along the track.

Non-skiers often find the lines of fencing difficult to understand. At Cairn Gorm, being a windy place, lying snow is blown around, but not in a random way. Loose snow blows on even a light wind, and rests in hollows or behind wind-breaks. Extra collecting places are provided by the fencing which causes the snow to drop on the lee side. By positioning the fences across the wind and parallel to the location desired for plentiful snow (particularly piste and tow lines) the wind can do the work.

Originally the fences were chespale, a combination of wire and split chestnut. I'm told Chespale is the only remaining commercial coppice used in the UK. Recent improvements have been to replace this with ranch-style board fencing. It is easier to erect and easier to repair, and captures snow better than chespale.

Unfortunately, the wind sometimes comes from the wrong direction, or blows too long and hard and not only the loose snow streams away in tatters, but the base layer is eroded into series of sastrugi ridges or is stripped entirely.

An earlier approach which was tried was to throw up bulldozed banks to provide sheltered areas, but they have several drawbacks. As larger piste-grooming machines have been introduced, they are sometimes unable to get between the bulldozed banks and immovable objects like tow towers.

The piste grooming machines finish the job done by the falling snow and drifting wind. A well-packed base of snow that hides all the rocks lasts much longer, to be topped up by new falls. A good ski season starts with the formation of a good base layer. Until then, skiers are dodging the rocks and wearing through to the ground, which is damaging to both ground and skis.

At the end of the ski season, I would usually take a tour round the ski area with a company manager and any other interested colleagues. We would look for damage to the ground caused by skiing and vehicles. We usually knew where to look, because some of us had been watching the progress of the ski season. Tow lines and pistes were the prime areas.

There were usually a few small items of recent damage which could be attributed to activity on insufficient snow cover by skiers or by piste groomers. The pistes are closed by Ski Patrollers when the snow gets too thin, but sometimes the damage is already done. The piste machine drivers are well aware of the potential for

*Damage. The Gunbarrel in June*

damage, but occasionally with an inexperienced driver or unexpected variation in conditions, the snow is thinner than required.

We often heard encouraging comments from outside observers. The vegetation became more natural and more complete almost every year, and the places where new damage occurred were few and far between.

It is not only damage that was highlighted by these inspections. We could resolve to close unnecessary gaps in fences, dig drains to guide water away, or get rid of loose boulders which obstructed the skiing or piste grooming. The list after a walk round could reach 80 or 90 items. The company's outside, fencing and Ranger teams worked away at them all summer.

# Repairing the damage

Repairing damaged ground is, as I said, expensive. In the early days, ground was left bare at the end of every construction operation, sometimes in large areas and for long periods. The Chairlift Company, then led by Tommy Paul, recognised this and engaged the best minds on the subject. Grass seed was the method of choice, along with some fairly hefty fertilizer. To prevent it blowing away, for a time, they used a bitumen mix which was sprayed on the ground. Some of this splashed on surrounding rocks and can still be seen today, often in drip-like run-marks.

Unfortunately, the grass seed they used was of varieties which either did not grow well or persisted too long. They were also extremely expensive. One year, HIE brought in half the entire UK production of seed of deschampsia flexuosa (wavy hair-grass), around 12 bags, which was very expensive indeed.

The seed mixes were adjusted and eventually came down to a two-species mix of sheep's fescue and Highland browntop bent. These species flourish for a few years, until the fertilizer is used up, then they fade away as other native plants take over.

The soil was analysed as part of the recent redevelopment, and found to need an unusual mix of nitrogen, phosphorous and potassium, with additional magnesium, to counter the deficiencies in the soil here. Despite this, the fertiliser costs about one-sixth as much as the seed, and it is usually applied at about twice the rate of the seed for good results.

For a while, our grass seed guru, Brian Robinson from Bolton, acquired pelleted paper-mache from America, in a bright blue colour, which retains water close to the seedling grass and prevents it drying out. On one occasion he had the greatest difficulty in convincing the border authorities he was not importing drugs!

One pleasant outcome of all this is the opportunity it creates for ring ouzel, the mountain blackbird. It appreciates the grassy areas for foraging on worms and insects, and reseeding is surely the main reason why so many ring ouzel territories are found on Cairn Gorm.

# Braeriach

*Braeriach as seen from Black Park*

It is entertaining, as a diversion, to think for a moment what might-have-been if Braeriach had been the site of ski development instead of Cairn Gorm. Many things would not have been much different. Aviemore would no doubt have been developed in the same way. There would have been a ski road through the Caledonian pine forest, probably passing close to a beautiful loch well-known for its wildlife. Though, if we had been heading for Braeriach, this would have been the small scenic Loch an Eilean, rather than the larger Loch Morlich.

The trouble with development is that it often gives rise to additional development, and it is doubtful that development of Loch an Eilean would have been acceptable for water sports enthusiasts, and Loch Morlich might well have followed in any case, with two roads being driven through the remains of the Caledonian Pine forest.

The Northern Corries of Braeriach hold snow as well as those of Cairn Gorm. There is less separation between them and it is likely that all would have been developed with uplift, starting from the relatively smooth Coire Beanaidh and working across the craggy corries to the west. A summer chairlift might well have been available to walkers, as it was on Cairn Gorm, probably up to the col between Braeriach and Sron na Lairige. This would have given a slightly longer walk along the clifftops to the summit than the walk to Cairn Gorm was from the top of the chairlift there. Beyond the summit of Braeriach, the level and undulating plateau holds lots of possibilities for wandering further, to the Wells and Falls of the River Dee, then the high level walk to Sgor an Lochan Uaine and Cairn Toul.

If this is not ringing alarm bells with today's readers, it certainly is with me. Development of Braeriach would have produced more problems and drawbacks at every altitude than the development of Cairn Gorm.

# Expansion plans

Faced with the difficulties brought on by the success of the ski development in the 1970s, the operator of the ski area, Cairngorm Chairlift Company, made two attempts to extend the development to the west. At the time, they leased the whole of Cairngorm Estate from HIDB, and they received considerable support from their landlords for these proposals.

To be fair, the overcrowding on the ski area was chronic. After queuing for an hour for uplift, a ten minute ski run would bring you back to the queue. The pistes had the same problems as an over-crowded swimming pool: Too many people trying to do too many different things in a small space. In particular there was a shortage of space for beginners. Expert skiers also felt under-stimulated by the terrain available.

The first great push was for the development of Coire an t-Sneachda and Coire an Lochain with lifts and tows. This was highly offensive to people like myself who took advantage of the high level starting point and ploughed our way out of the ski area and into one of the Northern Corries where we would find fairly natural conditions for climbing and walking. The prospect of mechanised uplift accompanying us into these wonderful places was intensely distressing.

In the end the proposal was defeated after a seemingly interminable public inquiry in Kingussie. A politician made a decision – and it was dropped. Great relief to me. Surprise and distress for the ski lobby.

A second proposal was to build a road to the foot of Lurcher's Gully and develop downhill skiing from there into this gentle, grassy place.

This is where I came in, with both feet. I offered to take people for a walk there to see it. I put up posters inviting people to meet me at the car park in Coire Cas and walk to Lurcher's Gully to hear what was proposed, and where. Quite a few people came out with me, on several occasions.

*Lurcher's Gully*

I found myself spending most of the time putting the developers' case as fairly as I could and watching the incredulous reactions on the faces of my companions. Several of them were skiers. They were most concerned about bringing a road to a fairly remote facility and keeping it clear in drifting snow when skiers were still out on the slopes. From the cross-section of opinions I heard, the case was indefensible.

To mountaineers and me it represented a pincer movement on the Northern Corries which could no longer be free from the prospect of future ski development.

I read through quite a few of the nature conservation arguments, of the sort that could be advanced just about anywhere. Apart from the unanswerable safety case, the whole proposal failed to take account of the cumulative interests of existing users, and of the still valid wild land qualities of the area.

I take no small pleasure from reminding people that in hindsight, the company was saved by these decisions from over-extending itself in a market that was about to get much smaller quite quickly.

This problem affected other ski areas, too, and instead of the precautionary principle being applied with respect to nature conservation, the economic arguments won the day for expansion, and now these ski areas are suffering the consequences.

I am certain that bankruptcy would have followed either of the extensions proposed at Cairngorm. I have even had this refuted by old-style developers, who claim that the old Chairlift Company knew a thing or two about expanding facilities and could manage its way out of any difficulties. Including snowless winters, apparently.

As a compensation and a consolation for those who supported the expansion of skiing, many of whom were feeling pretty sore after losing out twice, the Chairlift Company secured a small victory soon after. A series of snow fences was constructed, with planning permission from a sympathetic Regional Council, to encourage skiers to undertake expeditions out of Coire Cas and in to Coire an t-Sneachda.

The fences were the only artefacts of development visible in Coire an t-Sneachda, appearing as five straight lines, two pairs and a single, across the patterned boulder slope. This disruption of the natural rhythms and cadences of the scene were exactly what we feared from the wholesale development of the Northern Corries, yet this fencing went through the normal procedures with very little noise from the environmental lobby. We had taken our collective eye off the ball, exhausted by the protracted arguments about Lurcher's. The lesson was learned and Cairn Gorm was not ignored again.

I personally detested the Sneachda snow fences. Apart from the visual intrusion, they were a reminder of the wholesale development that had happened in the next corrie, like a creeper spreading round the corner of a house. Once, I had the rare sight of a piste grooming machine travel over the snow between the uppermost pair of fences down towards Coire an t-Sneachda, turn and disappear back into the ski area.

The purpose of building the fences was to provide a snowy connection between Coire Cas and the middle and lower reaches of Coire an t-Sneachda. The leased ski area was reduced in extent but included this adventitious project. It was not usually groomed beyond the fences, apart from the time I had witnessed. It was not patrolled, and increasingly, it was abandoned by skiers.

The fences may have annoyed some people like me, but most mountaineers treated the uppermost pair as a useful 'handrail' guiding them into and out of Coire an t-Sneachda. There were several instances of climbers coming across these fences in bad weather and being very grateful for the guidance they offered. This happened to me once, too

In Coire Cas, the presence of the Sneachda snow fences actually caused a problem for the ski area managers. The succession of climbing parties coming and going from Coire an t-Sneachda via the line of the Fiacaill ski tow and heading for the fences, left footprints in the snow that could not easily be filled or erased by grooming, disrupting the surface for skiing.

In snow-free periods, the erosion along the tow line, over the crest of the ridge and along the corridor provided by the snow fences, was some of the worst on the hill.

Unsurprisingly, I had a desire to see these fences removed. I pointed out to the Chairlift Company that they were falling down and if not maintained, they should be removed. I was surprised to find that I was pushing at an open door. The fences had been put up at a time when the situation demanded, and would be removed when the time was right. I didn't let up and was delighted that the removal of these intrusive fences was achieved in summer 2001.

*The White Lady in the heyday of the chairlift*

# Decline

One of the problems with development is that it requires renewal and updating. Things wear out, especially in a severe mountain climate, expectations change and possibilities expand.

Just as ski development arrived like an organism when conditions were suitable, it may well retreat like an organism up the hill if climate change makes the lower ground intolerable.

With the increasing unreliability of snow at lower altitudes, several ski tows have become virtually unusable. In the first twelve years I was working on the hill, the Aonach tow in Coire na Ciste was used just once. It had been built with its lower end too low for reliable snow. It was removed in 2009, though the tow hut, fences and bulldozed banks and ramps persisted for many years.

The Link tow in Coire na Ciste which gave access to the West Wall poma has been given a new lease of life near the Ptarmigan building for use by beginners. Here it was renamed the Polar Express and ironically referred to as "The Mighty Polar Express" as it is so short. The Fiacaill Tow has also been abandoned and removed.

The most catastrophic loss was the White Lady T-Bar. One of the oldest on the hill, this became synonymous with good days skiing the White Lady piste, one of the steepest and most popular. It was a noisy tow, its gearbox constantly in reverse, sometimes audible miles away over the plateau. It took skiers straight up the slope in a narrow groove which was increasingly difficult to groom. If anyone fell off the tow, the slope was steep enough for them to slide down the track, knocking lots of other people off the tow as well. One humorous article I read suggested that you weren't a real Cairngorm skier until you had pulled off this feat.

# The most catastrophic loss

One sunny winter's day, while spotting ptarmigan on Sron an Aonach for a BBC camera team, my son Duncan and I heard a loud noise from the return wheel of the White Lady tow. It had not been operational that day, and the engineers were giving it a quick turn to see that it was okay to run.

This was the last straw, and the bearing on which the upper wheel turned broke and the wheel dropped ten feet onto the ground below. Released from the return wheel, the cable sagged on all the towers, drawing a loop back down the hill until it was stopped by the highest tower.

The wheel had actually fallen on the designated Sledge Park. Fortunately there was no-one underneath the return wheel or the cable at the time. A rather shocked voice came over the radio. "The sledge park will be closed for the rest of the day".

As it was a new cable, there were high hopes that it could be re-used, but after months and then years of deliberation, during which an Internet campaign was launched by supporters to "Save the White Lady", the decision was taken to remove it. The cable went to scrap and the towers were progressively removed and stored, to substitute for other towers showing signs of terminal corrosion.

Decommissioning is the inevitable next process at Cairngorm. While it is likely that snowsports will survive, the zenith has passed, and the engineering skills and environmental consideration now exhibited by the operating company mean that they may consider marketing their decommissioning prowess to clients elsewhere in future.

# A second chance

Redevelopment is expensive and intrusive. Cairngorm should know, having just lived through a period of major redevelopment.

Clearly, the White Lady and Car Park chairlifts were not going to last forever. Technology moved on; so had users' expectations. The chairlifts were restricted to an increasingly impractical wind speed limit of 25 miles per hour. Parts were becoming difficult to source. A replacement was required.

An early debate considered what should replace the chairlifts. Another chairlift could increase capacity but would still have the same wind limit problem, still be outdoors in the open air with the rain, snow and drips of oily water falling on passengers. Gondolas were the solution adopted by the new development at Nevis Range. This protected visitors in enclosed bubbles, but was not proof against the wind speed problem.

The most expensive solution was a railway. It would be far more reliable, up and down. A railway could guarantee to evacuate beginner skiers using the easier slopes at the Ptarmigan when it became too windy for any other method.

The environmental lobby was most concerned – to put it mildly. Concerns included the amount of development money that would be diverted to Cairngorm, which could arguably be more effective if applied elsewhere, spread around in smaller amounts. I have some sympathy for this argument, as alternative energy development in the North languished for years as the railway was paid for, and only flourished when public money was again available in sufficient quantities.

There was widespread belief that the business plan proposed was unsustainable and the business would either need to resort to environmentally damaging practices to sustain a throughput of visitors or would become insolvent and require removal of the railway, at great extra cost to the public.

Personally, I don't think that those objections would have been much different if a replacement chairlift or gondola had been built instead. What I suspect opponents of the railway wanted, but didn't usually declare, was the cessation of mechanised skiing on Cairn Gorm. The building of a new piece of concrete infrastructure on the mountain made this seem less likely.

I was often asked my opinion on the development, and though I was prepared to admit that it was an awful lot of money, I avoided being drawn on the principle. I would work with the outcome, I said.

A second great concern to environmentalists, myself included, was the consequent trampling damage on high ground caused by people wandering off in all directions.

There seemed to be no prospect of fixing this problem while the chairlift continued to operate year-round on an open system. If a more reliable uplift system were to bring even more people to high ground in summer and winter, the erosion would become more serious still.

The Chairlift Company had a go at trying to persuade visitors that it wasn't worth the effort going to the summit from the Ptarmigan. I think this was based on several half truths (the view's not as good, there's less wildlife up there, you might get lost) and in any case the pilot scheme was carried out in a poorly-controlled manner. People would listen to the case, or not, and then do what they were going to do anyway.

It was my belief that even if you told people what to do, or made it a condition of carriage, they would do what they were intending unless it became impractical. The British public is often incompliant, and I congratulate them for it, but they are often guilty of failing to consider the consequences of their actions, either on the environment, or the effect on others.

During negotiations for planning permission for the railway all these issues came out. The regulatory authorities, particularly the Planning Authority, which was Highland Regional Council, and their statutory nature conservation advisers, Scottish Natural Heritage had a tricky line to steer. SNH, in particular, were minded to oppose the development, on the grounds that it could jeopardise the nearby designated sites for which it had a statutory responsibility. However, all wished to sustain a popular recreational facility and engine of economic activity.

The developers accepted the concerns about the increased impact that might ensue and proposed to limit access to the mountain from the top of the railway to those being accompanied by a Ranger on a walk. I didn't like this idea at all.

This would put the Ranger in the invidious position of lift attendant, travelling up and down the same limited course, reciting the points of interest over and over again, and, when some participants had had enough and wanted to go off on their own (either on a whim or deliberately taking advantage of the situation), the Ranger would be a gate-keeper without a gate, out on his or her own and possibly remote from assistance.

SNH didn't like this proposal either and rejected it.

The only other position the developers felt able to propose was to have a Closed System. Railway passengers would not be allowed to exit from the railway except to the Ptarmigan building and its panoramic outdoor terrace, until they returned to the Base Station, unless they were taking part in or watching snowsports within the Ski Patrolled Area. It was clear that this was the only solution that the regulatory authorities were going to accept, but it is possible for them to say that this was the developer's proposal, not their own.

There were real concerns that the Closed System on the railway would lead to demand for access to the highly protected area and people down at car park level, attracted by the railway, would spill out in great numbers. A whole array of measures, including punitively high car parking fees for non-railway users, a clearway order on the approach road and the closure of informal car parks was included in the first edition of the Visitor Management Plan which accompanied the planning application.

I was very concerned about all this when I first joined the Cairngorm Ranger Service. In 1997 I voiced my concerns to the Chairlift Company's representative in all these dealings, the Finance Director, Walter Edgar. When in battle, deploy your trained specialists. Leave the accountant to fret about the cost. He knew nothing of the practicalities and would not pursue my concerns.

All through the protracted negotiations on the Planning agreement and subsequent Visitor Management Plan and Baseline survey design, nobody thought to involve their newly-appointed Head Ranger in the discussions. I was told "Believe me, if you were cooped up all day with those scientists debating the minutiae of the baseline, you wouldn't want to have anything to do with it".

I wish I knew then what a complete and utter shambles they had been cooking up for me and my colleagues to deal with. I will come back to this later.

During the public debate about the merits of the proposed system, a group of conservation charities made a real effort to come up with an alternative. I had high hopes of this until I saw what they were proposing: The Glenmore Gondola. This would run from near Loch Morlich to the car park in Coire Cas, removing the need for people to drive up the hill road, and park in the car parks (which already exist). They would instead park in new car parks created in Glenmore, which is also a largely designated conservation site.

I felt they had completely missed the point of this redevelopment, as it made no contribution to replacing the ski lift infrastructure, but instead replaced the roads and car parks, which were not falling apart.

Other people advocated a railway from Aviemore, with parking in the town. Some indication of the problems this idea would have faced can be gained by considering the difficulty that was met when trying to create a quiet cycle path into Aviemore from Glenmore. Nice idea. Part of the difficulties anything would face was the degree of disturbance to the Caledonian Forest and the scheduled species of wildlife here.

The last stages were a legal challenge to the whole process in the Court of Session – which failed – and the granting of the money required to build the railway. The company celebrated, but did not invite their Ranger to the celebrations. Oh, well.

# Building the railway

The actual progress of the redevelopment produced some of the most difficult times, when the hill was ripped open and bled granite silt down the streams and slopes each summer. I was working with the contractors, project managers, the Chairlift Company and SNH to ensure that the construction site did not compromise the environment any more than the minimum necessary, and that casual users of the site – walkers – were not jeopardised by the works.

*The works*

# The hill was ripped open

It was particularly difficult to ensure safe passage for walkers round the works. We provided pedestrian diversions at the Base Station, later at the middle station and higher up. When the works reached the Traverse, there was nowhere safe for walkers to go, except to walk on the pile of gravel and rock which had come out of the adjacent trench. Fortunately, this period was short and produced no incidents or complaints.

The most spectacular aspect of the redevelopment was the cableway leased by the contractors, Morrison's, reputedly for a million pounds. This was used to carry loads of up to eight tons from the car park to the middle station and then on again to the top. Small plant and equipment was hoisted up. Hoppers of concrete went the same way, as did the long concrete beams shipped in from Creggan Concrete in Ireland. The low loaders delivering them were decorated with banners telling passing motorists that this concrete beam was "going to the top".

*Cable crane at the middle station*

During the summer, SNH's officer supervising the railway, Keith Duncan, was descending alongside the cable crane in lower Coire Cas when the towers were struck in succession by lightning, chasing him off the hill. He had the much gentler pleasure on a different occasion of hearing the ring ouzel, our mountain blackbird, using the towers of the crane as wonderfully elevated song posts. The ouzels bred every year the development thundered on below them.

The Ranger Service was decanted into a temporary cabin on the West side of the car park, and had a fine view of all this. Ruari Macdonald noticed one day that the builders putting up blockwork for the Base Station had missed out a window in the new Ranger Base. Fortunately, the project manager put them right and now we have the Macdonald window, without which the Ranger Base would be a very gloomy place.

The snow conditions in 2001 gave the best skiing for years until the contractor decided after Easter they had to recommence the construction process at the Ptarmigan.

I admire the engineers that work on these big civil contracts. They have a wonderfully confident can-do attitude. No matter how tricky the problem, they can find a piece of kit, or a technique to solve it.

There was too much snow on the access track to allow them to get up to the Ptarmigan so they sent up their biggest digger with its biggest bucket and cleared it. This gave rise to some of the most spectacular sights of the contract, walls of compacted snow six metres high towering over the track in the bright April sunshine.

*Six metre walls*

Development didn't end with the railway, of course. There was the fitting out and completion of the Ptarmigan and Base Station buildings, the demolition of the chairlift Bottom Station and the establishment of the mountain garden in its place. There were trails in Coire Cas and a replacement for the Shieling tow.

For now I shall pause in 2001.

# 11.                    The year 2001

A catastrophic air crash occurred in a snowstorm in 2001 when two USAF planes were on exercise in the airspace above the Lairig Ghru and both clipped the ground as they came over the ridge between the summit of Ben Macdui and the top of the Tailors' Burn. Both planes, each with a single pilot, ploughed into the eastern side of Ben Macdui, spreading debris far and wide.

There followed some of the snowiest weather of the winter, hampering recovery of the bodies and the wreckage. Military police and the Air Force Regiment (which I had never previously heard of) were dispatched to guard the wreckage and advise walkers setting out not to approach the clean-up operation.

And what an operation. The planes were eventually located at the foot of the slope below Ben Macdui. Snow-going vehicles were driven up from Deeside to dig and remove tons of snow and the contents. Fuel had been spilt in a large area and a huge amount of snow, with the fuel still in it, was removed to a place in Braemar where presumably it could melt and the fuel could evaporate or pond up without contaminating any further groundwater.

The smell of aviation fuel hung around the site for many years before it dispersed. Expanded plastic foam from the fuel tank blew over the plateau and was found miles from the impact site. Pieces of fuselage that had been thrown out by the impact were also spread around. It was a high price to pay for a couple of guys' adrenaline-filled training.

I'll put my cards on the table. Cherished mountainscape is no place to be exercising control of machines; air, sea or land. If we need to define what we mean by cherished, I would accept National Park designation as a starter, but it's much wider than that. We didn't have such a designation then, but we do now, and nothing has changed.

And why will it not happen? Because if it was possible to ban low-flying aircraft from National Parks in Britain, other communities not included in such a designation, such as Peebles, Pitlochry or Roy Bridge would be clamouring to join, and not all such communities could expect to be designated. I would feel a lot more comfortable if the low-flying limit was two hundred metres above the tops of the peaks, except for low-speed craft which have much less impact, and can sometimes only get past mountains by using through-valleys as passes.

2001 was the year of foot and mouth disease. Some animal keeper in the North of England cut too many corners and gave us a dose of a most disruptive disease at the coldest time of the year.

The whole country went mad with fear. Animal husbandry became the most important part of our economy. Nothing was too heinous to consider to prevent the spread of the disease. We looked on in horror as cows were slaughtered in their thousands and heaped up and burnt in ghastly pyres.

We all felt compelled to accept our own responsibility for preventing the spread of the disease. Cordons were placed around whole regions. Car tyres were disinfected on the A9 as traffic queued to enter the Highlands. Walkers were roundly condemned for continuing to take walks in the countryside. The economic damage to guiding companies and holiday providers depending on outdoor activities was severe. Many went out of business.

No-one took the trouble to explain how the actions we were forced to take were supposed to prevent the disease. (Or did I miss something, was it all on television?) How did my car tyres carry disease that was only present in England from the Highlands to, say, Perth?

As a Government Centre of Excellence, Glenmore Lodge was forced to close, although the equipment that people were bringing to the centre did not get used in areas of disease and could have been disinfected.

Reindeer are apparently very susceptible to foot and mouth disease. I had the proprietor of the Reindeer Company and her partner up in arms one day accusing me of jeopardising their herd and livelihood by not dissuading a walker from going along the path past their enclosure. I had taken the view that the separation between the path and the enclosure – over twenty metres – was sufficient for no-one to be worried. I hadn't counted on the woman going right up to the fence and patting the deer through it.

In the current climate I thought the visitor's actions were utterly uncalled-for, but to make it worse she cited me as her reason for doing something excessively stupid. If she had stayed away from the animals there would have been no cause for alarm. I suspect that even the 20 metre separation was too close for comfort, and the only acceptable walker was not there at all.

The reindeer people kept all their reindeer in their enclosure for the duration of the outbreak and put disinfectant trays at the entrance to the Northern Corries Path, where there were no reindeer.

Almost all the estates in the Highlands asked walkers and climbers to stay away. This was at the height of a superb winter for climbing and ski-touring. What this achieved was never evaluated or explained, but people largely responded compliantly.

To their undying credit, HIE decided that, because skiing equipment had no proximity to the disease, and because there were no animals on their estate that could catch it, Cairngorm Estate would not close. Glenmore Lodge could have come skiing, climbing, navigating, mountain rescuing, whatever, and we would have welcomed them, but instead they were closed down for the duration.

It was a bit quieter on the hill than normal. People didn't come out as much. A lot of DIY must have been done that winter. I suspect the casualty departments were much busier than normal.

At last estates began to realise the futility and unnecessary nature of their closures and began to be praised highly for boldly opening up again. One of the first was the Royal Estate of Balmoral, hurrah. No reference was ever made to the one estate that had never closed. Many stayed closed for ages, enjoying the peace and quiet.

I remember being stopped by a jobsworth in Flowerdale, near Gairloch, very concerned that I was walking up a track on the estate. I struggled to understand what threat I was supposed to represent, as I hadn't been anywhere near the disease, and there were no livestock present on the track or nearby.

Eventually he explained that I set a bad example to local people, and if they thought it was all right to walk up the track, they would all want to do it, and the disease would appear there, too. The understanding of the way the disease spread was woeful, and the lack of understanding was used blatantly as a way of keeping people out of places they had every right to be.

Months later, we were invited to a conference at Heriot-Watt University to hear about the lessons learned from the disease and response to it. It was 11th September, a date with no particular significance at that time. The proceedings were unremarkable. Outdoor recreationists of the general public were widely praised for their responsible attitude. This turned out to be significant in the run-up to the deliberations on the Land Reform Act. Landowners wanted a curfew on the new rights, and exclusions from areas they defined. These were seen to be unnecessary and we gained the best access rights in the world as a result.

The Heriot-Watt day was rather overshadowed by events in New York the same day. Annus horribilis indeed.

That was not all the Rangers put up with that year. One of the Seasonal Rangers was brutally assaulted in a shinty match and had to have his leg put back together again, which took nearly a year to heal. The other seasonal Ranger also had some time in hospital for an unrelated reason.

As the chairlift was airlifted away I cheered a small cheer. The chairlift represented an exploitive and careless way of treating the mountain, and we were promised a much more comfortable and reliable replacement, and the end of mechanised mass access for walkers to the tops.

With no uplift to run, the Chairlift Company all but closed down. On many days the only people on site were the builders and the Rangers. Irate visitors would come and hammer on the door of the temporary cabin into which we had been decanted. The opening gambit of one visitor, to my unfortunate colleague, was "You – are – useless!" I would love to have had the opportunity of devising some quick reply.

The problem was the lack of toilets. I pointed out to the company that the lack of toilets for visitors, whether or not the company had anything to offer, was likely to lead to problems in the car park. And so it did. And not just grumpiness.

For one period of the summer we had an unusually high number of thunderstorms. At one stage our telephone lines were struck by lightning, and the shock entered all the computers via the modem. This was in the days when computers were wired to the telephone service directly, and hardly anyone used surge-protectors.

My son was on a sailing course on Loch Morlich and witnessed lightning hit a tree, and saw the tree fall. I believe it was the same summer we had a lightning strike near the Northern Corries path which puzzled us later.

Air crash, foot and mouth disease, no visitor operation, lightning disruption and Twin Towers attacks. That was some year.

# 12. Gentler times

Almost as soon as it was finished, the mountain railway began to pay for itself. The number of days when the chairlift would have been suspended due to high winds was in stark contrast to the number of days when the train was suspended for the same reason.

The first few years of the railway coincided with warmer summers and less snowy winters. Enthusiasm for the railway was at its peak, and regularly over 150,000 people a year paid to use it, topped up by snowsports to over 200,000 in total. This was a change from the pre-funicular days, when snowsports was by far the major partner.

The bumper winters of 2009-10 and 2010-11 restored equality between the two markets, with half a million people riding for snowsports or not in just two years.

With the century wearing on, the numbers travelling the railway in summer is in slight decline, settling to around 120,000 to 130,000. Improved winter performance in these two bumper years has been the saviour of the commercial side of the company, but not before serious financial worries for HIE led it to take over all the fixed assets and write off the debts. This was portrayed as further financial support from the public purse, but there was some inevitability about it.

So what did HIE get for their money? They already owned the railway and took over all the buildings.

The Day Lodge was built by local workers in the 1970s, a steel frame with cladding that leaks heat and has dozens of stairs and no lift. It is seriously inefficient and all involved wish to see it brought into this century with a sustainable building.

For a while the then Chief Executive, Bob Kinnaird, promoted the idea of a National Centre for the Mountain Environment. It would have been an inspiring place, with plenty of visitors, good road access, good mountains, and passing on the messages I think are important. This quietly got lost along the way. Lack of vision, I believe.

The railway buildings are more attractive than the Day Lodge, though the size of the Ptarmigan building at the top of the railway appalled me when it was first proposed. I still don't consider the edge of the plateau to be the place to do either fine dining nor shopping nor interpretation when all you could see was the inside of the room you are in. I actually registered a formal objection to that aspect of the development, in the years before I worked up the hill. I wasn't nearly so concerned about the railway. My representation didn't get me anywhere, just a peculiar interview with my boss.

The Ptarmigan was one of the most complicated constructions imaginable, according to the lead engineer. His language was rather more colourful. Now it lies on the mountain, its shiny roof having dulled down to a neutral grey, looking for all the world like a big pavilion.

Snow blew into the roof voids and melted later, causing waterfalls down the stairs. The walls leaked in the lashing rain. It has cost a fortune to maintain and heat. The accommodation for Ski Patrol and technical maintenance teams is very sub-standard. It was a rather cheap job when a class act was required. We are still debating how to hang an extended terrace on the outside of the building to allow visitors a broader view, and how to provide a secure but more welcoming entrance for walkers arriving on foot.

The platform at the Top station was designed to allow trains to stop at level one, disembark passengers and move to level four to allow them to board again for their downhill journey. Despite knowing that both carriages have to move in opposite directions simultaneously, no equivalent platform was provided at the Base Station. So while the top carriage is disembarking passengers, the bottom carriage is in limbo, half in and half out of the Base Station, before both can move into their final positions. That was another cash saving.

In the Ptarmigan building, passengers make their way through the exhibition, and unless they use the lift, they climb stairs, pass through the shop, climb more stairs past the toilets and come out on the restaurant level, level four.

On the way they pass at least three fire exits which would allow unimpeded passage to the outdoors, where they are not supposed to go, but some do go anyway. They are either unaware of the conditions of travel of their ticket or don't care. The people working in the building get very weary of bringing visitors back in or being abused by them and failing to enforce the Closed System.

I would say that the fire exits are not passages to a place of safety in any but the most benign conditions. The safest practice in the event of a fire would be to go to a safe part of the building, as directed by staff. I am not convinced the exits are the appropriate response to the issue on a mountain, and they certainly provide a lot of headaches for the company. The numbers exiting the system are tiny, but it is annoying nonetheless.

*Ptarmigan building. Spot the place of safety,*

The Base Station building is much more straightforward, with an airy entrance hall for the carriage, partitioned off from the visitor concourse. Someone thought that the excellent chainsaw sculptures, mortared stone wall and English step-stile would embellish the place, linking it to the low ground by providing illustrations of forest wildlife. The one piece illustrating mountain birds features a golden eagle which for many years sported shades and earmuffs!

The lower floors of the Base station contain toilets and the Ranger Base. The Aonach Room at the back follows none of the original proposals. It was on the original plans as a store, and I wanted it as an environmental education centre. I have been able to do talks in it, but in summer the main function is as a meeting room. In winter it becomes the Ski Patrol first aid room, with up to four casualties

*Base station entrance*

simultaneously being attended to; screens, oxygen masks and emergency splints all in evidence. At these times there is nowhere to meet or conduct a talk.

The Ranger Base at the front of the building should be in a prime position, but Rangers find that it is often ignored or overlooked by visitors, or mistaken for the ticket office or toilets. I had a large sign over the window but one day the boss came in telling me to take it down, no reason given. We were able to get grant from An Comunn Gaidhealach for bilingual signs which declare it to be Ranger Base, Ionad an Maor-duthcha, and these went up later.

In frustration, I produced plans for a free-standing Ranger Base on the opposite side of the car park, where everyone walks past the door. When we were based across there at the temporary accommodation during the construction period, we found this location so much more public. People were always calling in. If we could design our own building, perhaps we would have a place to speak to groups, run training, display interpretation on screens and walls and office space. Is this not the standard of Ranger Base you would expect coming to the main visitor arrival point in a National Park?

All these hopes are on hold, as there are plans afoot for a re-designed Day Lodge, in which apparently the Rangers will be accommodated next to the Reception Desk, so they can be receptionists. They will be saved from this by lack of money again.

Other building assets taken on by HIE are at Coire na Ciste. Almost all are due for demolition as I write: A derelict café building which contains an important electricity sub-station; a timber-built shed with another sub-station in it; the mid-station of the chairlift and lower end of the West Wall poma. At the top of the chairlift is a derelict get-off ramp, which was a hazard to the public until it was properly closed off. Then there is the workshop called Base Four. Recently reclad and improved, it is amazing to think that in the early days, one could walk all the way up to Base Four and then buy a ticket at a window to continue on ski. Soon Base Four will be the lowest building in Coire na Ciste.

# An insult to the mountain

Quite honestly, Coire na Ciste was a mess, only now being cleared up. For years, the building and the lay-down area for fencing materials, unusable chairlift chairs, rubbish and a skip for disposing of burnable waste were eyesores often complained about by visitors. The chairlift stood for decades as a rusting testament to the hopes of a previous generation. The middle station boardwalks became full of dangerous holes and traps for the unwary. The curious walkway between there and the Ciste gully resembled something from Nepal, and was only recently demolished as it had started to fall down.

The whole area had a derelict air, an insult to the mountain. Plans for a mountain bike descent route involving revitalising and extending the lower chairlift and building adventurous bike trails in the floor of the corrie seemed to offer some hope of rejuvenation, along with a new café and improved management of the technical area. I'm not holding my breath.

## Natural Retreats

In 2014, HIE announced that they had assigned a 25-year commercial lease of the operation at Cairngorm to the UK company Natural Retreats. This meant the end of the old community company Cairngorm Mountain Limited, although the name Cairngorm Mountain was retained by the new operators to identify this locus for their operations. They already had many other operating environments, nearly all in connection with accommodation (notably John O'Groats in the Highlands) and in England, Wales, Ireland and the United States. This was to be their first ski area operation, as distinct from accommodation at a ski area, and, as far as I can make out, first Ranger Service.

# The end of the old community company

On reflection during my time at Cairngorm the Ranger Service was most valued when there was an external threat or a serious problem to overcome: The building of the railway and advising visitors how to get past the works safely; The monitoring scheme; Big events that require managing; Paths in a state that need repairing; Foot and Mouth disease; Plane crashes; Serious avalanche hazard; Maintenance works potentially threatening public safety.

When it comes to gentler times, the Rangers can turn their attentions more to bringing out the best in people through understanding and appreciation. That is when they do their best work for the future. But they get overlooked, in my experience.

# 13.          Living the dream

No-one lives at Cairngorm, everyone travels up the road.

They all go home afterwards to their houses, their meals and their beds with the mountain reigning their memories and their dreams for a while, occupying their prospects and plans and drawing them back.

Cairngorm is a long way, physically and figuratively, from where many people live. The environment of the mountain is familiar to many, but so foreign to most, that they can be forgiven for being taken aback by the rawness and brutality, the barrenness and sparseness, the elemental nature of the mountain.

Gradually people might take this on board. Until then, they are prone to approach the hazards and challenges with only the approaches they have learnt and adopted: cautious, cavalier or inquisitive.

## Love it or hate it, it is difficult to ignore a visit to Cairngorm

Their experience is based on what they perceive, how they feel and their innate disposition. It is impossible to generalise about everyone, but I will try to make some observations about many of the visitors who travel up the road, drawn by the mountain.

Love it or hate it, it is difficult to ignore a visit to Cairngorm. It is so different from normal everyday experience, it is bound to be memorable. New norms and experiences will be taken on and referred to later. Part of the appeal of mountains in any case is their otherworldliness. People go to experience the contrast with their normal lives. They come for a good time. They come because they want to, or because they travel in the company of someone else who wants to be there.

Compare working in such a place to working in a place where people only go under stressful conditions, to grieve, complain or be made better. I'm sure the professional people in these places are motivated by the opportunity to help or improve people's lives, and I'm grateful to them for it.

Working at Cairngorm is to help people have a good time in a place they have looked forward to visiting, and will look back on with satisfaction. Their experience is positive in prospect and positive in retrospect.

The only time this is interrupted is when something goes wrong with their visit. They are disappointed, annoyed, ill or injured, or something happens to a companion or a possession.

A surprising proportion of visitors bring problems with them. Often they don't realise that something that is not a problem in normal life becomes a real hazard in this unfamiliar context. People can live happily on the flat, or in the warm, or not far from the medicine cupboard, but when any of these norms change, they have to make allowances, and some of them forget.

## What do you recommend?

Rangers are frequently called on at the start of the day to advise people about what they might do with their time There is no charge for this advice, but it is often ignored.

In fact, advice is so often sought then ignored that it makes me wonder why people bother in the first place, but I'm always pleased to be consulted.

Very often people will come into the Ranger Base and ask what the prospects are for a walk.

"We'd like to do a hike for three to four hours" is common from Americans.

The Ranger doesn't say "I don't know how fast you walk", but "What sort of a hike do you have in mind?" It makes them feel more comfortable to use their terminology. Do they want mountain tops, mid-level or downhill through the forest?

To this they often say "We don't know. What do you recommend?"

Again, the Ranger resists the urge to say "You came here, what were your expectations? I can't judge your requirements or abilities", and instead something like "It's all good, I can't choose for you, you could come here every day for a week and have a different experience every time and enjoy them all." Clearly we are getting nowhere here, because the ones who want the advice aren't giving enough in return.

If the weather is exceptionally good or bad, that will have a bearing on their choice.

Perhaps: "It's blowing a gale on the tops, anything on the high ground is likely to be quite uncomfortable. Shall we have a look at the weather forecast? That might help you decide." Some people don't have weather back home. If it rains they take the day off work.

Generally it is a bad idea to recommend the High Tops to people who couldn't care less. True, the experience might well shake them out of their complacency and really open their eyes to the Cairngorms and Scotland, but there usually has to be some motivation there in the first place.

In general, people need the High Tops more than the High Tops need people.

There are other considerations. If the Ranger advocates a course of action, and something bad happens as a result of following the advice there might be a reasonable claim for negligence. The Ranger may well misjudge the visitor's capabilities and interest and at least disappoint them.

The Rangers at Cairngorm provide the best possible advice, but if things turn nasty, they have professional indemnity insurance through membership of the Scottish Countryside Rangers' Association. It has never remotely been needed.

The approach to giving advice to people who are genuinely puzzled by the opportunities available is to try to get them to act on their own preferences rather than advocate others.

The clueless visitor is potentially a self-defeating one. There is now such good quality information about anywhere you might like to visit, that it seems very adventurous – not to say reckless – to arrive anywhere with no ideas about why you are there.

# People need the High Tops more than the High Tops need people

Admittedly, I remember being in a fairly clueless position when travelling through Norway once. We had two days to drive back to Bergen and wanted to know a bit more about what we might see en route.

We didn't have a guidebook, and the road signs were not particularly helpful, so we called in at a village shop and looked to see what postcards of local scenes they were selling and found the names on our small-scale road map.

There are usually ways of finding out, so that at least you know what to ask for when you meet a local person who might be able to help.

One visitor arrived at the car park and leaned out of his car to ask someone "What *is* this place?", because he thought he was on the road to Deeside. With the advent of sat-nav this has become inexplicably more and more commonplace.

There was at least one incident when a 4x4 vehicle was driven by a visitor up to the Ptarmigan building in chairlift days because they thought they were on their way to Braemar. This must say something about the expectations of Highland roads among some visitors.

The opposite approach is less-often brought to our notice. The over-informed visitor is not often seeking advice. I suspect they more often just go and do their own thing. Occasionally they e-mail months in advance of their visit, with questions such as "Can you recommend a restaurant in Aviemore? Can you tell me what the weather will be like in September? And "Will I be able to hike to Perth?" The answer to all three is Yes. Or No. Or Call in when you get here. It's impossible to micro-manage a visit in advance.

Once people are resolved on what they want to do, that's when it is possible to help them. There are lots of examples of people declaring that they are off to climb Ben Macdui, and ask to be put on the right path.

In set-fair weather there are few concerns, save that they remember which direction they approach the final summit and retrace their steps. More than one visitor has continued in the mist down towards Deeside unintentionally.

In poor weather, their level of preparedness and understanding might make a straight answer an unsafe one.

A response might be "Before I tell you, are you okay with navigating in today's conditions?" And often "Do you have a map and compass, and know how to use them?"

There is an amazing resistance to buying a map, especially from foreign visitors. They say they are only visiting once and the cost of a map is a lot for them. Having found maps difficult to buy and very expensive on the continent, I wonder if they are just not familiar with them.

"Why would I need a compass?" ask some visitors. In clear weather it might not really matter, though clear weather can change. In cloudy weather at a summit such as Cairn Gorm, though, all directions are downhill. How would you know which was the correct one?

It's all very well if you are retracing your steps and recognising landmarks and features you saw on the way up, but what happens if you want to do a traverse, and come down a different way?

Having map and compass is only as good as the use made of them. A while ago we were working on one of the paths on the plateau heading towards Ben Macdui on a beautiful day, at the point where two paths run parallel for a while, but the other one peters out.

A call from the other path – some fifty metres away – drew our attention to a young man who was unable to make further progress as his path had petered out. He had a map and a clear view. We called him across to our path and explained his map to him. He might have been persuaded to turn back, even within sight of his objective, but a little kind advice and he was on his way.

I must tell you about the man in the kilt. A fit and determined man from Tees-side arrived recently, having appeared in the pub the night before insisting to anyone who would listen that he was going to climb Ben Macdui next day in the same Highland Dress he was wearing to the hostelry. I had four separate people warn me he was coming, but despite a barrage of advice from everyone he had met, he persisted in his plan. It was December, but the snow was very meagre and there was no ice; it was windy and with cloud just touching the higher tops.

I realised when he said "You only get cold if you have a cold heart" that I wasn't going to change his mind; the best I could do was to speed his safe return. He bought a map and we discussed his plan over a coffee. I said the wind would make it hard work, and there were a couple of places where it would really hit him. I was relieved when he said that if it was too bad he would turn back. Aha! An acceptance of possible frailty; that was a start. I said he should turn at 2 pm, not later (it was dark by 5). He planned to use his (cracked) mobile phone to light his way back.

He overtook some other walkers on the plateau more than once. Later they said he seemed to go off the route, but always came back to the path. He actually made his turn for home at the summit about 1.30 pm, a very creditable effort.

Back in the Ranger Base before 4pm, I was pleased to see him safe, not a spot on his silk or serge, a few mud-splashes on his leather-soled brogues. He was set on Ben Nevis now. I tried to minimise his blithe approach to hazard. Try to get someone to go with you; wear boots, not brogues; leave it till at least June. Ah, well, I tried.

Misreadings and mis-placings are legion, of course. One of the Rangers met a young man climbing to the top of Cairn Gorm who was convinced he had already traversed Cairn Gorm and was now approaching the top of Ben Macdui.

I met a lady at the top of Fiacaill a' Choire Chais who assured me that she and her friends had 'done' Ben Macdui in the mist, with no map. I wondered how she was so certain, as she didn't remember seeing the prominent viewpoint indicator.

Maps. I love 'em, but don't get me wrong. If you want a walk on the wild side and you are sure you can take anything the mountain is going to throw at you, including a benightment, try doing without one for once.

If you want to have any control over where you are going, your senses of observation jump into overdrive. It is a strongly liberating effect, but full of unexplained mystery (there are no name-boards or sign-posts) and uncertainty.

Perhaps big craggy hills with bad weather and a worse reputation are not the place to try this. It's amazing how many do.

Visitors often arrive with all the kit, and a good idea of what they want to do, but have doubts about the effects of the weather.

It's good to encourage them to get themselves into a location to achieve their goal (some people call it an attack point) if they feel confident enough at that stage.

For example, getting to Lochan Buidhe on the way to Ben Macdui is a good proportion of the way there, but the remaining miles can be an exhausting fight with the wind or knee-deep in snow, or in thick hill fog or whiteout that makes it a pretty unpleasant experience. Better to use Lochan Buidhe as a last point of decision to go on or to return by the other approach path.

At least if a decision has been made to abort up there, it has been made with the full knowledge of the conditions and their effect on the party, not by some doubtful Ranger back at Base.

On the Rim of the Northern Corries, the cairn at 1141m at the top of Fiacaill a' Choire Chais is another such decision point. On to Cairn Gorm, or (in the other direction) on to the Rim of the Corries, or back down the Fiacaill?

It's a touching faith people have in the Rangers' knowledge. There could be a "Do it *this* way" approach, but it's rare that the Rangers have an up-to-the-minute knowledge of weather and conditions. Even less can visitors' understanding and abilities be assessed in an instant.

I suppose the advice is pretty valid, because people often come back with their thanks. The Rangers all get out and about regularly on the hill, are familiar with the Loch Avon basin, and make at least one visit per year to the further away parts of the Cairngorms.

Most visitors have no need of advice from the Ranger. They might appreciate seeing the weather forecast or avalanche forecast or just having a chat about what they've been doing or what they've seen.

# It's a touching faith people have in the Rangers' knowledge

The problem is the Ranger Base is a little out of their way and embedded in the railway operation, which many of them have chosen to consider irrelevant. Some winters recently have seen queues for ski tickets which the operator decided to dispense from the Ranger Base. On those days I had to stand outside in the car park to talk to people because there was no room in the Ranger Base. On other occasions, I took up a position at the start of the Northern Corries path to advise climbers of an expected severe change in the weather or a high avalanche risk.

How much better to move the Ranger Base over to the other side of the car park where the mountain-goers would pass the door and there would be a view of the weather on the mountain and conditions on the main footpaths. It is the best position for the purpose.

So, that's the getting ready and going off stage. What happens when visitors are really out there, living the dream?

Help on the hill

Again, there is the full range of experiences, mostly positive, but sometimes disastrous.

Rangers often see instances of 'companion issues' where one, usually male, member of the party is leaving behind the other, usually female member.

These issues rarely involve anyone else. Occasionally, parties get split up and spend a long time looking for each other.

Rangers met a young man once on Cairn Gorm, going up to the summit by the Marquis Well path. He was hoping to find the top station of the railway and meet his friends there. The only trouble was, he didn't know what the top station of the railway looked like and couldn't see what the Ptarmigan building had to offer him in his quest. The railway is invisible from outside unless you look in through the platform windows.

*Out on the hill. Living the dream*

Another time, a party became separated on Cairn Lochan during a summer rain shower when the cloud had come down and they had not been able to meet up again. I offered to have a look for the missing party member, and found her on a different path, heading back. There was no rescue needed, she hiked off the hill at such a pace, I could hardly keep up!

There are only rare occasions when the Ranger who is out and about intervenes deliberately with someone enjoying the mountain. Usually it's the other way around. A visitor will come over and speak first to ask advice.

The 2003 access legislation, with the Scottish Outdoor Access Code, has clarified many situations, and given people a strong sense of their right to do what they please. Some of them are aware of the responsibilities that go with this, others are not.

Some of the things the Ranger would always intervene in are fires, damage and building in stone. A senior academic of a Scottish University was drilling holes in the ground in Coire an t-Sneachda one late summer day, to place temperature sensors in an attempt to discover permafrost. I asked him to stop until he had the relevant permissions, which he did. He never found his permafrost.

A family had a portable barbecue on the peat near the Northern Corries Path one dry summer, oblivious of the fact they were sitting on thousands of tons of combustible fuel. They were asked to put it out.

I have not been able to intervene with any of the stone-builders who like to leave their mark on the mountain in the form of cairns, shelters and message arrows, nor with the hooligans who enjoy trundling large rocks down slopes to see how far they go, but I would have liked to. The last builders of a shelter I dealt with cost us several helicopter lifts, so large and sprawling was their construction.

# Mountain biking raises a lot of hackles

Some issues are a little more borderline. Mountain biking raises a lot of hackles. People don't like to see mountain bikes being used on the high tops, and I agree with them about the party of 48 that was seen on Ben Macdui in summer 2011. Bicycles do leave marks in soft places (but so do walkers), and skid marks on steep places. Considering the numbers of mountain bikes accessing the mountains – very few – I am not convinced they cause a major problem.

## Dogs – a boon or a nuisance?

Dogs in the countryside can also be a boon or a nuisance. Our wild animals – particularly birds – are easily disturbed by dogs. We have seen dogs chasing ptarmigan away from their nests and sprinting after hares. Hardly a year goes by without physical damage to reindeer – which actually belong to someone, like sheep do – caused by dogs.

The signs at the start of the paths might seem a bit harsh. Others have criticised them for being too dog-friendly. The signs ask for dogs to be kept on leads all year, and Rangers will approach people on the hill to ask them to do this. One visitor refused point-blank, saying his Labradors had never been on the lead in seven years, so he would take them away and not come back.

Visitors arriving and seeing no sheep often think that their dogs can enjoy a good run-around without disturbing anything. In the breeding season dogs represent a threat to ground-nesting birds, but these are not obvious to their owners.

In winter the birds and hares are living at the edge of what is possible. Being flushed out of shelter might use up energy needed for surviving, and might be fatal. Ptarmigan, in particular, make every effort to avoid flying in the cold air. During the moult period, they find it difficult to fly at all.

There are quite a few other activities the Rangers see but rarely intervene. Sometimes it's important to be ever so diplomatic, or people will think they are living in a surveillance society when they thought they were enjoying a day on the hills.

## What about the children?

What do you say when children are being dragged along, hardly able to keep putting one step in front of another, or led off from the railway onto the plateau, or carried shoulder-high on steep, rocky ground? My inclination is to consider

*On the way to Ben Macdui*

these as child abuse issues: adults showing cavalier disregard for the interests and well-being of the children, overcoming their objections with aggressive or superior demeanour or just ignoring them.

When thinking about taking small children over to Ben Macdui, try to see it from the point of view of the child. It's a long way, and not very entertaining for the small one. They will probably be bored and complaining. That is usually enough to remind the parent that it is supposed to be fun, and even if they are only concerned for their own enjoyment, a complaining child is not an accompaniment to enjoy.

There is a fine line between intervening and interfering with child-welfare issues. "Hello. The little one's struggling a bit, isn't he?" and "Are you on the right track?" might be the right sort of approach.

# Sometimes it's important to be ever so diplomatic

Another issue that has caused me to approach people is the wearing of crampons long beyond the need for them. This has caused damage to the fragile vegetation on the plateau, and is quite damaging for the crampons, too. An opening gambit here is "Hello! Don't you like your crampons? Walking on the rocks like that blunts them. You might as well take them off and save them for somewhere you need them. That way you'll not be doing so much damage to the mountain, either."

Most of the time, though, Rangers are too few and far away and the only way we will have less damaging behaviour is through education and advice. Perhaps even this book might do some good. What we need is an attitude towards the mountain, an environmental ethic that will guide all we do.

I am fortunate in having a broad interest and a great exposure to the mountain and the issues, so that what is necessary and acceptable is obvious to me, but I have to accept that it is not obvious to everyone.

Is it worth making a counsel of perfection?

- We accept that human activity in the mountains is a natural and necessary part of human experience and has become part of the ecology of the mountains.
- Humans are very similar to wild animals in being attracted to places which serve their needs, and make trails to these places just as animals do.

- Humans, as well as animals, wish to pursue their activity guided by themselves, not overseen by some external authority, which they may see as threatening.
- To achieve a sustainable relationship with the mountains humans must understand the environment they are in and act accordingly. Until this is the case there will be a need for external influence on them.
- Sustainable activity by humans depends on accepting the limitations of the environment on any activity and on leaving no trace of their presence. The trails they make are the only acceptable exception to this.

*Guided by themselves, not overseen by some external authority*

Let's eavesdrop on a selection of visitors as they make their way through the day – any day – at Cairngorm, and in the Cairngorms. Don't worry if they sound critical of the Ranger or come away with opinions that are not true, they are only fictional in any case, but they are based on what people really do, say and presumably, think.

# Many dreams

**0632** First light. The team is here. Some have been out all night. Still no sign. Plans are adjusted. Callsigns practised. Small groups set out. Four dogs. Avalanche probes and shovels, but they hope they won't need them.

**0635** Ski Patrol are the early starters. There is a lot to do before the first tow turns a wheel, especially after the wind of the night before. Rime ice inches-thick has to be chipped from the cables and wheels. Climb every tower, ice hammer aloft. Poles, ropes and nets marking the runs, signs helping people find their way to the tows, or closing off areas. All buried by last night's drift. Time to dig them out. Time to find them in the debris pushed aside by the piste grooming machine. No time to repair them.

220

**0640** They stir, stretch and stand up. It has been an uncomfortable night, but at least they know where they are, not lost. Now it is a decent morning and they can continue down Strath Nethy to walk out to the road. There had been a bit of an error of judgement last night, but no harm done, and no bones broken. It was when they started falling over all the boulders scattered across the glen they decided to call a halt and wait for daylight.

**0815** The chef struggles against the wind from his car to the building where he clocks in. Then he heads for the train. He will be fighting a roasting kitchen all day making macaroni cheese and millionaire's shortbread. Breaktimes he will stand outside the building for a cigarette. He knows what the fuss is about but he isn't interested. His job is people's food.

**0918** Filling in a route sheet in the Ranger Base is all very well, the walker thinks, but as she hasn't decided where she's going yet, she just puts "Route Undecided".

**0919** Four young men, one in sandals, are hopeful that the Ranger can tell them where to find the Shelter Stone Crag. They have heard there are some hard routes they would like to try, but have no map and are a bit taken aback when the Ranger tells them that they are hopelessly under-equipped, and the crag is over two hours away. They pine for the road side crags of Cheddar.

**0920** The first day of the student's dissertation fieldwork. Now all those plans can be put into action. Tape measure – check. Camera – check. Map – check. Notebook – check. GPS – check. Time to go. The study supervisor was a bit hard on the plans, but he has seen it all before. One day's fieldwork for every two days' bad weather is what he said. If today's the fieldwork day, better make the best of it.

**0925** The Swiss lady speaks English so the others push her to the front to ask the Ranger about walking to Ben Macdui. His face falls when she asks if there would be restaurants along the way. She assumes it lost something in translation?

**0932** The ski instructor faces the tenth day on the trot passing on his skill on snow. A different school party each day, some pretty private clients in the afternoons, some pretty awful private clients, too. Youngsters with grace and attention. And some with two left feet and an attitude. He turns on the smile and the charm.

**0935** The old forester has read his paper. He steps off the bus and looks around. So many changes. So much concrete and tarmac. He fades away to the mountain paths he has seen grow from nothing to black scars, now tidied up and gentrified. The world has caught up with his simple pleasures, but there is no harm in taking them anyway. He knows a little-used way up where he won't be overtaken by anybody.

**0954** He doesn't really mind where he puts his fish and chip van. Village car parks, summer shows, youth hostels. This gig is just a bit further to drive, it's a bit of a hill climb to get to it and the old truck is not pulling as well as it used to. He and the boy will be on their feet for five hours and serve one hundred and thirty customers. That's a tidy day's takings. And tomorrow they'll do the same.

**0955** The young mother stares dejectedly at the yellow sheet. The sign in the Ranger Base says to fill in a sheet before you go on the hill. All they wanted was a nice little walk to Ben Macdui. Anyone would think it was a major expedition. What's this? Describe the route? Well, isn't it obvious? She didn't know what it was like, so she couldn't describe it. All this stuff on the form about emergencies and bad weather was beginning to make her feel dizzy. They couldn't possibly do this walk. Just trying to fill in the form had completely put her off. They would go for a hot chocolate and a ride on the train instead.

**0956** Delay upon delay, and here they are, waiting at the snow gates at nearly ten o'clock, the sun beaming down and not a breath of wind. The guy on the gate explains that it's very busy up there, and there might be some parking places. He lets them through. There is another guy waving them into the first car park. They know this is a mile from the train. The queues are going to be horrendous. A seven o'clock start and still having to wait for the shuttle bus to get round to the start of the skiing. So frustrating!

**0957** The American walker was very pleased to get the proper advice from the Rangers. They could be expected to know about their patch. "Now, could you tell me where I might expect to see puffins?" he asked.

**1010** The Ranger had been most insistent that the German visitor take a map and compass. No, he wouldn't bother with the map, or the compass. These were not the Alps, just little undulations. He is quite confident.

**1020** The sign says Ranger Base, but it is queued-out with people in ski gear, standing in a line that stretches round the building. They are waiting for tickets they have paid for over the Internet. Two friends approach, carrying climbing gear. They hoped to get a word with the Ranger to find out what the climbs were like, but it doesn't look as though they'll be able to get near. Like Father Christmas' ******* grotto, one of them says. Then they hear two people talking about the weather forecast and realise one is the Ranger. He has come out of his office to talk to people. Probably because they can't get in to talk to him.

**1022** It had been her favourite bicycle. He couldn't bear to let anyone else ride it. He needed some space, some really wild space. Loch Avon. He was taking the bike and would throw it in the loch. No. He couldn't do it. He would just take the bike and leave it there. It would have a beautiful view. Forever.

**1025** The Welsh walkers are disappointed to find that their full winter kit was regarded as inadequate by the Ranger. He said they needed ice axes and crampons, which to them seemed a bit of an overkill in March.

**1026** This will be the last trip with the Alphorn. The first in Scotland. It is a devil of a luggage. Several people eye him suspiciously as he walks slowly up to the corrie. The crags frown, the wind is light, perfect. He puts the antique brass to his lips and blows. The frowning crags give him back his music over and over again. He is quietly satisfied.

**1032** The teacher is getting a slight headache, but knows she cannot help it that the coach bringing them up the hill was slow, and they are late. It is blowing a gale. She knows she has asked all the children to have full waterproofs with them, but last year the group had deliberately left them behind so they did not have to go for a walk in the rain with the Ranger. She does not know it will be the same this year. And next year she will forget again. Fieldwork is almost impossible here, she tells herself.

**1040** This Closed system is an outrage, but he knows what they will do. They will travel up the train; listen to all the announcements about not leaving the building. He knows which door they went out of last time. They will have a pleasant walk to the Summit of Cairn Gorm and then down to the top of the cliffs to gaze on Loch Avon. They will walk back to the top building. She will feign injury and they will take pity on them, and allow them to travel down the train. Just like last year. So much more comfortable than the chairlift.

**1046** The man is confident. These little hills will soon get knocked off. Cloud on the tops? That's nothing. The Picos (de Europa) are the most cloud-girt mountains in Spain; these rounded lumps won't give any problem. Usual white shorts and trainers will be sufficient. Quick skip over to the highest peak and back, should only take the morning.

**1050** A French visitor was having none of the Ranger's advice about what to wear. It was March, and the Ranger was saying he should have winter boots and gaiters; he should have different clothing and a map and compass. To make it worse the Ranger then refused to tell him how to get up to Cairn Gorm!

**1057** Three friends, all male students at Dundee University, have been planning to go to Ben Macdui for weeks. Two are teasing the third about having his lunch in a carrier bag. They call in to see the Ranger. He advises to put the carrier bag in the rucksack one of the others is carrying. They show the Ranger their map. It is a library edition with a hard cover.

**1106** It might look fine, the man said, but you never know. Yes, sure, there's blue sky, but still he isn't going to take it from Sara that it might be okay. They go in and ask the Ranger. He looks at the weather forecast with them. Light winds, no hill fog, hmm. Might be okay? Better leave a route plan anyhow. These foreign mountains, not like the Alleghenies back home.

**1120** "It is possible to climb Cairn Gorm?" asks the diminutive lady. It's a lovely day, the Ranger says. Possible?, he thinks. Do it today while you can!

**1135** The annual walk to celebrate John Roy Stuart has chatted its jolly Gaelic way up the trail to the car park and is now heading for the summit. There they will unfurl the green banner they are carrying and celebrate an early mountaineer and Jacobite who kept his ardour warm with an annual defiant flagwaving remembered even today.

**1200** Okay, perhaps this isn't going quite as well as we planned. The Ranger didn't tell us we couldn't get the whole family to Ben Macdui, he just left us to find out ourselves. How far have we come? We've been going two hours and we've just reached Coire Cas. And we've got masses of the best equipment, too. Gaiters, ice axes. Perhaps we'll aim for Cairn Gorm, that's only another couple of hours away, at this rate.

**1210** They have never seen this much snow in the corrie before. It must be three feet deep at least. They have struggled and plodded their way up from the car park for two hours and only now are they approaching the crags. The sweat is pouring off them as the leader's step drills into another deep footprint, like a post hole. He retreats to the previous step and tries a little to the left. And again. This is exhausting. A skier appears, walking on his skis as if there is nothing unusual about the level of snow. He gives them a cheery wave as he strides on past towards the corrie.

**1230** The two men from Blackburn, in Lancashire, are quite chuffed with their thumbsticks. They have just completed an ascent of the Goat Track in full winter conditions using nothing more technical than the hazel sticks. Sure, one of them had taken a bit of a slide at one point, but he dug his toes in and soon stopped. Then he had been on his knees most of the rest of the way up, but was none the worse. Then some guys wearing the full winter kit, crampons and all, had come over and they had asked them for directions to Ben Macdui. The guys hadn't said much, but it wasn't until they left them at the bottom of the big slope down again that they realise they have been escorted off the hill for their own safety.

**1235** The two friends had enjoyed their walk up Ben Macdui. It was a pity the view had been robbed by a spot of cloud, but now they had finished their sandwiches at the cairn, the sun was beginning to shine through. A rainbow halo formed around the sun, as it does in these conditions, but because the light wind was pushing the cloud over them, it was never stable, brightening, dimming. They can't explain what happened next, nor could anyone else they told the tale to. The blue and green colours faded from the halo, leaving the red orange and yellow colours, which expanded out from the sun as the clouds blew over, to be replaced by another halo, also expanding outwards, and another. This went on for several minutes until at last they started back down from the summit, and the cloud cleared completely.

**1237** It might be snowy but the wind is light, the sun is shining and the proud father has his young son in a baby buggy on the mountain path, being avoided by skiers and crampon-wearing walkers. These baby buggies will go anywhere, he thinks.

**1243** The coach disgorges forty-eight passengers, most of whom head straight for the toilet. Then they wander back out into the sunlight and shade their eyes to watch the railway carriage and explain to each other how it works.

**1245** The coach party is queuing for the train. Very different from Dorset, they keep telling each other. The mountains stick right up through the forest. Not many villages. They can't remember the last time they saw a good village pub. There had better be some good scones at this café they were going to. The driver called it Tarrmigan, but they've seen it spelt with a P, so there's no knowing who's right.

**1246** It is a lot rougher ground down to Loch Avon than he remembered. Who said that about the Cairngorms being smooth hills? He is getting a severely sore shoulder from carrying the bike. At last. Near the stream that flows from the corrie, one of her favourite places. The bike's final resting place. So much easier walking on without it. Like floating. Now this is a fine place, perhaps he'll wander round to the Shelter Stone. Such a great wild place.

**1254** Mum, dad and two tiny tots are struggling up the hill track in icy conditions in late November because they have seen some snow further up and they have a circular plastic sledge they think will give some good fun.

**1300** The Spanish visitor is disgruntled with the hills. Nothing like as good as the Picos, he says to himself. Once in the cloud he has seen nothing and asks the way down. He did not like the attitude of the walker he had asked, something about his footwear. White trainers are perfectly acceptable in his opinion. A bit tricky on this gravel, but he'll be glad to get down out of the cloud. It's very cold.

**1315** The three friends are back. They are very relieved about this, because somewhere out there they have had a really hard time with the wind. They never anticipated such a gale. Before they set out they had called in to ask the Ranger about going to Ben Macdui, but he had said try Cairn Gorm first. They had made it to the Ptarmigan building only with the greatest of difficulty, and not ventured any further up. Macdui was a planet further away.

**1318** Fantastic clear weather. Crisp snow underfoot, not a rock to be seen. Blue sky and not a breath of wind. Ken would have enjoyed this. They are carrying him up Cairn Gorm for the last time. The cairn at last. Ken's son opens the lid and tips the grey ash over the white cairn. Ken would have been proud. The only blemish on the landscape for miles around.

*Family fun*

**1323** The family of five have different ideas about this walk. Dad wants a good mountain walk in the snow, and is pleased that the skiing people have let them use the train to get up the mountain. He leads them over Cairn Gorm and now is descending towards the plateau. Mum is very unsure and tells him so regularly. The two boys are having a good time but can't keep their feet in their wellies and regularly crash into each other, the rocks and their dad's striding legs. He remonstrates with them very roughly and carries the little girl high on his shoulders. He has not considered that should he fall, she will hit the ground with exaggerated force. They progress like a bickering caravan down onto the plateau utterly devoid of anything that might help them, save other walkers. The Ranger looks on open-mouthed.

**1405** They came all the way up from Aviemore in the little van they have driven from Barnsley. The road had delivered them to a vast car park with a dismal building and loads of old chairlift seats and rolls of fencing. There is no sign of the railway. No-one is there. Pylons march off into the mist, strung together with a cable. What is this place meant to be? they ask again. No answer. There is no mountain railway here. They get back in the van and drive back to where the road shrugged them off. They never even look at the uphill alternative, but retrace their journey and are puzzled for the rest of their holiday.

**1406** The old guy is sitting with his back to a rock. No answer when the two climbers pass. They greet him again. No answer. He just had his last breath sitting looking out on peace.

**1412** The German visitor had had no need of map and compass, until now, which is a good job, as he thought these little hills needed no such elaborations. Now he wasn't so sure. Perhaps he could ask for directions. No! That would be a weakness. He would just keep on walking, this mist was sure to clear before long.

**1422** The four students from Singapore are very excited by their first visit to snow. They are delighted to hire skis, boots and poles. They go outside onto the snow and carry their skis over to a flat bit. They clip in their boots to the ski bindings. One of their number takes photographs as the others pose, make happy V-signs with their fingers and grin. One falls over and pulls two of the others over. They all laugh. They take more pictures and then take off the skis and return everything to the hire department, having had a great time on them.

**1440** What's this? "Area Closed. Keep Out" They can't do this to us, one of them says. Huh. Ski areas. Says the other. The little wooden sign makes an arc through the air as it is tossed aside, the square mark in the snow soon trodden on as the walkers proceed as, they perceived, was their right.

**1452** It is a busy day on the ski area. There are lots of people out on the snow around the Ptarmigan building. Every train brings another one hundred or so. The young man is looking for his group leader who has gone into the building. In his haste he has completely forgotten that he is still wearing the crampons they lent him this morning. The open double doors of the building are jammed full of people streaming out from the train onto the snow. A very officious voice cuts across his attention, as he is looking for a space in the crowd to push through the doors into the warm building. "You're not coming in here with those on", he hears, "You're a serious hazard to everyone, go and take them off before you come back!"

**1511** The rainbow has been hanging over the far end of the empty car park for most of the day. The bus driver has driven into it five times already. Drizzle from the permanent cloud roll shatters the sunshine from above it. A catabatic wind howls down the slopes, drives the drizzle, shatters the sunshine, makes it all happen.

**1522** The leader had looked at his map and looked at his compass but still has no idea which mountain they are on. This walker might know. They would ask him. Oh, he's a Ranger. He says we can get down by going down that path. The leader wonders why he didn't suggest they carried on going up?

**1535** The cortege sweeps right to the top of the car park, ribbons singing. This is a wonderful day, an exciting place, the best day of her life, and the bride is glorious.

**1540** The Welsh walkers are pleased with themselves until they start trying to come down from Cairn Lochan. They had not needed the ice axe and crampons the Ranger had advised until then, but find the way barred by long sloping sheets of ice, with rocks at the foot of the slope. They stamp into the snow at the edge but can't make an impression on the grey ice. The bare ground had been their friend up till now, but it runs out at the snow and ice, and there is no way through. Wearily, they turn back up the slope and start to retrace their steps.

**1542** The management call this the waste water treatment plant, but there are other names for it. It needs a daily visit, it only takes a few minutes, and someone has to do it. It is only two hundred yards down the hill but they take the Land Rover. They might need to dose it with some chemicals to restore it to neutrality but it's settled down a lot lately. The biggest problems are when there are thousands of people and lots of – er – effluent.

**1552** Three low-flying jets streak up past the picnicking families at about sixteen feet, leaving in their wake nerve-shattered people, bawling babies, shrieking car alarms, activated by the shockwave, and the pervasive smell of aviation fuel. The boys do like to put on a good show at these popular spots when they are over from the States.

**1601** Grim realisation dawns. The man has just locked the keys and his 17-month old boy in his car, and the little boy is frightened by the expressions of the people looking in at him. The toddler grasps the keys pulls them out of the ignition and then drops them. The tot retreats into crying, and can give no further assistance. A hammer and chisel are borrowed. A back window is smashed, to the hysterical sobs of the child.

**1603** The paper bag just blows away. There is no way she can chase it, it bowls over and over down the car park and out of sight. Later that she realises that her two postcards and change of a tenner are in the bag.

**1610** At last the coach pulls into the car park. The Japanese tourists are past anticipating the thrill of a ride in the train. They are bored and thirsty and want the loo. The driver is wondering how he is going to get them back to Newcastle without exceeding his hours. He has totally underestimated the distance. The journey has taken three hours longer than he expected, and he hasn't had the next piece of bad news yet. They are too late for the train.

**1633** "Mission accomplished" the man says pointedly to the Ranger on return from Ben Macdui with his son. What a fuss! A little low cloud, wind and rain. Anyone would think they should have gone somewhere else the way the Ranger was going on. Nathan had really enjoyed the walk, haven't you, Nathan. Nathan? Come on, pick up your feet, boy. Perhaps he's a bit tired, maybe that's why he's just looking at the ground. So? a little character-building. He'll be well on his first round of Munros by the time he's ten years old.

**1645** The parents of a young man walking the Lairig Ghru are beginning to get concerned about his non-appearance and go and ask the Ranger. He is reassuring. It's a long way, he says, will take about ten hours, when did he set out? Where was he due to finish? He could have been delayed by all sorts of things, not paying attention to the time, spending too long enjoying himself. It would be several hours before the Ranger would be getting alarmed, but then it would be a job for the Police, so here's their number…

**1655** The American walker is quite lost. The fog is so thick, he can't make out where he is and uses his mobile phone to summon assistance. He is put through first to the Police operator, then to an officer in Aviemore, finally to a Ranger in a nearby Ranger Station. He describes the pile of stones beside him. Miraculously the Ranger appears to recognise his description and tells him to walk away from the wind. The call ends. The ground is terribly steep, like walking over a cliff, but it never breaks into really steep craggy rocks, just goes on, boulders, and more boulders, down and down. Then he is questioning his own judgement. The boulders seem to be built into steps, leading down. They are! Another ten minutes of steps and path and he is down below the cloud. Phew! That was some job. He wonders where the Ranger was, and how he knew.

**1658** The Bangladeshi family from Acton hasn't seen snow before. They are all excited that it is falling, mixed with rain, and stand looking at it for two minutes before the lady of the household shivers and they walk up to the front door. It is closing time. They have driven since eleven o'clock and they are too late for the train.

**1730** The car park is deserted. Two vehicles still sit there, the day is nearly done. The wind never abated, the train never ran. Everyone else went home, went for tea, took the day off.

**1744** The German visitor is still sure he did not need a map or a compass.

229

He knew all along that this path would lead him to the top of the second highest mountain in Britain, and here he is. It would have been much better if the mist had lifted, but the wind was rising, and would soon push it away. He knew a thing or two about mountain weather from the Alps, and these small mountains couldn't be as dangerous as that. They didn't even put up any direction indicators, so the routes were clearly obvious.

Twenty five minutes later, he is pleased to be proved right again, and the rising wind has indeed stripped away the cloud. His path is clear in front of him, leading all the way down this ridge. He does not remember seeing that lake on the way up, but no matter.

**1900** The man and little boy reach the summit of Ben Macdui, having started from Coylumbridge that morning. It is a lovely summer's evening and they were going to enjoy their high-level camp. The boy was limping on blistered feet. He would be asleep before the tent was up.

**1955** "Look at this honey, I got video of the Head Ranger of the Cairngorms National Park telling us we've not got the right kit to go up the mountains. He never batted an eyelid, just went right ahead and gave it us straight. I'll plug the camera into the TV here."

**2010** Good walking leads the German visitor right down to a valley, passing a hut he is sure he did not notice on the way up, and now he is approaching great trees in the evening light. These mountains certainly go on a bit. He is not so sure now that he will reach the car park in the next ten minutes.

**2045** The idiot the German visitor met going in the opposite direction told him that he had come off the wrong side of Ben Macdui and was now heading to Braemar, which he would reach in another hour or two. That was just not funny. This would not have happened in the Alps.

**2300** The minibus driver waits, and waits. The walkers are still not back. The light in the sky is long gone and no small lights puncture the vast darkness. The driver agonises and uses his phone. He gives details and waits.

**0054** They can still use the phone, thank goodness. It is pitch dark and they've no idea where they are. A text comes through. "If u hav a camera, useit now". What's that supposed to mean? There's nothing to see. The man holds up his phone and operates the camera.

The flash is seen four miles away. "They're down in Strath Nethy" says one of the rescuers over the radio. He sighs. The dustbin of misadventures, is his opinion of Strath Nethy. It's going to be a long night, but at least they're safe.

# Spoiling the dream

As you can see, there are many dreams, and much expectation. So many people come to Cairngorm and single-handedly spoil their own dream, or those of others. They forget the effort and expense they have undergone to have an enjoyable holiday, and then they fall into a row with a companion, an objection to paying what it takes to make the most of the experience, or just moan about anything unexpected or different from home.

Then there are people who have no idea of the impact their actions are causing on other people or the mountain. What is the person who drops paper handkerchiefs all along the Northern Corries Path thinking? Perhaps they think someone else will clear them up, or the wind will blow them away, or they will biodegrade. Perhaps they don't think any of these things.

How is the visit of the ardent dog-lover to be remembered in these mountains, when the dog spends most of the time racing around, investigating every unfamiliar scent in great excitement? I have spoken to innumerable dog owners who are genuinely surprised that this is not acceptable, and who put the dog on the lead for as long as it took to get out of my view. Sometimes the incidents when wild birds are actually caught verge on the point of becoming hunting with dogs – and that's illegal.

There will always be some litter, it goes with the territory. People genuinely accidentally drop things and they blow away or fall in the snow and are lost. But sometimes, clearing some obviously deliberately discarded rubbish I wonder if that represent's the former owner's opinion of this place. A rubbish dump.

# What more do they want?

From what we hear, visitors often want more or different from the Cairngorms. They are not necessarily going to get what they want, but we might learn something by listening to them.

Ever since the railway facility opened, the Tourism organisation has awarded it four stars. This is very creditable, but as the second most-visited destination in the Highlands, there should be an ambition for five. What's the problem?

Despite all the good work being done on staff training and facilities, the single thing that would make more difference than anything else is the sense of arrival.

Driving up the road is quite an adventure. The come-down is the car park which resembles a hillside airstrip. Look at any big visitor facility: Culloden, Glencoe Visitor Centre, Balmoral, to name but three, and their car parks are landscaped and screened. Parking bays are divided from each other and there are places to linger and enjoy the outdoor environment.

There is a very good reason for Cairngorm's main car park being devoid of internal structure, save the strips of tarmac. Snow has to be cleared from it several times every winter. Snow ploughs are big, powerful machines, not suited to sculpting the detail of a highly-designed area.

Speed is the essence of the snow-clearing operation. People are waiting to drive up the road to their work, or to ski. They get in the way if they are allowed up before the car park is clear. The road comes first, then the car park. Then people can come and work, or play.

It's quite common for the staff to arrive at the snow gates at the bottom of the road and find that there is a delay before they can be allowed up. On these occasions, I would assess the delay and sometimes decided to walk. Once when this happened, the gates opened soon after, I was only part-way up. On the next occasion we were forced to wait, the Chief Executive said "Off you go, Nic, it always opens up just after you've set off".

On arrival, staff may find a small part of the car park cleared, and the wide plough working on the rest. Recently there was a timber barrier erected on the downhill edge of the car park. It was damaged in several places by the press of snow on it. Anything else we built in the car park would be similarly damaged.

There have been some efforts to improve the car park, but the present layout is almost ideal for the environment and purpose, even if rather an intrusion in the landscape.

# Visitors want more or different from the Cairngorms

I suspect the average visitor is quite happy to see a few other visitors there, but would prefer it if they didn't get in the way. On weekends and holidays, it is inevitable that other visitors will be there in large numbers, especially in winter. The resulting queues are because too many people want to do the same thing at the same time.

Cairngorm became notorious for queues at the height of its popularity.

Queues for tickets, queues for ski hire, queues for uplift, queues for catering and again for the loo. I'm not a great one for crowds and have a fortunate lifestyle that makes it easy to avoid them, but I can't help looking at the throngs of people on busy days and feeling sorry for them. Then I think that if they really found it too awful to contemplate, they would plan to come at some other time, or go somewhere else, or take up something different.

What else would you like when you visit? Good weather? Can't do much about that. A walk on the mountain at the top of the railway? I'll come to that in a minute. Signposted and circular trails around the mountains? That's a difficult one.

Circular routes are the exception rather than the rule on Cairn Gorm. The trails have developed where people have walked, and spread out from Coire Cas on routes arranged almost like the fingers of a hand, one to each destination. It is only when you reach the plateau edge that you get the chance to circle round and join from one main route to another.

The two routes on the summit of Cairn Gorm form an ideal circuit for the Walk at the Top but more by luck than planning in their construction.

As if to emphasise that they do form loops, the trails in Coire Cas are often referred to as Loop trails.

There are interpretive signs around Coire Cas, but no-one wants signs to direct people to take themselves off into potentially hazardous places. The provision of guided walks is a completely different matter. The experienced guide, often a Ranger, can manage the walk in a way to maximise the enjoyment and informativeness, and minimise the hazards.

There is a persistent expectation among visitors for regular signposting on trails. This probably arises from experience elsewhere. Setting aside the liability issues again for a moment, what would the effect be of placing such waymark signs around the hills, as they are already around the forests below?

The group that might benefit from them could dispense with relying on their map and compass, and rely instead on someone else's signage, hoping that it is accurate and competent, and hadn't been turned round, broken, defaced, buried in snow, caked in rime or vandalised. They might hope, too, that the destination was feasible in the overhead and underfoot conditions, within the time available. A sign would not be able to advise on this.

The group that had adequate skills and knowledge and didn't need the signs would see the proliferation of unnecessary man-made objects into remote and un-cluttered places. They might well take a dim view of this (in fact I know they would) and act to remove these intrusions. The story of the Summit Path markers comes to mind.

The people who put up the markers would have a constant job making them, carrying them up, along with the poles, and ensuring they remained in place and fit for purpose. It would take a small army.

The net effect would be a diminution of wild values and the rule of self-reliance.

The biggest complaint from visitors to the railway is that they are not allowed to set out on their own for a walk at the top of the train ride. This is the main provision of the Visitor Management Plan, and is not likely to change.

## The Visitor Management Plan (The VMP)

You might be a bit surprised that I have come back to this subject, but the Visitor Management Plan doesn't operate as it was written. The Closed System was completely closed at first. People could walk up – and did – and look in through the windows of the Ptarmigan building, even at their family members, and couldn't take advantage of the shelter, toilets, catering or anything.

The argument had been that if Cairn Gorm was uniquely graced with such inducements to climb, the fickle public would flock to it, and then spread far and wide, causing all sorts of trampling damage and disturbance.

*Sign in, please, then you can go out again later*

I think the attraction of the railway was much less of a big deal than the most optimistic – or pessimistic – observers expected.

The first amendment to the VMP was to allow walkers in at the top station. That was patently sensible. Before that they had to be refused entry unless they were in distress. To ensure that the walkers were allowed out again, but train passengers were not, the operator was required to provide a separate entrance (which became known as the Walkers' Entrance) and a signing-in facility. They would sign in, and only those who had signed in could go out.

The second amendment was much more controversial, but made sense to me. There were actually two parts to it. One was that the Company could promote (signpost and mention in literature) the Windy Ridge Path, which was an omission from the original VMP.

The controversial bit was to allow walkers who had come in to the Ptarmigan building to buy a ticket to ride down the train. This would have the effect of removing them from the fragile part of the mountain so they wouldn't have to walk down the trails, and was presented as a further measure to reduce pressure on the mountain.

To find out whether this measure would again encourage lots of people to walk on Cairn Gorm and the European Sites, every customer was asked if they had been into the European Sites and whether they would have come walking on Cairn Gorm today if there had been no Down Train ticket. In other words, to judge the extra walking generated by this facility.

Most respondents did not walk in the European Sites (when they found out what they are) and would have come anyway.

The next amendments were about letting people out of the building at the top, but in small parties, accompanied by a guide. The groups could use the footpaths in the ski area and climb to the top of the mountain. The "Walk at the Top" as it became known, was popular from the start, and remains so. Train passengers can visit the summit and find out what it is that they are supposed to be protecting by being cooped up in the building. Walkers who start from the car park may also join the walks if they wish.

An extension to the walks was permitted to allow the operator to take train passengers with a mountain bike and ride down the main track with them. This is considerably more adrenaline-fuelling and there have been a few accidents. In my opinion, this will be worthwhile when a purpose-built mountain bike descent route is built, but until then is an exercise in hanging on to the brake levers and jumping the stone drains in the track.

Standing accused of operating a monopoly on offering walks, the operator suggested they would extend this facility to train passengers guided by other suitably-trained guides such as wildlife guides. This makes sense. On a holiday sampling the wildlife delights of the area, ptarmigan, dotterel and snow bunting are important prospects. Making the guide double up his guiding with a guide from the operator's organisation is just an unnecessary cost. So it won't happen. If the holiday can sample the high ground on the same routes as the operator uses, following the same conditions, more people get to understand a bit about the area, and there is no damage to the wildlife or habitats the operator is obliged to protect.

There are still many accusations of scamming the public: only taking them out if they pay to be guided, but doing it free is not viable, and letting some go out free, no matter how well-behaved they are, would mean letting them all out. I'll come back to this in the next chapter.

# 14.  Monitoring, watching paint dry

Like so many epics in life, the prospect of getting involved in the monitoring scheme at Cairngorm posed no terrors at the time, but grew gradually to be a monster. The monitoring scheme dominated my work while it was being drawn up and has been present in my work ever after.

I am all in favour of monitoring. Even if the operator and HIE weren't obliged to do it (by the Section 50 agreement), they would be doing it anyway.

When a place is nearly perfect and it's almost impossible to improve on it, the people looking after it can't busy themselves improving it, they watch for change, and this is called monitoring. This is to find out if it is still up to the standards expected, and to reveal new aspects of its quality, and discover areas of concern where intervention may be needed.

*Fiacaill Coire an t-Sneachda – nearly perfect*

237

These topics could be summed up by the expressions:

"Yes, it's still a great place."

"We never knew such a species/process/thing occurred here/this region/this time of year etc"

And "This gives us some concerns, and we need to do something about it."

Monitoring is watching something in an organised way. (Scottish Natural Heritage) SNH knows about monitoring. They drew up a method for writing a monitoring scheme just before we wrote ours. Unfortunately, no-one told us, so we were left to draw up a scheme for the most contentious high-profile development in the country from scratch. Most of the work fell to me, but everything I did had to be approved by two disagreeing parties. So it was not much fun.

What were we supposed to monitor? Our finance director came back from a protracted meeting about the overarching Section 50 agreement and proudly announced that we were to monitor a whole list of topics, including bryophyte springs and geomorphology. I think he was pleased he could pronounce these technical expressions, they would make him feel almost scientific. I can't think why else he would be pleased, because this would be bad news for his finances, and, as I shall explain, a huge waste of money.

Why were we to do all this? The overall purpose was to see that the development and management of the railway did not adversely affect the integrity of the adjacent European Sites, the Natura sites, which are also SSSIs. This is a good thing.

So, we were looking for changes in these sites. To start with there had to be a Baseline survey, and in the absence of any knowledge of the topic, the Chairlift Company commissioned Universities and Consultants to carry out a Baseline Survey of all these topics. At no point did they involve their newly-appointed Head Ranger. I might not have been considered impartial, but at least I could point out the lack of the emperor's new clothes.

I actually wonder whether SNH knew all this, and considered that the developer and their allies needed to pay some blood money to some institutions and organisations to make it all look good.

To focus attention, a map of the area to be surveyed was provided. For reasons I haven't been able to fathom, the survey area included the ski area, which has never been part of the Natura sites. It also included the cliffs of the Northern Corries, where everyone agreed, only climbers went, and the railway was not going to affect them in the least. The monitoring area also included Loch

Avon, Loch Etchachan and Ben Macdui. Later on we found that much of this was not really affected by developments at Cairngorm. The monitoring area was huge.

The changes we were supposed to be looking for were only those brought about by the building and management of the railway. We weren't looking for changes brought on by the number or effect of large sponsored events, or the growth in mountain biking, climate change or other external events.

We had to monitor all the Baseline topics: Habitats, Footpaths, Bryophyte Springs, Dotterel, Visitors, Geomorphology and Soils. And we had to repeat an aerial survey and a visitor opinion survey at intervals. We would report to SNH and the Highland Council (THC), but in order to introduce an element of independent scrutiny, SNH and THC would ask an independent Reporting Officer to comment on the data and advise them on changes to the monitoring scheme or management of the railway.

The original idea was that a Monitoring Group of stakeholders would agree in advance what management action was to be taken if any change detected was not within a Limit of Acceptable Change (LAC). These limits had to be stated in the original monitoring scheme document, and we had to state what might be considered in response to any breach. The dreaded Reserve Powers (a clearway on the road, closing car parks, or car park charges) were the main methods required.

We laboured long and hard over devising how the process would work, only for it to be abandoned a few years later. The Monitoring Group never met, as the only two stakeholders that needed to be satisfied were SNH and THC, because the matters were statutory ones for them, not matters of opinion. So the whole LAC system was scrapped.

During the drafting process, the document was batted back and forth between veteran ecologist Neil Bayfield and me for 8 or 9 drafts till he withdrew and I was left to try to find acceptable wording for SNH and THC on one hand and CCC on the other.

I would show the most recent draft to SNH and they recommended changes. I would show the redrafted edition to CCC and they would ask for changes. Up and up the edition numbers crept, nearer and nearer the date for the inaugural run of the train. This could have been a show-stopper.

To everyone's relief, the 24th draft was accepted by the board of SNH and the relevant committee of THC with less than a month to spare. It had been a marathon.

Now it fell to Cairngorm Chairlift Company to carry it out. There was a strong expectation among the Universities and researchers that had carried out the Baseline survey that this particular "dripping roast" would be a nice little earner for them to carry out the monitoring. I wonder what sort of service we would have had from them. If the Baseline was anything to go by, we would be none the wiser and much the poorer.

The only good thing we could have expected from commissioning the baseline surveyors to carry out the main monitoring scheme would have been that they would have had to sort out the mess they had created. Much of the Baseline was unrepeatable, and never used. And I can't imagine that the constant effort to improve the techniques and reduce the overall volume and cost of monitoring would have even occurred to the successors of the people who set it up.

My decision (mine? I think it was mine, but no doubt it was taken by someone else on my recommendation) to undertake the monitoring in-house came as a nasty jolt to at least one of the academics who had carried out the Baseline. I mentioned that we were going to take on an Ecologist and she gulped. I had just blown a hole in her budget projections which included income from CCC for carrying out the monitoring scheme.

CCC, and soon CML, were fortunate that Dr Cathy Mordaunt offered her services. She was already known to the company as the secretary to a group of mountaineers concerned about the effect of the VMP on their interests. They were different from many other such groups because they were willing to keep talking to the company about it, and not just campaign.

Cathy's doctorate study was in the very field we needed – mountain habitat analysis and fieldwork. She had done her work on Aonach Mor, and she even lived locally, in Nethy Bridge. Cathy took herself and all the documents off to an office in the Shieling and read herself into understanding the job better than anyone else. I can only imagine some of the shocks and disappointments, missing photographs and field sheets she had to chase up, incomplete work she had to ask about and newly-devised techniques that couldn't work.

# Paths – getting started

The most acute difficulties were in repeating the methodology invented for surveying paths and habitats and used in the Baseline survey. It is a point of scientific rigour that the same techniques and measurements are made consistently. If they are not, how could anyone compare them and make a judgement about whether anything had changed?

Different techniques had been devised for 'diffuse' paths and 'non-diffuse' paths. I argued strongly that there is no path which never has anyone stray off it, so all paths are diffuse to some extent. The Baseline surveyors had also found some 'semi-diffuse' paths, so help us.

Cathy's discussion of the footpath survey was diplomatic but to the point. Baseline surveyors had not had accurate maps of the footpaths they were supposed to be surveying, did not make careful records, made inconsistent notes, or none, made typing and transcription errors and took poor-quality photos with a hand-held compact camera. Cathy's list goes on and on, listing 13 major problems.

The footpath methodology was abandoned on the advice of SNH. This presented a problem for the monitoring scheme. If there is no Baseline, who can say what it was like before the railway was commissioned, so then and now can't be compared. We could still compare now with some time in the future, though, and this is still a valid reason for trying again.

## Paths – the next try

SNH and THC agreed to adopt the industry-standard Amber survey technique for monitoring the condition of footpaths. This is designed to be used for planning future repair works, though the monitoring scheme does not have that objective. The monitoring scheme is intended to see whether change is happening, not what should be done about it. It

*The path to Coire an t-Sneachda*

doesn't help that most of the problem footpaths are not on Cairngorm Estate, so all we were doing was looking at problems on other peoples ground (with their permission), and reporting on them. When they eventually came to be fixed by the Cairngorms Outdoor Access Trust (COAT), they undertook their own Amber surveys in any case.

The Amber survey depends on each section of path being measured, its physical characteristics such as bare width, trampled width, long gradient and cross-slope measured, and loads of photographs taken. Later development saw this data mapped with GIS, so improving and deteriorating paths could quickly be identified. It is still a cumbersome system, requiring a large database and associated photo files.

## Paths – the results so far

Here is the first result to report: The paths are not getting worse as a result of the management of the railway. The paths are, in fact improving. The most obvious improvements are on the paths that have been rebuilt, but many others are recovering spontaneously. The vast majority are stable and one or two are showing signs of greater wear and tear.

# The paths are, in fact improving

Interesting though this result is, it is not news. The Cairngorm Ranger Service carried out transect measurements across paths for several years before I started with them, and I continued the practice. Although the sample points were small and spread out, numbering about 16 to 24 per path, every path showed a decrease in the amount of bare ground, and a corresponding increase in the amount of vegetated ground, even on paths that had had no help from us.

This observation even applied on the Fiacaill a' Choire Chais, the broad ridge leading up to the plateau that was nearly 99% bare in 1996, and dropped little by little every year. I was a bit at a loss to understand why, but put it down to the damp, mild summers promoting vegetation growth. They may also be benefitting from improved snow cover (which protects the vegetation) and increased nitrogen deposition, a pollution issue which is benefitting plants.

Two paths are actually disappearing. One is the path to the site of Jean's Hut in Coire an Lochain. Since the hut was removed, fewer people go there. Beyond it, the Twin Burns path that climbs steeply from Loch Coire an Lochain to the plateau is also greening over. Neither can be attributed to any mountain railway management.

If the original footpath survey was an obvious turkey, at least it didn't leave a legacy that was actually making things worse.

## Habitats – getting started

The Baseline surveyors laid out, in each sub-area of the monitoring area, eight transects using thick wooden pegs to mark the end points and along each transect small wooden pegs and two steel pins to mark the location of each of two squares called quadrats. Each quadrat measured half a metre on a side and had to be surveyed painstakingly, noting the amount of each type of vegetation or bare ground.

*A quadrat*

There were strict rules on which broad vegetation type could be used to locate a quadrat, and if the wrong type turned up, a different place was chosen. This was to avoid habitats impossible to survey such as boulderfield, or which show no change, such as *nardus* grassland or areas already heavily trampled. The idea was to try to find out what light, diffuse trampling pressure was doing to the vegetation of the Natura sites.

# The development of the railway certainly did have an impact on the Natura sites

The pegs and pins do not stand out on the plateau, and were located only by six-figure grid references (narrowing the search area to at least 100 metres by 100 metres, if accurate). It took Cathy up to 3 hours to find some end-points, after which they were declared lost. For those she successfully located she upgraded their grid reference with the newly-improved GPS signal that was available. We were to be very grateful later on that she had done this, as her ten-digit grid references cut down the search area to a minimum of one square metre, though it was more usually six to eight metres square.

Cathy reckoned that normally one day in the field needed one day in the office to make sense of the data, to organise it and store it in a way it can be found and used again.

Unfortunately, she had to spend about four days in the office retrieving the data from the Baseline survey, as it had been locked into an Access read-only database as text, not numbers, so she had to fiddle around for hours of repetitive work before it could be used again. We began to suspect the Baseline was not reliable and competent here, either.

When Cathy found that some of the iron rods marking the quadrats were missing, she did not replace them, because she regarded them as an alien intrusion, spilling ferrous ions into the soil and possibly modifying the vegetation. The rods were supposed to be stainless steel or galvanised, but corners had been cut. So the habitat monitoring was actually damaging the habitat.

Cathy estimated that 120 kilograms of iron and 150 kg of wood were acting as markers for this piece of dubious scientific monitoring. The development of the railway certainly did have an impact on the Natura sites in the introduction of all this foreign material, much on land not owned or managed by the developers, and without the knowledge of those who did.

There were more problems with this survey. The statistical 'power' to demonstrate change was very poor. No limit of acceptable change could be set, because no-one could be sure whether a little change was significant or not.

More and more errors came to light. Original Baseline fieldwork sheets were spoiled by rain, rewritten, copied, errors made and then stored in a way they couldn't be corrected. Three years of painstaking and expensive work amounted to nothing.

Again the Baseline was discarded, with all it could have told us about what the habitat was like before the railway was developed, because it was done in a way that could not be trusted to give a meaningful answer.

## Habitats – the next try

From 2005 the monitoring scheme moved on to using the technique of step-pointing. This is an ingenious method, involving the surveyor walking round quite a large representative area (still no cliffs, bogs or *nardus*) and recording the plant type that appears at a mark on the toe of their boot.

Each step therefore points to the next random sample. Actually it's a bit difficult to be completely random, because the surveyor is going to have to put weight on that step, and although methods have been devised to avoid bias in choosing where to put the step, it creeps in unintentionally. So there are difficulties of achieving consistency between different observers.

We settled down to 500 steps as a sample size for these large areas, walking up and down, up and down across a rectangle defined at the corners by landmarks and GPS, and made clearer by walking poles stuck in the ground. We marched up and down reciting into a voice recorder or noting in a notebook "1; 0; 1; 5; 6; 4…" which means "Plant; Bare; Plant; Lichen; Hepatic Crust; Rock…" and so on. Then on the subsequent day in the office, all the zeroes, ones, twos and so on were counted up and a relative population size calculated for each.

## Habitats – the results

*Pin and peg removal*

Though our consistency (and especially my inconsistency) has been inexplicably variable, it is gratifying to see the bare ground in these big areas of plateau decrease year on year, and the plants and things that would suffer from trampling increase. While this might be because of the continuing run of wet, mild summers, the steepness in the decline of bare ground mirrors the decline in the number of people out on the plateau, and I am optimistic.

We still have to come to terms with this mountain of iron and wood that was put up there. Using the ten-figure grid references and GPS, backed up by a metal detector, we visited about half of the 28 sub-units and removed pegs and iron pins from about 100 transects.

# I am optimistic

While I was searching near the summit of Cairn Gorm, I came across a strong metal detector response from among rocks, but not quite in the right position. I dug out of the gravel a huge horseshoe, with the nails still sticking out of it. It was probably a forestry horse. I wonder if the animal had an arduous walk back down to the forest after throwing its shoe near the summit. It was well-buried.

## Bryophyte springs

Bryophyte springs are places where water oozes out of the ground and mosses and liverworts dominate the vegetation. This habitat was of particular interest to someone setting up the monitoring scheme and a separate study was launched. There was concern that if recreation patterns were to change as a result of the management of the railway, these places might become more trampled and damaged.

I'm not sure how this might have happened. Bryophyte springs are dire hazards for walkers. The vegetation mat is quite distinct from the surroundings, and is always wet. One stumble into a spring early in your hillwalking career is enough to teach you to avoid them at all costs. The surface looks solid but does not support the weight of a walker, and the wet layer may be shallow or over knee deep, it's impossible to tell until it's too late.

*A bryophyte spring*

Fortunately for us the monitoring is easy, with fixed points used for photography. So far the photographs show change only in the amount of wetness. No one is going near them.

## Soils and geomorphology

Another two topics of the monitoring scheme go together, though I am at a loss to describe the process by which the management of the railway might impact on them.

Presumably the regulatory authorities (SNH and THC) agree and have decided that soils do not need to be monitored regularly.

Geomorphology, being the subject I enjoyed most during my studies at university, is one I should welcome.

The Baseline was set up by taking pictures of variable quality of the large-scale features of the plateau and Northern Corries. Cathy made a second visit in 2006. Again, she corrected errors, located viewpoints and took accurate GPS readings.

This made it all much easier to repeat in 2011, though I nearly failed completely. Only two days of good weather were required. I thought July 4th was going to be my first one, but by the time I got to the first of the points to re-photograph the geomorphology, I was nearly being blown off my feet, and abandoned the attempt.

*Geomorphology*

I tried again two weeks later and managed to photograph half of the points on the list. I had to wait till November 7th for the next day of sufficient quality, with good sunshine and lack of cloud shadow, to complete the survey. By then, of course, the sun was much lower in the sky, shadows lay on many of the slopes of interest and I am not particularly proud of the result.

The sort of influences people really could have had on the geomorphology have not been included in the monitoring scheme, presumably because the Baseline surveyors didn't think of them. Lots more people going up on the hill than before might collect – or bring – rocks to add to a summit cairn, or to construct waymark cairns along the way, or even to make a rock garden of lots of little stone sculptures. People might make dams in rivers, with ponds or overspills. They might delight in scree-running on gravelly banks which occur around the plateau. There could be a resurgence in the practice of smashing up quartzite rocks in the search for Cairngorm crystal. No matter. There is no baseline, and no monitoring.

# Dotterel

The only bird which is on Schedule 1 of the Wildlife and Countryside Act that occurs regularly in the monitoring area, is dotterel. Arguably, changes to the recreation patterns caused by the management of the railway could lead to additional disturbance of this bird while nesting on the high ground.

But so could a number of other factors: Late snow; Summer rain and cold conditions making the chick chill or starve from lack of invertebrate food. Problems with its migration pattern and winter resort, too, could have an influence. They can be put off by pet dogs or wild ravens quartering the area regularly, and they can easily move somewhere else.

Although poor breeding in the UK is unwelcome, it is known for dotterel to guard against this and cope quite naturally. It makes us wonder what a well-managed system could do to harm the interests of the birds.

Despite dotterel numbers not being a good measure of the degree to which management of the railway affects them (or not), the operator paid thousands of pounds annually for a team of expert ornithologists to walk the plateau each year and count dotterel, apply a carefully-calculated correction factor and report on the health of the population.

This work is a continuation of a long-running research project called the

Cairngorm Montane Ecology Project. Is it mean to suggest that the scientists seized on the monitoring scheme as a way of continuing a pet project?

Yes, a bit mean. SNH were quite happy for the operator to have a break from paying for this monitoring, and the ornithologists were going to carry it on without being paid. But when CML were given temporary permission for the Walk at the Top, responsibility for monitoring dotterel came back to CML before it had even gone away.

Important to the analysis of the breeding success of the dotterel is a survey of late snow lying on the plateau. Rangers took this on in the last few years. Big variation was recorded: May saw full cover on the plateau in 2010 and very little in 2011 and 2017.

In the first three years of the monitoring scheme the Ranger Service carried out the dotterel survey in-house. This was one of the least well-delivered of all our tasks ever. We depended on an experienced team member who had previously worked for RSPB and who assured us it was well within his competence.

It didn't help that 2004 was almost certainly a dead loss for the birds, when no recruitment at all was achieved, caused by late snowfall and then cold, heavy rain.

Looking back over his records for 2002 and 2003, however, it was clear that not only was the task too great for a single fieldworker acting alone, but that he had not followed the specification for the survey and had not kept adequate records of his methods. There was, therefore, very little confidence in his results, nor in their ability to demonstrate any slight change in the population caused by the management of the railway.

*Dotterel (circled) and walkers*

As an aside, we were all very concerned about the complete failure of dotterel to breed in the Cairngorms in 2004, but we didn't see this as reflecting on the monitoring scheme or the management of the railway, nor of the actions of recreationists and their dogs.

The Ranger Service prepared signs forewarning walkers, especially those with dogs that they were approaching an area of the plateau particularly suited to nesting dotterel, and while people were still encouraged to look out for them, it was stated that by sticking to the path, the least disturbance was likely to be caused.

We placed the signs at the North and South ends of the path across the Miadan Creag an Leth-choin and watched.

To our consternation, the pair of dotterel nesting on the extensive flat area chose to nest within seven metres of the path, in a quite bizarre example of the confiding nature of the species. Up to a hundred people a day passed close by, and the birds managed to raise the normal number of two chicks.

I was observing the area one day when a man appeared quartering the plateau, armed with a tripod and a movie camera. His manner was not peaceful, he appeared frustrated at not being able to find what he was looking for, but he didn't know where to look, and I didn't make a point of telling him. He passed within seven metres of the nest but didn't see the bird, eventually moving off to some other part of the hill.

Later a slow-moving couple with a black Labrador came along the path. I could see them stop regularly and the man look through his binoculars. Eventually they found the dotterel on its nest. I heard the man's exclamation of delight. The woman put the dog on a lead. It hadn't been wandering off in any case. Without approaching the bird, they watched it through the binoculars, photographed it from a distance and soon turned to go back down again. I could sense the triumphant spring in the man's step.

If the dreaded human disturbance does not prevent dotterel breeding even this close to a popular path, and yet a poor summer – and fewer walkers – sends them away, it is clear that dotterel are not a suitable subject for assessing the effect of the railway. No-one would wish these lovely birds any harm, but the feeling is that the operator and HIE are watching them because they need watching, not because the railway requires it.

SNH came round to the same view a while later, and, although the operator and HIE are happy to assist the ornithologists with their survey, it is no longer an annual expense.

Considering that I was the main author of the monitoring scheme, it gives me little pleasure to be sticking the boot in. So with some relief, I can turn to some success stories at last.

After the monitoring scheme was written, I was introduced to the fundamental distinction between variables which represent a pressure for change and those which are a response to the pressure for change. If the pressure mounts, eventually, the effects will be noticeable, but if there is no pressure for change, there should be no worries, even if the things, like dotterel populations, change for some other reason. All the topics described so far can be thought of as response variables, and they amount to detail, but not the big picture.

# It's all about people

## Aerial photography

The over-view of the response to environmental change is provided by the aerial photography. This was carried out in 2000 and 2006, and provides a clear view of the big important environmental changes.

The obvious drawback of aerial photography is that it needs good weather, and as I have already mentioned, 2011 was not a year for that either. So although HIE commissioned an aerial survey in 2011, it couldn't be flown, and by 2012, SNH decided it was no longer needed.

In my opinion, the aerial photography gives the best early-warning of problems with the environment. It is easy to see footpaths growing longer, extending into previously unmarked areas where before there was no real path. It's even possible to make out wear and tear on the vegetation leading to bare patches or changes to geomorphology on a landscape scale when comparing photographs from successive surveys.

This might lead to more work to check for any real change on the ground.

So what is it that brings about this environmental damage or change? What are the things that bring about pressure on the environment?

It's all about people. What they do, what their dogs do, what the peoples' attitudes are which lead them to do certain things, and how many of them there are. We have been quite good at measuring this.

# Vehicle numbers

From 1997 to 2010 Highland Council operated a traffic counter in the approach road. It was ripped out by a snow plough during our big winter and took eighteen months to replace, but it's working again now.

Cathy carried out a check on the occupancy rates in the vehicles and came up with a reasonable estimate of the number of people coming up the road.

There are a number of cautions on the figures. All vehicles are counted alike, though coaches usually carry a lot of people and cars usually only a few. In a season when lots of coaches are visiting, an average figure might be an under-estimate. It's not possible to tell that all the people in the vehicles stop in the car park, but there are several other methods of counting them. Only the people who come purely for the car park and café, and who never go on the train or for a walk, are likely to avoid all efforts to count them.

# Ticket sales

As you might imagine, sales of train tickets and snowsports tickets are closely monitored for commercial reasons. There is a long-standing record for Cairngorm and, understandably, it shows a jump in 2002, when the summer market was rejuvenated by enthusiasm for the new railway. There has been a steady decline since, replaced by a jump in the winter market in 2010.

The operator also counts how many people come for a Walk at the Top and how many buy a down-train ticket. These numbers have risen steadily, but are small in comparison to the overall numbers.

# People counters

For many years, the Cairngorm Ranger Service has maintained automatic people counters on the paths leading out from the car park. We also looked after one on the path to the Chalamain Gap before it was transferred to the Forestry Commission, and now there are eight automatic people counters on the paths in the Northern Corries.

The counters are made by an inventor in North Kessock, Rolf Schmidt, who still gives us lots of help and advice, and sometimes even remembers to charge us for his work. His other claim to fame is that he built and operated a solar-powered boat on the Beauly Firth in which he gave people sightseeing rides. He's a clever chap.

Unfortunately, vagaries of the environment often conspire to make his people counters less reliable, and we have done a lot of work to keep them going. This has particularly been taken on by the Cairngorm Rangers, but I have had the biggest share of calibrating them. I should explain how they work.

You probably won't notice when you pass one of the people counters. There is nothing to see, it's buried in the path. As you step on the gravel overlying the counter you will compress a rigid sandwich formed by two layers of board, between which is a snake-like length of tubing. The air in the tubing gets pressed out and the pressure is detected by a sensor, and transmitted as an electrical impulse up a short wire to the recording unit.

When I started, the Mark Two recording units had an exchangeable component on which data was recorded. It was an Electronically-Programmable Read-Only Memory, or EPROM. It had to be sent away to be read, and a paper copy of the results would come back.

The newer Mark 3s have black data pods which are exchanged wholesale. The in-situ pod is disconnected and the new pod is connected, then the whole pod is taken back to the office for downloading. This allows it to be dried out, the battery can be tested and the data downloaded directly onto computer.

Better still, now the Mark Four counters allow immediate download of a USB data stick to a small portable computer.

With all types, the data shows, in tabular form, how many people were detected crossing the counter in each hour of each day since it was connected.

This ever-vigilance is one of the automatic counter's greatest assets. We can go away and leave it for a month and come back and find out what's been happening day and night.

*Downloading a people counter on the Lochain - Lurcher's Ridge path.*

Needless to say, errors creep in, and there is also the problem of calibration.

The errors are often self-inflicted. If the counter is not located correctly, people can walk round it too easily (it counts none), or they can walk across two at a time (and only one gets counted). If the gravel covering is too thick, it takes a heavyweight to trigger it, if too thin the counter is exposed. If there is a stone underneath then only one spot is sensitive. If there are voids underneath the pad it also loses sensitivity. And we haven't even got on to water ingress, battery life and interface problems.

When we were only checking the counters once a month, a slight error could go undetected. A weekly check has proved much more reliable.

# The problem of calibration

The counters need to be calibrated. That means finding out how many people the counter counts when 100 people go past. How long do you think it takes for 100 people to pass on one of Cairngorm's paths?

It can take two hours on the Summit Path on a busy day, and twelve or more hours on the Fiacaill Path in Coire Cas.

The calibration factor should be a fairly constant rate, so once it is calculated, it can be taken as correct for a couple of years unless the counter or the site is disturbed, or the pattern of use changes significantly.

In theory, if 100 people are seen to pass and 80 are actually recorded, the counter records need to be multiplied by 100/80 or 125% to reveal the correct numbers. If the correction factor is greater than 200% or less than 50%, the data are suspect, and something needs to be done to restore a better performance. This probably requires changing the counter or the site, so any calibration will have to start again.

As the Mark 3 counters had no external display, we had to start calibrating on the dot of the start of a new hour and finish exactly an hour, or more hours later.

So one mild November day, I saw two people pass the counter on the path on Fiacaill a' Choire Chais and noticed some more coming down the ridge that were going to be too late to count for the hour I was observing. There was a stiff breeze, but I could probably hide from it, but did I really want to wait another hour to see what happened?

I decided yes, and was rewarded with eleven people passing within the first ten minutes of the new hour. This was a good contribution towards the target of 100. Then, as the sun went down, and I got colder and colder, the rest of the hour passed and not a single further person passed the counter. I sat for 50 minutes to check.

In theory, it should have been possible for me to observe more than one counter at once, but I would need to be very alert, and use binoculars unless they are very close by. That afternoon, the only other counter needing attention was on the windy side of the ridge, and I couldn't face the cold wind, especially as the other counter – on the Sneachda path – was notoriously quiet.

These calibration sessions called on all my resources of diligence and patience. They are very undemanding compared to the observation surveys which we used to do, and I'll explain later, because I was only watching one or two points, and sometimes very little happened. For an hour.

The report on a couple of the people counters for 2010 shows how frustrating this work can be:

*Northern Corries path: After emerging from snow in May, it was presumed this counter was working satisfactorily, but calibration was included in the work programme as it is an important counter. This started in August 2010 to take advantage of greater volumes of traffic. It was found to be under-counting beyond the acceptable range of tolerance. The counter was removed, rebuilt and had a new sensor fitted. It was re-laid with a very light cover of aggregate, and was considered very close to the surface. However, further calibration indicated that it was still undercounting at the year end. Therefore no acceptable data have been collected by this counter in 2010. Three hours were spent [calibrating] in August before the counter was rebuilt and re-seated, and four hours afterwards. All this work produced no usable data. Will require renewing and recalibrating in 2011.*

And

*Windy Ridge path: Snow-free from 23/5/10 but a fault was not recognised until late July when 8 good days' data were produced, coinciding with a calibration exercise. A second lapse was not detected until September when 30 good days' data were produced. ... Successfully calibrated during six hours of observation in July and August 2010, but following later failure will require recalibrating in 2011.*

All the time recorded for these two counters was wasted, as none of the calibration could be applied to any other period, so the counters on two of the busiest paths produced no data in 2010. Four other counters performed satisfactorily, and of the remaining two one was not bad and one gave nothing.

In 2011, I had much better news to report. All the pods, the sensors and some of the pads had been serviced, and the calibration almost completed for the busier paths.

## People counters – the results

So, how many people do use the paths?

In 2009, the Northern Corries Path counter gave a calibrated count of 42,472 people passing between April and November. (It was frozen the rest of the year). This has become the most popular path by far since before the demise of the chairlift.

# The most popular path by far

The Summit Path used to be the most popular, because it was well built and the Northern Corries Path was a horrible bog-trot with a granny-stopper at the start. The Summit Path trended up to 20,000, but even before the open system ended, it had been overtaken by the more-accessible Northern Corries Path.

As an answer to those who complain that thousands of pounds were spent on the Summit Path and "no-one can use it", I would point out the recent counts from automatic counters. In 2009 this gave 16,763 and in 2010 it gave 15,533 people. Some of these people will be on return trips, and about 1100 people counted in 2010 were on Walks at the Top, so it's still a popular path.

Third in order of popularity – but gaining – is the Windy Ridge, which in 2008 had 10,714, and in 2009 had 12,995. This has now been rebuilt from bottom to top, and will attract more downhill traffic, and we can confidently recommend it as the best direct way to the summit if asked.

For a while there was a counter on the Northern approach to Ben Macdui, but it was unsustainable. The path was so wide, it had to be covered with two adjacent pads. It took ages to calibrate, and was a long way out to maintain. What was worst, it was covered with snow for seven months of the year, but still gave a count of 4000 in the remaining five months. We eventually gave up and brought it all back in.

The counter at Windy Col on the edge of the plateau above Coire Raibert was maintained by land-owners RSPB until Cairngorm Ranger Service took it over in about 1999. It too has a long dormant period, but in the six months of its summer, it regularly records over 3,500 passes.

The Sneachda Path, as I remarked already, is quiet in the summer. If accurate counts were possible in the winter, it would be a different story, but the summer period rarely sees more than 5,000 passing. There was one winter when the path was clear but the cliffs were frozen. This led to records of over 300 passes per day, which certainly boosted the annual total. I suspect this would be typical, but the frozen path makes it invisible to us.

# Some very high counts at midnight in December

There are other types of people counters, of course. We used to operate a beam counter on the Summit Path, in an ideal location between the posts of the top fence. Everyone had to pass between the posts and would break an infra-red beam and be counted. Unfortunately, so did snowflakes, and there were some very high counts at midnight in December, for instance.

The posts are more intrusive than pressure pads, and the possibility of mischievous multi-counting discouraged us from using beam counters.

The people counters were incorporated into the monitoring scheme because they are a recognised way of measuring the number of people on the paths. In terms of whether they have shown a change in the pressure on the environment, the jury is still out. No-one can say yet.

## Asking people where they go

The Baseline study coincided with a Mountain Recreation Survey, in which walkers were asked where they went. They were asked a lot of other things, too, such as which map they carried and whether they had been before.

Both surveys suffered from the same problem. Despite being shown a map, many people – a large minority – had no idea where they had been. This is very concerning and, for me, calls into question their motives and methods (but never mind that).

Other people knew where they had gone but either they or the surveyors made such a hash of marking it on the maps offered, that the information was lost.

# No idea where they had been

When we came to repeat this survey we asked lots more questions, about whether the respondent knew about the access restrictions at the top of the railway (they did), and whether they approved of them (they did) and whether, if permitted they would like to undertake a walk from the top station (they did).

Hang on a minute! (We didn't say) You know about these restrictions and why they are there, you approve of them but you would still like to go for a walk. That's inconsistent!

Yes, if the system was unmanaged, Cathy calculated that 77,000 visitors would make a very short walk from the top of the railway. A further 61,000 would go to the top of Cairn Gorm and 21,000 would go down the hill. None of these would go into the European Sites, but the trampling around the Ptarmigan building, where ptarmigan and dotterel have actually returned to nest and dwarf cudweed and dwarf willow still flower, would have a serious effect on the environment for everyone.

Worse, 33,000 annually would go for a walk of two hours or more, vastly increasing the number of people on the plateau each summer. (5000 at present)

Now we all know that people are quick to say they will do something if they had the chance, and not do it when they get the chance, but an increase like that is not going to melt away in a mass attack of indifference. To me this was the strongest endorsement yet of the tightly managed access system at the Ptarmigan.

# Watching where people go

I wanted to be sure that our surveys were correct and devised a method of observing recreation patterns for long periods from viewpoints scattered around the Monitoring Scheme area. I carried out two years of surveys in 1997 – 1999, including in winter. This observation survey method was incorporated in the original Monitoring Scheme and continued for five summer seasons from 2002 to 2006.

*Observation survey*

I tried to describe, for each period of watching, where people came from, where they went, how many of them there were in a party, counting adults, children and dogs, and whether they crossed people counters, whether their dogs were out of control and other things.

The observation survey became a bit of a marathon, too. It was only possible to carry it out in good visibility, when wind speeds were not too great to hold binoculars steady and count people, sometimes at a great distance. We used viewpoints which together allowed us to observe almost all the monitoring area, though some of these were gradually dropped as we found better places or we realised nothing was happening in the areas observed.

The only year we made a serious attempt to survey the Loch Etchachan basin was in 2003, a summer of above-average warmth and sunshine. Fortunately, we established that 75% of the recreation there emanated from Deeside, so it was hardly of concern to the railway development, and we could safely ignore it.

One of the best viewpoints is at the cairn on the ridge between Coire Cas and Coire an t-Sneachda. In the preliminary years it was the main viewpoint, giving a good view of all the paths setting out from Cairngorm and as far as the plateau.

It was too busy, though, and I had to decide which of the prospects to view. The decision was often made for me by the weather. I would turn my back to the wind. The same applied to the two viewpoints at the top of Fiacaill Coire an t-Sneachda, too. We could look North-West or North-East into quite contrasting basins, and there was always enough walking activity to keep the observer busy on one or the other.

One day, staring intently through binoculars trying to count the several dozen people passing up the ridge to the West of Coire an Lochain, I greeted two middle-aged men who were traversing the ridge I was on. They wanted to know what I was doing, and I made a stock reply of "recreation survey" and hoped they would accept that. They wanted to talk, and I was in the middle of counting. It was one of those busy days when it was near-impossible to keep track of everyone, and I was resorting to making periodic audits of the state of play at certain time intervals.

The guys got quite abusive about me sticking to my task, accusing me of being stuck-up, which in one way I was. If you knew me, you would know I would talk to anybody, but no-one has the right to anyone else's attention. I hope they enjoyed the rest of their day. I did. It was the only time in this work that I could sit with no shirt on.

The rising panic of busy days was often a distant memory, though. Sometimes it was really quiet. I would devise mind games to keep me waiting for the next walker to appear, putting off snacks and lunches till something started happening. One day I made a real effort to get up there early and observe from 8am on Miadan Creag an Leth-choin. Despite the beautiful summer weather there was no-one else there for a whole hour. I started back down at 9 o'clock just in time to see, in the distance, the first people setting out from the car park.

## Results of the observation survey

The most interesting aspect of the results was that it demonstrated very clearly how the number of people changed along the path, for instance, from the car park to Ben Macdui. Numbers at the start are very great, and decline steadily. When there is a flat area where people dispersed, the numbers reached a low point, but where the paths came together again, they bucked up. More people joined the path at Lochan Buidhe, and the final sections were quite busy again, but only a third as busy as the initial sections.

Enjoyable and vexing as the observation survey was, it gave us the only reliable evidence of what was actually going on out there, and what the trends were. The Reporting Officer clearly hated it and dissed it every year. Eventually SNH allowed us to drop it. So we invented something even less open to statistical analysis, which demonstrated more clearly than anything else where people were going.

# Satellite technology

If we could track where people walked throughout their day and present the tracks of where they had been on maps, surely that would demonstrate where people went.

It occurred to me that if we lent a walker a small GPS unit and they carried it round and we downloaded

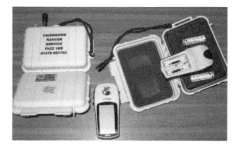

*GPS and box*

their track when they got back, we would have an accurate map of where they had been.

Perhaps we are straying a little further from the purpose of the monitoring scheme, and we only included this as a trial, in 2006, but what a graphic result it produced.

All we had to do was buy the GPS units, package them securely, and hand them out to walkers setting out, and make a note of who they were and whether we could get in touch with them if they forgot to hand it back.

We didn't need to watch them, we could get on with something else. We didn't need good visibility, they worked in good weather or bad, and they could go as far as they liked, as long as they came back.

One guy went to Beinn Bhreac and back in a day. It was so far away we had to search a map for it. It stands above Glen Quoich on Deeside.

Another appeared to make an instantaneous visit to Rockall, but that was a glitch in the machine, of the sort we became used to spotting. Sometimes it looked as though the unit had been attached to the dog which had then sprinted around chaotically for a while. It gave me a cautious approach to relying on this particular model of GPS for navigation.

Nevertheless, the overwhelmingly clear picture that emerged was as shown by the map and published in the journal Countryside Recreation.

The main paths are like thick ropes, with a few maverick lines between them. On the rim of the Corries there is great divergence on the plateau round the head of Coire an t-Sneachda. Many walkers avoided the undulating nature of the route by contouring round the side of hills on the way. There is divergence, too, on Cairn Lochan as people head to and from the Ben Macdui direction.

Two main approach routes towards Ben Macdui converge by Lochan Buidhe

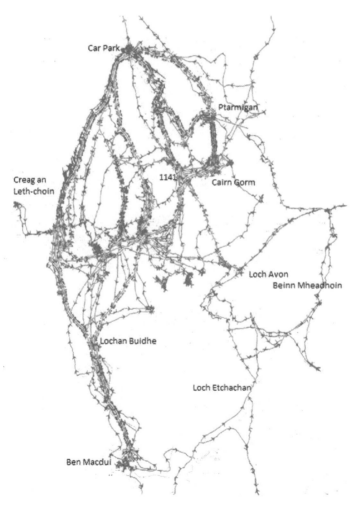

*Traces of walkers' routes recorded by GPS, summer 2007*

and continue as a thick trace to the peak, but few indeed continue to Loch Etchachan. Loch Avon and Beinn Mheadhoin are similarly rarely visited.

Fascinating stuff! Though I described it all for you earlier on, it's clear where people go, and where they don't go.

# Other monitoring – Weather

From long before my days at Cairngorm, the Rangers have been recording the weather every day. The Met Office supplies the equipment and Cairngorm Mountain are (officially volunteer) observers at the Cairngorm Chairlift Climate Station, number 0591. This means a 9am trek (10 am in summer) up to the white box in which the thermometers reside.

| Date | Cloud (oktars) | Wind direction (degrees) | Wind strength (knots) | Visibility | Present Weather | Dry bulb (C) | Wet bulb (C) | Max temp (C) | Min temp (C) |
|---|---|---|---|---|---|---|---|---|---|
| 29/2/13 | 8 | 270 | 15/18 | 8 | 02 | 2.1 | 1.2 | 3.3 | -0.6 |

| Grass temp (C) | 30cm temp (C) | State of ground | Snow depth (cm) | Rainfall amount (mm) | Day of Snow | Day of Hail | Day of Thunder | Day of Gale | Cloud height (m) |
|---|---|---|---|---|---|---|---|---|---|
| D | 2.4 | 13 | 3 | 2.3 | 5 | 0 | 0 | 0 | 1000 |

The process of taking the weather readings is an interesting daily ritual, resulting in an entry in the pocket book that might look like the one shown.

Oktars are eighths of the sky, so when 8 oktars of cloud are reported, the sky is covered by cloud. Even a chink of blue would see it reduced to 7, and it is a rare day indeed when Rangers record cloud 0. There is scope for cloud 9, too, when the sky is obscured by mist.

The Met Office uses knots, which read a bit lower than miles per hour, but as there are at least five scales for wind speed measurement in common use in Europe, I suppose they had to choose one. The split value indicates that it was 15 knots, gusting 18 knots. When it gusts above 20 knots, it's a serious concern for walkers and climbers, even though they do not have an anemometer to check. They can tell it's a windy day before they set out.

Visibility is measured on a scale denoted by code numbers from 9 (Excellent) down to 0 (thick fog) and less. The codes for Present Weather are from 00 to 99, and cover every imaginable condition, including some never recorded at Cairngorm (such as sand storm). The most commonly recorded, summer and winter, is code 02, indicating no change in the sky in the last hour.

The box contains four thermometers shaded from the sun. The air temperature, measured by a dry bulb, is compared with a thermometer with a strip of wicking material which keeps it saturated, from which the humidity measurement can be calculated. The maximum temperature was probably achieved the previous day (though this is not always the case in winter), and the value is later recorded against the previous day's figures. The minimum temperature usually occurs a few hours before the readings.

The minimum temperature at ground (grass) level is shown, unless it is covered by snow (D for drifted over) and so is the actual temperature 30 centimetres underground. This last one is fascinating, changing slowly and steadily with the season, but never recording less than zero degrees at Cairngorm.

Codes come into play again for the state of the ground, 13 indicating complete cover of compact or wet snow. There was a depth of 3 cm. Whether or not it fell as rain or snow, the water yield is measured, which may involve taking it back to the Ranger Base to melt.

A "Day of" is a record of whether the day had snow, sleet, hail, gales or thunder. For good measure cloud height is recorded because it is easy to compare with land features of known height. If the cloud is above the tops or below the station, it cannot be measured, of course.

There is also a narrative entry along the lines of "Moderate breeze, hill fog, good vis. Reset min thermometer" or some such.

Although this daily visit is interesting, and doesn't take long, it can sometimes result in second visits to the box to replace instruments that have been disrupted by wind, making them inaccurate. Occasionally there is a breakage, so the observer has to send off for another thermometer. Although they are only 30 cm long and about 1 cm in diameter, I have yet to see a thermometer arrive in the post in a box less than 80x15x15 centimetres, packed with "plastic macaroni" packaging. They are quite fragile.

Cairngorm is an interesting intermediate station between the valley (where there is a station at Aviemore), and the summit of Cairngorm, the Met Office and Heriot-Watt University weather stations endure the harshest conditions.

So rather than the extremes of heat and cold (in Aviemore) and snow-lie and gales (at the summit), the Cairngorm station is in between in most matters.

# Results of the weather readings

The installation at Cairngorm is a Climatological Recording Site; the data is used to draw conclusions about the changes and trends in the climate. Individual readings are of less importance, in the long run, than the sequence of data. We have a few insights into the trend of the data long-tem, but it is the extremes that always draw most attention, and these are based on individual readings, chance or extreme events and these may be significant or not.

The highest temperature ever recorded in the period is 27.1 Celsius, on 27th June 1995, which is not bad for 640 metres above sea level. The lowest temperature was minus 12.2 Celsius. This is most unimpressive, as the Strath gets much colder. Our cold air streams downslope and ponds up in the valley, where it is always colder on really cold nights.

The highest minimum was on the night of 20th July 2006, when a stuffy 17.8 Celsius was recorded, and the lowest maximum temperature during an entire day was -7.1. This is unremarkable at this latitude and altitude, as the warming effect of the winter sun is quite small, and the temperature depends more on what the air mass is like than how much the sun is shining. It annoys me when in winter radio and TV presenters say that the rising temperatures represent an improvement in the weather, as it usually means moving from fine, dry, cold weather to gloomy, damp, mild weather.

On average, the mean daily maximum rises from 3 Celsius in midwinter to 15 in midsummer, which is not a great rise. The average night time temperature will rise from below minus one in winter to around seven in summer.

It might not surprise you to know that the average number of days in a year when there is an air frost is 111, and the average number of snowfall days is 74, and snow lies at the weather station on 97 days.

This is the least thundery part of Britain. There averages only 7 days when thunder is heard every decade. Hail is hardly more common, at 8 days per decade, though ice pellets and frozen rain are more common. The reason is the lack of opportunity for thunder clouds to develop, likewise hail clouds.

Wind is often a problem at Cairngorm, with 36 days of gale per year. A gale is a wind of more than 35 knots for at least an hour. Calm days can be few and far between, usually totalling 3 or 4 a month, and fog persisting at the weather station at 0900 GMT occurs on average 29 days per year.

# Climbers

If there is a near-perfect resource which is heavily used for recreation, it makes sense to try to find out what impact the recreation is having on the resource. This seems obvious in the case of footpaths, but it took me a while to realise that we needed to do this for climbers on climbing routes as well. This arose when someone exclaimed that there had been "200 people in the corrie!" and I thought that claim needed to be substantiated.

So I started counting winter climbers in Coire an t-Sneachda and Coire an Lochain as often as conditions and my time permitted. This turned out to be ten to twenty times a winter, and as far as I know remains the only observation of mountain recreation over a large number of years.

As I adopted the practice of counting for a minimum of 30 minutes, at least some of which is between noon and 1 pm (the peak time), a consistent method has allowed me to compare days and route choices accurately. I have also seen some astonishing congestion on routes, occasionally with over 20 people trying to get up one of the large gullies. Some popular routes have become notorious for being climbed by multiple groups simultaneously, a dangerous proposition.

It also provided me with first-hand information to pass on to climbers about the prospects for their own climbs subsequently.

By the end of winter 2016 there had been 199 counts of climbers in Coire an t-Sneachda. Only once had the total number of climbers exceeded 200, the

*Good conditions for counting climbers on Mess of Potage*

greatest number seen on any one occasion in a year was usually around 150. This is still a lot of people, leading to some congestion on routes. This happens when climbers have to queue, or climb closely behind another party, or even climb alongside them.

In the years 2006 – 2016, the average number of climbers active in the corrie peaked in 2008 to 2010 at 47 to 54 climbers, but numbers have since declined to average 32 in 2016. This is not only a measure of the popularity of Coire a t-Sneachda as a climbing venue. There are many other places where people may climb, and counter-intuitively a high number climbing in this reliable location may indicate poor conditions elsewhere, and vice-versa.

Looking back at some of the counts is eye-watering. The most crowded routes are usually the more popular and easier ones, such as Runnel, overcrowded on a quarter of all counts.

Aladdin's Couloir had 28 people climbing it at the same time, when a comfortable number would be no more than 8. I've counted 21 people in Aladdin's Mirror, where there are several different lines feasible, and 6 could be accommodated comfortably. Another 21 climbers were in Jacob's Ladder all at once; more than 6 is a crowd.

The most disproportionately crowded route was 20 people in Crotched Gully on 29th December 1999, five times the number I would consider the upper limit for safety. Runnel had 19 people on 20th January 2008, a chaotic scene: ropes crossing, parties overtaking each other, and fortunately no-one dropping anything on anyone else.

Why climbers crowd these routes is a bit of a mystery. There are dozens of routes in the next corrie with less than a tenth of the traffic. Climbers often pursue a popular route they have aspired to, or one that is in condition. Some are attracted by the activity of others, and others are impervious to all signs of hazard, such as other climbers of unknown competence ahead.

## Snowholes

Another fragile resource heavily used for recreation is the hollows on the plateau where reliable snow banks are suitable for digging and staying in snowholes overnight. As I said earlier, the Snow White facility allows snowhole users to return their waste hygienically, but Rangers still need to keep an eye on whether this is working.

It is difficult to know how many people that need to use this facility actually do so, except by reviewing the state of the snowholing sites regularly in the winter and the following spring and summer as the snow melts. The system does not eliminate the problem, but it has reduced it by over 90% and publicised the need for environmentally responsible activity very effectively.

# Overnights in the car parks

Until I started counting units such as camper vans and tents which were in the car parks when I arrived in the morning, no-one had any idea of how much interest there is in spending the night in the Cairngorm car parks. They offer a quiet alternative to the crowded commercial campsites in the valley, but have no facilities. There may even be a move one day to provide facilities and charge for them, but the operator seems unconcerned or unaware of the opportunity.

Counting 'units' – camper vans or tents – is quite easy. I can do it on my drive to work. Calculating how many people that represents is more difficult, and not something I'm going to start inquiring about. Numbers of units were as low as 61 in the whole of 2000, and have grown exponentially to over 1000 in 2016. Some days the Ciste car park is like the Ciste camper van park, with a dozen or so vans spread around. In the epic winter of 2009-10, the vans at the upper end of the Coire Cas car park were hemmed in by walls of snow and sported yard-long icicles from their roofs.

# Wildlife

One other major topic of monitoring you would expect the Ranger Service to be aware of is the wildlife of Cairngorm. The Rangers are supposed to know a lot about it.

Well, yes, this is true, but there are, in fact, lots of other people who know lots more. The Rangers make notes on anything seen or reported and publish records in the form of an annual report every year. Even the highlights would take too long to recount, bearing in mind this is a remote, impoverished and stormy mountain resource where the species need to be specialists, and vagrants are often wrecked here and usually overlooked.

So we get excited about a robin in the garden, or a chiffchaff singing at the Ciste car park. In 2017, snipe and swallow nested near the Base Station for the first time on record. All are common species lower down, but rare for Cairngorm.

There have been a few lucky wrecks, too. A young gannet was grounded near the car park and a Manx shearwater near the Ptarmigan building. Lucky, because if they had chosen a corner of the mountain just a few hundred metres further away, they would never have been rescued. I have found a redwing and a goldcrest on the plateau at different times. Unfortunately, I was too late.

Plant life is mostly in a very steady state on Cairn Gorm, but because of the disturbance brought about by the activities of the development, several species have unintentionally arrived and survived. They now reach their highest stations in the British Isles on Cairn Gorm.

For instance, there is hazel at the car park (630m), coltsfoot at the Middle Station (750m), ragwort on the Traverse (1000m) nettle at the top of the M1 tow (1090m), and rosebay willowherb above the Ptarmigan building (1120m).

Some native plants appear very high up, too, with chickweed wintergreen above Ciste Mhearad (1150m) and deer-grass (a sedge) above the Marquis Well at 1200m.

Don't get too worried about seeing dandelion in the Northern Corries and attributing its presence to unnatural conditions brought on by the effect of walkers. It is also in inaccessible parts of the Highlands where nobody goes. It is just a very successful coloniser with wind-borne seed.

So that was the highlights of the monitoring. There are lots more topics, of course: snow patches on the plateau which eventually melt (or not); water heights in streams; mountain bikes on high ground; avalanche dates and debris; sporadic cairn building; weather phenomena, the list is a long one. You would expect the Rangers to watch what's happening, otherwise, how would they know?

# 15.

# What Happened Next?

I can't say much about what happens next, because it's still happening.

One of two things is going to happen to the developments on Cairngorm: Either snowsports will remain strong and development will continue and improve; or snowsports will become weaker, and efforts will be made to diversify and strengthen the summer offering, eventually to the exclusion of the winter one.

While all this is happening, there will be more organisational change, and that will make life interesting, but not necessarily comfortable.

## Decline

If Cairngorm suffers further poor snowsports seasons and poor summers, it may be obliged to reform its business model to a much more slimmed-down operation. The other ski areas would recognise this. There was a time when, if a coach party arrived at the Glencoe ski area, it would be all hands to the pumps. There may even be an engineer working out on the ski equipment called in to help clear tables and empty bins.

Cairngorm is very fortunate that if a coach party arrives, the fitters can carry on with their work, there will be enough catering staff to cope, and if not, a couple of people from the admin and management team might well come and lend a hand.

I've lost count of the hours of labouring the Rangers have done to try to make up for the lack of an adequate squad to maintain the hill track, drains, fences, re-seed the damage caused by commercial skiing operations, rope off areas where fitters are working and pick litter round the car park. There is a cost, of course, to the other work Rangers, and only Rangers, can do.

But if Rangers are just standing in as labourers, couldn't the Company save money by employing labourers instead? Many Ranger tasks could be reallocated to other staff, but managing the estate beyond the ski area depends on Rangers entirely. Many other functions just wouldn't happen, because there is no-one with the time, or interest, or capability, even before we consider liability issues and insurance.

When you arrived at the busiest visitor location in the National Park, did you expect there to be a Ranger Service? Even if you hadn't been here before, wouldn't you expect this to be one of the things National Parks do? Is this something that is dependent on there being good snowsports? Most visitors are still summer or casual visitors, not snowsports enthusiasts, and in any case, is the Ranger Service provided for the snowsports visitor?

Many people objected to the building of the railway because they believed the safeguards to the environment would not be strong enough to survive a financial downturn. In other words, the operator would open the doors at the top to get more people up the railway, and would return to the trampling and disturbance that characterised the old chairlift open system.

Bob Kinnaird (our CEO) answered this early on, and his point is still valid. If the operator was in such dire straits that they would consider reneging on legal agreements and opening the doors at the top, the financial benefit would be insufficient to save the company. It would go under anyway.

The Walk at the Top has been a good way of providing managed access at the top of the railway. If winter conditions were to recede significantly even from these highest parts, there might be an extension of the season for the walks. While I could imagine an Easter Sunday Walk at the Top proving popular, the daily provision of these walks is likely to be insufficiently popular to depend on them as a financial lifeline.

So, faced with a severe budget decline, if the operator decided it couldn't find the money to run a Ranger Service, who could? HIE is probably good for support, but their budgets are under pressure too, and the National Park Authority would not welcome the prospect of being seen to lose a Ranger Service at the Heart of the National Park.

HIE has a record of bringing the Ranger Service back into their management but that was when they had a more generous budget. To my surprise, the new operator has taken over the entire running of the Ranger Service, including paying for it, thus returning to the arrangement before 1997 when I joined.

My opinion is that the Ranger Service is key to delivering the visitor management plan and monitoring scheme which are not going to go away. It is wholly a cost to the operator. However, HIE and the National Park need the Ranger Service to exist, so I suspect the Ranger Service would survive even a severe slimming-down.

What would the decline be like? Suppose instead of 100 snowsports days there were 60 or even 30. The lower slopes would never come into condition. This is what happened in 2017.

The lower tows would be maintained for a few years but eventually there would come a really big bill. A new rope or a gearbox, for instance. Hard decisions would have to be taken.

In the cases of the Aonach tow and the Ciste chairlifts the decision was taken to mothball the uplift and eventually abandon and remove it. This took 15 years of ugly dereliction and hazard to birdlife. Without adequate investment, the uplift would atrophy from the most snow-free areas upward. It's not a prospect that fills me with any pleasure at all.

*The snowless scene of March 2012 - sign of things to come?*

One way of counteracting the effects of a lack of snow on the low ground would be to install a modern high-speed chairlift from the car park to the middle or upper slopes of Coire Cas. This has already been discussed by skiers and ski area managers at length. It could replace redundant or inoperable surface tows, could provide uplift over snow-free terrain and summer-time uplift for casual visitors, in addition to the train.

A new chairlift might be much more attractive to investors if snowsports were seen to have a bright future, as they might, but I am sure that the same concerns would be raised about it as were raised about the development of the railway, and for the same reasons. With an existing precautionary agreement to protect the neighbouring Natura sites, it would be the obvious thing to extend or replicate it for a new uplift.

A new chairlift in Coire Cas could give easier access to the Natura sites than the railway. So there would be VMP number 2 and monitoring to accompany it. This does not sound like a scenario for less work for the Ranger Service. Quite the opposite, in fact.

And what if, in addition to the loss of snowsports opportunities, there was a diminution in the conditions for winter mountaineering? The last two places to feel the effects of this would be Ben Nevis and the Northern Corries of Cairn Gorm. Before any final demise, then, all attention from winter mountaineers would be concentrated on these two places. Cairn Gorm would be even busier for a while.

In the 1920s there was no winter climbing, it was too warm. If the 2020s was a similar period, what then? People would still come to walk and birdwatch, rock climb and geologise in the winter. There would be smaller numbers of casual visitors than in summer, but the opening up of the months of short daylight to people not equipped or interested in snow and ice would present opportunities for organised groups – clubs, schools and colleges – which are concentrated in the summer months at present.

The loss of winter is regarded by many people as a threat to our native wildlife. In a place where winter specialists can thrive to the exclusion of everything else, wildlife would see some significant changes.

We would expect to see the movement uphill of the climate and habitat zones. What used to be regarded as a 400m habitat (forest) would be seen at 600m, and the scrub zone would extend upwards towards 1000m. Ptarmigan territory would be squeezed into the top parts of the mountains. Dotterel might be unable to cope with increased numbers of crows living comfortably much higher than at present. Greater coverage of mat grass and other higher plants would severely curtail the tremendous lichen diversity on the mountains.

The loss of winter conditions on Cairn Gorm would be a bleak prospect, making them so much more like everywhere else. They would still have their attractions, of course, people would still come in great numbers. There will still be a Ranger Service even if winter is a distant memory.

If the foregoing scenario is too miserable to contemplate, let's think about something more cheerful.

# Resurgence

*Kilted skiers in a line, March 2010*

How about more winters like 2009-10? More snow, more snowsports, and protection for the ground from November to May. Lots more money coming in would allow redevelopment of Coire na Ciste with new chairlifts, and perhaps a new chairlift in Coire Cas to replace the lower tows.

Everyone can have fun imagining spending money they don't have. I would invest in improvements to the Base Station, with a new reception facility at the front corner replacing the Ranger Base, and I would demolish the Day Lodge and relocate most of the services in the Base Station. The Day Lodge could be replaced with a smaller visitor and catering facility with a remit to interpret the mountains.

I would shift the Ranger Service into a new Ranger Base on the opposite side of the car park, where the walkers and climbers that Rangers need to meet pass close by. I would make it a walk-through facility at car-park level, with offices and education space below, storage below that and 24-hour toilets at lower car park level.

While I'm in the mood, why don't we make a two-level car park, so that vehicles parked on the lower level are sheltered from the weather by the upper level?

I've heard the arguments for relocating car parking to Glenmore and providing cable-car, railway or road transport up the hill. This is not something I would advocate. Glenmore forest is another Natura site, and hasn't capacity for a large suite of car parks. Who can guarantee to run the transport up and down the hill at the times when people want it, even early morning or into the evening? If a railway or cable way is to be built, how can it avoid damaging more Natura sites, ancient forest, capercaillie leks, meltwater gorge and all?

# Reorganisation

We have seen the change of CCC to CML, and the appointment by HIE of Natural Retreats as their commercial operator.

I never thought the new business would want to be saddled with the costs of the environmental responsibilities of the landowner, along with the Ranger Service, but I was wrong and Cairngorm now enters a new period with Cairngorm Mountain Ranger Service provided by Natural Retreats on behalf of HIE.

HIE still wish to complete a transfer of Cairngorm Estate to a new owner. Owning land is not an easy job. HIE has all sorts of bits of land all over the Highlands, mostly to do with industrial estates. I would be surprised if together they amounted to a greater area than Cairngorm Estate. The Estate does not 'fit' with HIE's portfolio, nor with its modern purposes.

A few years ago, HIE had high level discussions with a view to disposing of Cairngorm Estate. The only viable interest was from Forestry Commission (Scotland), FCS. Negotiations continued for a while and then ended by mutual consent. HIE embarked on a period of investment in the infrastructure of the Estate, possibly to rectify perceived obstacles to a transfer.

While I welcome these investments, it is perhaps unfair to claim that they were motivated by a wish to sell the Estate. They might just have been managing the Estate routinely. I hope so, because there is no net benefit to the public if one public agency 'sells' assets to another, except that the purposes of the agencies on behalf of the public might be better met in the new arrangement.

The fact that this piece of land is with HIE and that bit is with FCS and another with SNH is merely to subdivide the public ownership of land into artificial pockets. Rangers might work cordially with neighbours in FCS and SNH, but they are separate in every other respect.

If public land was owned by the government through a single agency, there would be no need for HIE to struggle to justify having Cairngorm on its books. All such areas could share resources and staff, have one representative at meetings, one set of statutory notifications and one management structure. Rangers and maintenance teams could be shared around more fairly, concentrating on core work rather than be drawn into other work to make up for local shortcomings.

I'm not saying this change is inevitable, but we should all expect big changes in public services in the 20-teens. The referendum in 2014 was just the start of it, there is no reason why Scotland has to follow the rest of Britain's way of doing things, and in a small country, it is excessively wasteful to divide up public agencies and have them duplicate similar functions. Something will happen, nothing is more certain.

Now. I'm sorry to disappoint you, but as I hinted above, I didn't stay at Cairngorm for ever. I left at the start of July 2017 to pursue my other interests, such as living with my wife, hill walking guiding, and writing and playing music. The date was the 20th anniversary of my starting there.

I think I deserve a rest. Nearly 40 years in service, and 20 of them at Cairngorm. I think I held the line on most things. Now it's someone else's turn.

# 16.     The big "SO WHAT?"

So, thanks for coming for a walk, it's been fun. We've had a stroll round the Cairngorms and some of the issues that get thrown up.

I'm not going to get all hyperbolic with you and say it's the best place in the world, or the most fantastic mountains, the best wildlife or walking, but it is very special, indeed.

There's nowhere else like it.

*Evening*

Perhaps we get a bit too modest about our little island, a bit overwhelmed by the Alps and the Andes, Yellowstone and Rift Valley, Himalayas and Great Barrier Reef. I've only been to one of these and, yes, they're great, but that doesn't mean we can't be proud of what we have in the Cairngorms. It stands up on an international stage. Loads of people tell me this every year, and I'm not going to contradict them.

Even on a European scale, there are things in the Cairngorms they can get excited about in Venice and Paris. Britain compares reasonably well in European terms for the conservation effort, but you have to have the things to conserve in the first place. For an island that has been subject to several successive clear-outs of its natural populations (by Ice Ages), there is still a good diversity, and the process of loss and rejuvenation is far more complex than on the continent.

The process of trying to understand the natural world has been well advanced by curious minds in Britain – especially Scottish ones. Now the natural world of the Cairngorms is as highly investigated, cherished and understood (by people who don't actually need to know for their survival) as anywhere.

In Britain, the Cairngorms are an extreme. Only one point is higher, but this apart, the Cairngorms holds so many British superlatives, that everywhere else you go will feel like coming back from the extremity. You will probably be able to say that your accommodation in the valley was higher than your local English hill. The snow-lie in the Cairngorms is ten times as long as the snow-lie in the West Midlands. The average top temperature in the Cairngorms is more than seven degrees below that of the East Midlands. Red squirrels are common in the Cairngorms. A village of 1500 people is a big place in the Cairngorms. And so on.

The Cairngorms, moreover, are not a run-up to or a half-way house on the way to anywhere. They are not at the furthest extreme of the land mass, but people travelling past them don't often stop off. This is partly to do with excellent modern roads and the lack of obvious opportunity, but also, I would suggest, that if you are coming to the North, you either do the Cairngorms properly, or you don't do them at all.

They have an other-ness to them which distinguishes them from most of the Highlands. They sit back, aloof from the world, retiring behind long steady up-slopes. They do not wave their peaks around the sky shouting look at me, but calmly doze under the cloud or the stars as if it is not necessary to make a fuss to be known as special. Sure, there are some brash young slopes with steep gullies and shattered crags. In fact these surprise the viewer rather than characterise the mountains. The cragginess does not intrude onto the skylines often, and the mountains become known as steady, rounded masses.

The novice could be forgiven for being under-whelmed on first view. Had this been Glencoe, or Torridon, the first-time visitor's eyes would be out on stalks. With the Cairngorms, the fearsome reputation could well precede the first view, and give the impression of a quiet but daunting adversary rather than a lofty peak to climb, and be seen to climb, all the way up.

Within these famous mountains, surely there is no room for quiet discovery. The straths are surely taken up with every last mortal vending their wares, for accommodation, whisky shops, visitor centres and guiding services. Surely the National Park was brought in to retain some semblance of the natural world among all this.

Not a bit of it. The straths are truly spacious. So much land is not available to be settled, as it floods too frequently. There is not a big city of half a million on the eastern boundary and another on the west, as with the Peak District. It is too far to commute from most of the Cairngorms to even a small city.

You can wander into the woods and come across a cottage that looks as if it had been there for a hundred years – because it has – with no sign of a vehicle track up to the door. Little sleeper-built bothies in the woods with corrugated iron roofs still stand. People genuinely walk for days without crossing a road, and agonise over perceived failings no more damaging than a quad bike track, used once.

In a society dominated by urban life, time-poor and cash-rich, the Cairngorms is a place to come to find out what really matters. It will lodge in your memory indelibly.

Truly, there is nowhere else like it.

# Epilogue

# Cairngorm Rangers

Cairngorm Mountain Ranger Service is employed (and paid for) by the ski area operator, Natural Retreats Cairngorm Mountain, on behalf of the landowner, Highlands and Islands Enterprise.

The original Cairngorm Ranger Service in the 1970s comprised one Ranger, Jo Porter, and one or two Seasonal Rangers. Owing to a disagreement between the employers and Countryside Commission for Scotland about the number of Rangers that was appropriate for such a job, this Ranger Service was discontinued, and Jo was made redundant. This was by no means the only controversy to assail Cairngorm during this time, as I have related. The facilities operator then had their own Ranger Service, which expanded as a summer service and transferred to ski operations in the winter.

The present Cairngorm Ranger Service, the third incarnation, came about because the landowner wanted a professional year-round service, and appointed me as the first senior representative; and Ruari MacDonald as Seasonal Ranger in 1997. Jim Cornfoot was recruited soon afterwards, and for several years, I soldiered on through the winter on my own and Ruari and Jim went over to join the Ski Patrol in winter. Jim was later appointed Interpretive Officer for Cairngorm Mountain Limited and later still came round to be my line-manager as Cairngorm Land Manager.

In 2000 we recruited a second full-time, year-round Ranger in Ewan MacLeod. When he left in 2005, we continued briefly with a winter seasonal Ranger, Rex Sircus, and recruited one of the current Seasonal Rangers, Heather Morning, to the vacant year-round post in 2006. With Heather leaving to take on the post of Mountain Safety Adviser for the Mountaineering Council of Scotland, we were back down to two again, and carrying a vacancy indefinitely. Things are not static, Attila Kish came to join us in 2010, but with his departure, I was left on my own for most of the winter, with the intolerable choice of having a Ranger Service presence or a day off. Jonny Porteous joined the team in 2015, but left in 2016, and the future is again unclear.

The additional word Mountain was added to our title in 2010 to emphasise our connection to Cairngorm Mountain Limited and, of course to our location.

# References

## Mountaineering

*Mountaineering in Scotland* and *Undiscovered Scotland*, W. H. Murray. All mountaineers going to the hills in Scotland should have read some of Bill Murray's classics.

*The High Mountains of Britain and Ireland* (2004) Irvine Butterfield

*Hamish's Mountain Walk.* (1978) Hamish Brown, published by Gollancz. Hamish dashes through the Cairngorms on his non-stop climb of the Munros but sees some rare sights.

*Classic Rock* (1978, but new edition recently), edited by Ken Wilson, published by Granada. Some of the best Cairngorms routes illustrated in early chapters.

*Cold Climbs.*(1983) edited by Ken Wilson, published by Diadem. Classic photo of Jean's Hut and Coire an Lochain, among others.

*The Cairngorms* (2007) edited by Andy Nisbet and Alan Fyffe. The SMC climbing guide that gives a full listing of the winter and rock climbing routes in the Cairngorms

*Where do the walkers go?* Bullivant, N. (2007), Countryside Recreation v15 no 1, p19 – 22 http://www.outdoorrecreation.org.uk, navigate to Journal archive for vol 15-1.

# Mountain Rescue

*Friends In High Places* (1988) By and about the Cairngorm Mountain Rescue Team, 1963 – 1988. This is where to go for the best description of early rescues in the Cairngorms.

*Cairngorm John* (2009) by John Allen with Robert Davidson, published by Sandstone Press. Many mountain rescue incidents from 1988 to 2009 contemporaneous with this book

# The Cairngorms

*The Cairngorms.* (1992) Adam Watson. The best of the SMC District guides, published by the Scottish Mountaineering Trust which reinvests profits in selected mountain projects

*A Camera In The Cairngorms.* (1948) W.A. Poucher. Classic black and white photography that brings home how little the Cairngorms have changed

*Rothiemurchus. Nature and People on a Highland Estate 1500 – 2000* (1999), edited by T.C. Smout and R.A. Lambert.

*A High and Lonely Place.* (2000) Jim Crumley's polemic masterpiece. I am sure he would disapprove of much I describe in my book, but he is an eloquent observer on the moral high ground, and I was down in the fight.

*Caring for the High Mountains – Conservation of the Cairngorms.* (1990) edited by J.W.H. Conroy, Adam Watson and A.R. Gunson, produced by the Centre for Scottish Studies and Natural Environmental Research Council. Conference proceedings giving a fascinating insight into the entrenched positions of the pre-National Park era. Probably difficult to find, now

# Nature and ecology of the Cairngorms

*The Ecology, Land Use and Conservation of the Cairngorms,* (2002) edited by Charles Gimmingham, published by Packard Publishing.

*Ecology and Land Use in Upland Scotland,* (1969) D N McVean and J D Lockie

*The Nature of the Cairngorms. Diversity in a Changing Environment.* (2006) edited by Philip Shaw and Des Thomson, published by Scottish Natural Heritage

*Wild Land. Images of Nature from the Cairngorms.* (2005) Peter Cairns and Mark Hamblin, published by Mercat Press

*The Cairngorms, a Landscape Fashioned by Geology* (2006) British Geological Survey. An excellent summary booklet incorporating the latest research into the formation of these mountains

*Crystal Mountain (2012)* Roy Starkey. The cairngorm crystals, hunters and history, lapidary and jewellery. Fascinating

McCallum Webster, M. (1978). *Flora of Moray, Nairn & East Inverness.* Aberdeen University Press

The Rangers' work would be so much harder without: mwis, the Mountain Weather Information Service www.mwis.ork.uk/scottish-forecast/EH,

The sportscotland Scottish Avalanche Information Service http://www.sais.gov.uk/northern-cairngorms/

The Met Office observations http://www.metoffice.gov.uk/public/weather/observation and rainfall radar (which you can search on this site)

There are no maps in this publication, the Ordnance Survey 1:50,000 sheet 36 Grantown, Aviemore and Cairngorm is widely available, as is Harvey British Mountain Map Cairngorms and Lochnagar (1:40,000) and Ordnance Survey 1:25,000 sheet OL57 Explorer, Cairn Gorm and Aviemore.

Picture credits. All pictures from the collection of the author unless stated.

Page 94 summit path summer 1984 Cairngorm Chairlift Ranger Service

Page 109 Dotterel female Cathy Mordaunt,

Page 170 Curran bothy, Andrew Ker

Chapter 10 Tea hut, Queue, Railway construction cable crane, road clearance and White Lady, Cairngorm Chairlift Company

Page 249 dotterel and people, Cathy Mordaunt

# Index

# Kit List
(NB, not all of these items are recommended!)

Sandals 113, 221
Shawl 113
Silk (clothing) 145, 214
Sunshades 13

Tent 80, 127, 230, 268
Thumbstick 224
Torch 13, 145, 162

Training shoes (trainers) 17, 74, 223, 225

Waterproofs 12 - 13, 145 - 147, 156, 223
Wellingtons (wellies) 17, 154, 226
Windproof 145
Wool (clothing) 12, 16, 145, 147
Wrist loop (for ice axe) 156

# Mountain Peaks and Places

# People

# Wildlife and Geology